HARPERCOLLINS
BUSINESS
GERMAN

HarperPerennial
A Division of HarperCollins*Publishers*

HarperCollins books may be purchased for educational, business, or
sales promotional use. For information, please call or write: Special
Markets Department, HarperCollins Publishers, Inc., 10 East 53rd
Street, New York, NY 10022. Telephone: (212) 207-7528; Fax: (212)
207-7222.

First HarperPerennial Edition

ISBN 0-06-276517-5 (pbk)

92 93 94 95 96 HCUK 10 9 8 7 6 5 4 3 2 1

Editorial Director
Lorna Sinclair

Editorial Management
Vivian Marr

Editors
Stephen Clarke

Diana Feri
Hildegard Pesch
Dagmar Förtsch

Assisted by
Elspeth Anderson   Lucy Dawes   Susan Dunsmore
Joyce Littlejohn   Carol MacLeod   Val McNulty
Megan Maxwell   Helga Michaelis

We are indebted to the following for their
specialist contributions:
Sandy Anderson   Ray Carrick   Marion R Chalmers,
Pieda plc   Colette Clenaghan   Kate M Crooks
Jack Denny   Alec Dickie   Catherine Girvan
Jim Irvine   Hugh McGhee   Charles Ranstead
Stewart Reid-Foster   Janet Richardson
Lesley Robertson   Peter Stafford
David Swarbrick   Brian Turtle   Gary Weir

CONTENTS

INTRODUCTION	vii
THE GERMAN ALPHABET	viii
NUMBERS	ix
THE TIME AND DATE	xiii
ACCOUNTS AND PAYMENTS	1
ADVERTISING AND MEDIA	9
AT THE BANK	16
BANKING AND FINANCE	18
BUYING AND SELLING	28
COMPANY STRUCTURES	36
COMPLAINTS	41
COMPUTING	45
CONFERENCES AND PUBLIC SPEAKING	54
ECONOMICS	64
ENGLISH ABBREVIATIONS	70
ENTERTAINING	77
THE ENVIRONMENT	83
THE EUROPEAN COMMUNITY	87
GERMAN ABBREVIATIONS AND INSTITUTIONS	91
AT THE HOTEL	104

IMPORT-EXPORT AND SHIPPING	110
INDUSTRIES AND TYPES OF COMPANY	118
INSTITUTIONS AND ORGANIZATIONS	120
INSURANCE	124
INVESTMENTS	129
JOB APPLICATIONS AND RECRUITING	134
THE LAW AND CONTRACTS	143
MAKING CONTACT	151
MANUFACTURING	163
MARKETING AND PR	167
MEETINGS AND NEGOTIATIONS	173
IN THE OFFICE	180
PERSONNEL	184
PROJECT MANAGEMENT	191
PROPERTY	194
RESEARCH AND DEVELOPMENT	201
STOCK MANAGEMENT	204
TAXES AND DUTIES	205
TRAVEL	208
GERMAN-ENGLISH GLOSSARY	221

INTRODUCTION

Your Collins Business German dictionary is a handy quick-reference guide that will be an invaluable aid when doing business with the German-speaking world. It has been designed to provide you with the German vocabulary necessary to communicate clearly and efficiently in a wide range of business situations, whether you are working from your own office or in a German-speaking country. The information it contains will enable you to translate both out of and into English and is arranged as follows:

ENGLISH INTO GERMAN

TOPICS

These cover areas of general business interest (e.g. **IN THE OFFICE, COMPANY STRUC-TURES**), specific business fields (e.g. **ACCOUNTS AND PAYMENTS, INSURANCE**), and subjects which have an impact on business (e.g. **THE EUROPEAN COMMUNITY, THE ENVIRON-MENT**). Each topic consists of an alphabetical list of the most widely used items for that topic, along with a selection of useful phrases arranged alphabetically by the key word they contain, and their translations.

Some terms could be assigned to several different topics but to avoid duplicating information we have listed them in only one place. However, topics are cross-referred to related topics, so if a term that you might expect to find under one topic is not there, you should look for it under the other topics referred to at the top of the page.

For appropriate topics, such as **ENTERTAINING, MAKING CONTACT** and **TRAVEL**, where cultural information is as important as the vocabulary itself, we have supplied useful background information and tips.

ABBREVIATIONS

This is a list of the most widely-used abbreviations and acronyms in general and business English. For acronyms of the names of national and international organizations, you should consult either **INSTITUTIONS AND ORGANIZATIONS** or **THE EUROPEAN COMMUNITY**.

GERMAN INTO ENGLISH

GLOSSARY

The glossary at the end of the book contains over 4,000 words and is an alphabetical list of the German translations from the topics. For the most commonly used words, basic meanings as well as business-specific meanings are translated.

ABBREVIATIONS AND INSTITUTIONS

This is a list of essential German abbreviations and acronyms of the kind that you are likely to come across in a range of business material, from articles in magazines and newspapers to shipping documents and forms.

ABBREVIATIONS USED IN THE TEXT

acc	*accusative case*	**m**	*masculine*
adj	*adjective*	**m(f)**	*masculine or feminine*
adv	*adverb*	**n**	*noun*
dat	*dative case*	**nt**	*neuter*
f	*feminine*	**pl**	*plural*
f(m)	*feminine or masculine*	**prep**	*preposition*
gen	*genitive case*	**vb**	*verb*
inv	*invariable*		

THE GERMAN ALPHABET

	Phonetically	*Pronounced approximately as*
A	[aː]	**ah**
B	[beː]	**bay**
C	[tseː]	**tsay**
D	[deː]	**day**
E	[eː]	**ay**
F	[ɛf]	**ef**
G	[geː]	**gay**
H	[haː]	**hah**
I	[iː]	**ee**
J	[jɔt]	**yot**
K	[kaː]	**kah**
L	[ɛl]	**el**
M	[ɛm]	**em**
N	[ɛn]	**en**
O	[oː]	**oh**
P	[peː]	**pay**
Q	[kuː]	**koo**
R	[ɛr]	**air**
S	[ɛs]	**ess**
T	[teː]	**tay**
U	[uː]	**oo**
V	[fau]	**fow**
W	[veː]	**vay**
X	[ɪks]	**iks**
Y	[ʏpsilɔn]	**oopseelon**
Z	[tsɛt]	**tset**

NUMBERS

CARDINAL NUMBERS

0	*null*
1	*eins; ein(e)*
2	*zwei*
3	*drei*
4	*vier*
5	*fünf*
6	*sechs*
7	*sieben*
8	*acht*
9	*neun*
10	*zehn*
11	*elf*
12	*zwölf*
13	*dreizehn*
14	*vierzehn*
15	*fünfzehn*
16	*sechzehn*
17	*siebzehn*
18	*achtzehn*
19	*neunzehn*
20	*zwanzig*
21	*einundzwanzig*
22	*zweiundzwanzig*
23	*dreiundzwanzig*
30	*dreißig*
31	*einunddreißig*
32	*zweiunddreißig*
40	*vierzig*
50	*fünfzig*
60	*sechzig*
70	*siebzig*
80	*achtzig*
90	*neunzig*
99	*neunundneunzig*
100	*(ein)hundert*
101	*(ein)hundert(und)eins*
102	*(ein)hundert(und)zwei*
110	*(ein)hundert(und)zehn*
150	*(ein)hundert(und)fünfzig*
182	*(ein)hundert(und)zweiundachtzig*

200	*zweihundert*
300	*dreihundert*
400	*vierhundert*
500	*fünfhundert*
600	*sechshundert*
700	*siebenhundert*
800	*achthundert*
900	*neunhundert*
1,000	*(ein)tausend*
1,001	*(ein)tausend(und)eins*
1,500	*(ein)tausendfünfhundert*
2,000	*zweitausend*
10,000	*zehntausend*
100,000	*(ein)hunderttausend*
200,000	*zweihunderttausend*
250,000	*zweihundertfünfzigtausend*
a million	*eine Million*
two million	*zwei Millionen*
a billion (1000 million)	*eine Milliarde*
two billion	*zwei Milliarden*
a million units	*eine Million Stück*
two billion units	*zwei Millarden Stück*

To divide thousands and above clearly, a point may be used in German where English places a comma: English 1,000 = German 1.000 or 1000; English 2,304,770 = German 2.304.770.

DECIMALS

In German, a comma is written where English uses a point: English 3.56 (*three point five six*) = German 3,56 (*drei Komma fünf sechs*). Note that a German number cannot start with *Komma* — *null* must precede it: English .07 (*point nought seven*) = German 0,07 (*null Komma null sieben*).

FRACTIONS

half	*halb*
half a kilogram (½kg)	*ein halbes Kilo(gramm) (½kg)*
1½	*eineinhalb, anderthalb*
1½ kilos	*eineinhalb Kilogramm*
2½	*zweieinhalb*
⅓	*ein Drittel*

$\frac{2}{3}$	*zwei Drittel*	
$\frac{1}{4}$	*ein Viertel*	
$\frac{3}{4}$	*drei Viertel*	

ORDINAL NUMBERS

1st	*erste(r,s)*	1.
2nd	*zweite(r,s)*	2.
3rd	*dritte(r,s)*	3.
4th	*vierte(r,s)*	4.
5th	*fünfte(r,s)*	5.
6th	*sechste(r,s)*	6.
7th	*siebte(r,s)*	7.
8th	*achte(r,s)*	8.
9th	*neunte(r,s)*	9.
10th	*zehnte(r,s)*	10.
11th	*elfte(r,s)*	11.
12th	*zwölfte(r,s)*	12.
13th	*dreizehnte(r,s)*	13.
14th	*vierzehnte(r,s)*	14.
15th	*fünfzehnte(r,s)*	15.
16th	*sechzehnte(r,s)*	16.
17th	*siebzehnte(r,s)*	17.
18th	*achtzehnte(r,s)*	18.
19th	*neunzehnte(r,s)*	19.
20th	*zwanzigste(r,s)*	20.
21st	*einundzwanzigste(r,s)*	21.
22nd	*zweiundzwanzigste(r,s)*	22.
23rd	*dreiundzwanzigste(r,s)*	23.
24th	*vierundzwanzigste(r,s)*	24.
25th	*fünfundzwanzigste(r,s)*	25.
26th	*sechsundzwanzigste(r,s)*	26.
27th	*siebenundzwanzigste(r,s)*	27.
28th	*achtundzwanzigste(r,s)*	28.
29th	*neunundzwanzigste(r,s)*	29.
30th	*dreißigste(r,s)*	30.
31st	*einunddreißigste(r,s)*	31.

See also **THE TIME AND DATE**.

PERCENTAGES

2½% two and a half per cent *2,5% zweieinhalb Prozent*
18% of the people here are over 65 *18% der Leute hier sind über
fünfundsechzig*
Production has risen/fallen by 8% *die Produktion ist um acht
Prozent gestiegen/gefallen*

THE TIME AND DATE

SAYING THE TIME

The major complication when saying the time in German is expressing *half past*. Where an English-speaker says *half past 4*, a German-speaker will say *half to 5*, i.e. *halb fünf*. So *half past 5* is *halb sechs*, and so on. You can avoid this problem using *dreißig*, e.g. 5.30 can be said *fünf Uhr dreißig*. Apart from this, saying the time in German is simple. One says *nach* (after) for *past* and *vor* (before) for *to*, e.g.

10 to 11 *zehn vor elf*
5 past 8 *fünf nach acht*

WRITING THE TIME

The time can be written using full stops as in English, with *Uhr* written after the figures, e.g. *9.30 Uhr, 10.15 Uhr, 11 Uhr*.

THE 24-HOUR CLOCK

German speakers use the 24-hour clock more frequently than is common in Britain. For German speakers, *zehn Uhr* implicitly means *ten in the morning*. When arranging meetings and travel times, it is therefore best to use the 24-hour clock or to specify *morgens, nachnittags, abends*, e.g.

	SPOKEN	*WRITTEN*
at 10am	*um zehn Uhr (morgens)*	*um 10 Uhr*
at 11.30am	*um elf Uhr dreißig (morgen)*	*um 11.30 Uhr*
at 4.20pm	*um vier Uhr zwanzig (nachmittags)*	*um 16.20 Uhr*
at 9.25pm	*um neun Uhr fünfundzwanzig (abends)*	*um 21.25 Uhr*
at 11pm	*um elf Uhr abends, um dreiundzwanzig Uhr*	*um 23 Uhr*

QUESTIONS AND ANSWERS

what's the time? *wie spät ist es?*
what time do you make it? *wie spät haben Sie?*
have you the right time? *haben Sie die richtige Uhrzeit?*

it's 1 o'clock *es ist ein Uhr*
it's 2 o'clock *es ist zwei Uhr*
it's 5 past 4 *es ist fünf (Minuten) nach vier*
it's 10 past 6 *es ist zehn (Minuten) nach sechs*
it's a quarter past 9 *es ist viertel nach neun*
it's a quarter to 2 *es ist viertel vor zwei*
it's half past 8 *es ist halb neun*
I make it 2.20 *nach meiner Uhr ist es 2 Uhr 20*
my watch says 3.37 *auf meiner Uhr ist es 3 Uhr 37*
it's just after 3 *es ist kurz nach drei*
it's nearly 9 *es ist fast neun (Uhr)*
about 8 o'clock *etwa acht Uhr, ungefähr acht Uhr*

what time does it start? *um wieviel Uhr fängt es an?*
when does it end? *wann ist er/sie/es zu Ende?*
when do you open/close? *wann machen Sie auf/wann schließen Sie?*

at exactly 3 o'clock, at 3 sharp, at 3 on the dot *um Punkt drei Uhr*
at midday *um die Mittagszeit*
at midnight *um Mitternacht*
until 8 o'clock *bis acht Uhr*
from 1.30 to 4.30 *von ein Uhr dreißig (1.30 Uhr) bis vier Uhr dreißig (4.30 Uhr)*
how long will it take? *wie lange dauert es?*
how long does it last? *wie lange dauert es?*

ten minutes *zehn Minuten*
a quarter of an hour *eine Viertelstunde*
half an hour *eine halbe Stunde*
three quarters of an hour *eine Dreiviertelstunde*
two hours *zwei Stunden*

when do you need it? *wann brauchen Sie es?*
I need it for 9am tomorrow *ich brauche es morgen früh um neun Uhr*
by Wednesday at 4pm *spätestens Mittwoch um sechzehn Uhr*
at/by 6 o'clock at the latest *spätestens um sechs Uhr*

THE DATE

WRITING THE DATE

The full date may be written exactly as in English, e.g. 11.7.91. or 11.7. If writing it out in full, the style is this:- *11. Juli 1991* or *11. Juli.* The number representing the day of the month is usually followed by a stop, and is always written before the month.

July 1 *der 1. Juli*
May 2 *der 2. Mai*
on June 21 *am 21. Juni*

When writing, the numbers do not change even when the date is preceded by *vom, am* or *zum*, e.g.

on November 25 *am 25. November*
from June 14 to 18 *vom 14. bis zum 18. Juni*

The days of the week and the names of months are written with capital first letters, as in English.

Montag	*Januar*	*Juli*
Dienstag	*Februar*	*August*
Mittwoch	*März*	*September*
Donnerstag	*April*	*Oktober*
Freitag	*Mai*	*November*
Samstag, Sonnabend	*Juni*	*Dezember*
Sonntag		

SAYING THE DATE

the second of January *der zweite Januar*
the fifteenth of October *der fünfzehnte Oktober*
on the second of January *am zweiten Januar*
from the fifteenth to the twentieth of October *vom fünfzehnten bis zum zwanzigsten Oktober*

When saying the year, you must say the *hundred*, e.g.

1993 *neunzehnhundertdreiundneunzig*

You do not need to say *in*, e.g.

in 1992 *neunzehnhundertzweiundneunzig*

QUESTIONS AND ANSWERS

what's today's date? *welches Datum haben wir heute?*
today's the 12th *heute ist der zwölfte (der 12.)*
about the 4th of July *um den 4. Juli*
in (or **during) the 1960s/70s/80s/90s** *in den sechziger/siebziger/
    achtziger/neunziger Jahren (60er/70er/80er/90er Jahren)*

when? *wann?*
when do you need it? *wann brauchen Sie es?*
until when? *bis wann?*
since when? *seit wann?*
how long? *wie lange?*
how long have you worked here? *wie lange arbeiten Sie schon
    hier?*
how long will it take? *wie lange dauert es?*

yesterday *gestern*
today *heute*
tomorrow *morgen*
I need it for tomorrow *ich brauche es morgen*
the day after tomorrow *übermorgen*
last/next week *letzte/nächste Woche*
last/next month *letzten/nächsten Monat*
last/next year *letztes/nächstes Jahr*
every day/Friday/week/month/year *jeden Tag/jeden Freitag/jede
    Woche/jeden Monat/jedes Jahr*
every other day *jeden zweiten Tag*
on Monday *am Montag*
on Fridays *Freitags*
until Thursday *bis Donnerstag*
since Saturday *seit Samstag*
from Monday to Friday *von Montag bis Freitag*
by Wednesday *spätestens Mittwoch*
one Thursday in October *an einem Donnerstag im Oktober*
in 2 days *in zwei Tagen*
they finished it in 2 days/weeks/months *sie hatten es in zwei
    Tagen/Wochen/Monaten fertig*
I've worked here for 2 years *ich arbeite hier seit zwei Jahren*
I'm in Switzerland for 2 days *ich bin zwei Tage lang in der
    Schweiz*
it will take 3 days *das dauert 3 Tage*

1   ACCOUNTS AND PAYMENTS

See also **BUYING AND SELLING**

absorption costing	*Vollkostenrechnung f*
account	*Konto nt*
(on) account	*(als) Anzahlung f*
accountancy	*Rechnungswesen nt*
accountant	*Bilanzbuchhalter(in) m(f)*
accounting	*Buchführung f*
accounting period	*Abrechnungszeitraum m*
accounting procedures	*Buchführungsverfahren nt*
accounting standards	*Bilanzierungsrichtlinien fpl*
accounting system	*Buchführungssystem nt*
accounts *(books)*	*Bücher ntpl*
accounts *(book-keeping)*	*Abrechnung(en) f(pl),*
	Buchführung f
accounts (department)	*Buchhaltung f*
accounts payable	*Verbindlichkeiten fpl*
accounts receivable	*Forderungen fpl*
accrued charges	*aufgelaufene Kosten pl*
accrued interest	*aufgelaufene Zinsen mpl*
administrative expenses	*Verwaltungskosten pl*
all-in rate	*Inklusivpreis m*
allocation of overheads	*Geschäftskostenaufteilung f*
allow *(discount)*	*geben*
allow *(time)*	*zugestehen*
allowance *(on balance sheet)*	*Abschreibung f*
allowance *(tax)*	*Steuerfreibetrag m*
allowance *(discount)*	*Preisnachlaß m*
amortization	*Amortisation f*
annual report	*Jahresbericht m*
anticipated profit	*erwarteter Gewinn m*
appreciate	*eine Wertsteigerung erfahren*
appreciation	*Wertsteigerung f*
appropriation	*Bereitstellung f*
appropriation account	*Gewinnverteilungskonto nt*
arrears	*Rückstände mpl*
assets *(property)*	*Vermögenswerte mpl*
assets *(on balance sheet)*	*Aktiva pl*
audit *n*	*Wirtschaftsprüfung f*
audit *vb*	*prüfen*

to keep the accounts *die Bücher führen, die Buchführung machen*
the total amount payable is ... *die zu zahlende Gesamtsumme beträgt ...*
to fall into arrears *in Rückstand kommen, in (Zahlungs)verzug geraten*
to carry out a complete audit *eine Revision durchführen*

auditor	*Wirtschaftsprüfer(in)* m *(f)*
average cost	*Durchschnittskosten* pl
average fixed cost	*durchschnittliche Fixkosten* pl
average variable cost	*durchschnittliche variable Kosten pl*
backdate	*rückdatieren*
bad debt	*uneinbringliche Forderung* f
balance n	*Bilanz* f
balance vb	*ausgleichen*
balance in hand	*Kassenbestand* m
balance sheet	*Bilanzaufstellung* f
bank(er's) draft	*Banktratte* f
bill n	*Rechnung* f
bill vb	*fakturieren*
bill of exchange	*Wechsel* m
bills payable	*Wechselverbindlichkeiten* fpl
bills receivable	*Wechselforderungen* fpl
book-keeping	*Buchführung* f
break-even analysis	*Break-Even-Analyse* f
break-even point	*Break-Even-Punkt* m
budget n	*Haushaltsplan* m
budget vb (prepare a budget)	*den Haushaltsplan* m *aufstellen*
budgetary control	*Haushaltskontrolle* f
budget period	*Haushaltsperiode* f
capital account	*Kapitalverkehrsbilanz* f
capital budget	*Investitionsplan* m
capital charges	*Kapitalkosten* pl
capital employed	*arbeitendes Kapital* nt
capital expenditure	*Kapitalaufwand* m
capital formation	*Kapitalbildung* f
capital gains	*Kapitalgewinn* m
capital goods	*Kapitalgüter* ntpl
capital-intensive	*kapitalintensiv*
capital investment	*Kapitalanlage* f
cash account	*Kassenkonto* nt
cashbook	*Kassenbuch* nt

your salary increase will be backdated to May *Ihre Gehaltserhöhung wird auf Mai rückdatiert*
to balance the books *die Bilanz machen*
the books/accounts don't balance *die Bilanz/Abrechnung stimmt nicht*
to be £1 million in the black *mit £1 Million in den schwarzen Zahlen sein*
to keep to budget *das Budget einhalten*
to go over budget *den Etat überschreiten*
we are budgeting for losses/sales of ... *wir veranschlagen Verluste/einen Umsatz von ...*

cash flow	*Cash-flow m*
cash-flow statement	*Cash-flow Aufstellung f*
cash reserves	*Bargeldreserven fpl*
certified accountant	*öffentlich zugelassener Wirtschaftsprüfer m, öffentlich zugelassene Wirtschaftsprüferin f*
chartered accountant (CA)	*Wirtschaftsprüfer(in) m(f)*
circulating capital	*Umlaufkapital nt*
collateral	*Sicherheit f*
consolidated accounts	*Konzernabschluß m*
consolidated balance sheet	*konsolidierte Bilanz f*
consolidation	*Konsolidierung f*
cost *n*	*Kosten pl*
cost *vb (have a price)*	*kosten*
cost *vb (calculate cost of)*	*Kosten pl berechnen*
cost accountant	*Kalkulator(in) m(f)*
cost accounting	*Kostenrechnung f*
cost-benefit analysis	*Kostennutzenanalyse f*
cost control	*Kostenkontrolle f*
cost-effective	*kostenwirksam*
cost-effectiveness	*Kostenrentabilität f*
costing	*Kalkulation f*
cost-plus pricing	*Berechnung f der Herstellungskosten plus Unternehmergewinn*
credit *n (loan, deferred payment)*	*Kredit m*
credit *n (in account)*	*Guthaben nt*
credit *vb*	*gutschreiben*
credit balance	*Kreditsaldo m*
credit control	*Kreditkontrolle f*
credit limit	*Kreditgrenze f*
credit note	*Gutschrift f*
creditor	*Gläubiger(in) m(f)*
credit transfer	*bargeldlose Überweisung f*
current assets	*Umlaufvermögen nt*
current cost accounting	*inflationsbereinigte Bilanzierung f*
current liabilities	*kurzfristige Verbindlichkeiten fpl*
daybook	*Journal nt*

in duplicate/in triplicate/in 5 copies *in zweifacher/dreifacher/fünffacher Ausführung*
to do something as a cost-cutting exercise *etwas zur Kosteneinsparung tun*

debenture	*Obligation f*
debit	*Soll nt*
debit balance	*Debetsaldo m*
debit note	*Lastschriftanzeige f*
debtor	*Schuldner(in) m(f)*
defer	*aufschieben*
deferred	*aufgeschoben*
deposit *(advance payment)*	*Anzahlung f*
deposit *(in bank)*	*Einzahlung f*
depreciate	*im Wert m sinken*
depreciation	*Wertminderung f*
direct cost	*direkte Kosten pl*
distribution costs	*Absatzkosten pl*
draft accounts	*vorläufige Abrechnung f*
drawer	*Aussteller(in) m(f)*
due date	*Fälligkeitsdatum nt*
earned income	*Arbeitseinkommen nt*
earnest money	*Angeld nt*
economize	*sparen*
entry	*Eintragung f*
equity capital	*Eigenkapital nt*
estimate *n*	*Voranschlag m*
estimate *vb*	*schätzen*
estimator	*Schätzer(in) m(f)*
ex gratia payment	*Kulanzzahlung f*
expenditure	*Aufwand m*
expenses	*Spesen pl*
external auditor	*außerbetrieblicher Wirtschaftsprüfer m*
fee	*Gebühr f*
final demand	*letzte Zahlungsaufforderung f*
financial statement	*Bilanz f*
financial year	*Geschäftsjahr nt*
fixed assets	*feste Anlagen fpl*
fixed charge	*feststehende Belastung f*
forecast *n*	*Vorausberechnung f*
forecast *vb*	*vorausberechnen*

to agree to defer payment for 60 days/until the end of next month *einem Zahlungsaufschub von 60 Tagen/bis Ende nächsten Monats zustimmen*
we have noted an error and would be grateful if you would amend your invoice *Ihre Rechnung weist einen Fehler auf, und wir wären Ihnen dankbar, wenn Sie diese entsprechend berichtigen würden*
we are sorry for this error and enclose a credit note for the sum involved *wir entschuldigen uns für den Irrtum und fügen eine Gutschrift über die entsprechende Summe bei*

forward contract	Terminabschluß m, Terminkontrakt m
frozen assets	eingefrorene Guthaben ntpl
general audit	Buchprüfung f
gross profit	Bruttogewinn m
gross sales	Bruttoumsatz m
half-yearly	halbjährlich
idle money	brachliegendes Kapital nt
incidental expenses	Nebenkosten pl
income	Einnahmen fpl
income and expenditure account	Gewinn-und-Verlustrechnung f
instalment	Rate f
integrated accounting package	integriertes Buchführungspaket nt
interim accounts	Zwischenkonten ntpl
internal audit	betriebsinterne Buchprüfung f
internal auditor	betriebsinterner Wirtschaftsprüfer m
investment income	Erträge mpl aus Anlagen fpl
invisible assets	unsichtbare Vermögenswerte mpl
invoice n	Rechnung f
invoice vb	fakturieren
labour costs	Lohnkosten pl
ledger	Hauptbuch nt
letter of credit	Akkreditiv nt
liabilities	Passiva pl
liquidity	Liquidität f
management accountant	Bilanzbuchhalter(in) m(f) für besondere Bedürfnisse der Betriebsführung
management accounting	Buchführung f für besondere Bedürfnisse der Betriebsführung
marginal cost	Grenzkosten pl
materials	Material nt
monies due	ausstehende Gelder ntpl

to invoice a customer einem Kunden m/einer Kundin f eine Rechnung ausstellen
to invoice goods Waren in Rechnung stellen
on your invoice dated 15 October auf Ihrer Rechnung vom 15. Oktober
please find enclosed our invoice no. 151058 anbei unsere Rechnung Nr. 151058
to go into liquidation in Liquidation treten

monthly instalment	*Monatsrate f*
national insurance contributions	*Sozialversicherungsbeiträge mpl*
negative cash flow	*Überhang m der Zahlungsausgänge mpl*
net assets	*Reinvermögen nt*
net loss	*Nettoverlust m*
net profit	*Nettogewinn m*
non-payment	*Nichtzahlung f*
operating costs	*Betriebskosten pl*
operating profit	*Betriebsgewinn m*
operating statement	*Betriebsergebnisrechnung f*
outgoings	*Ausgaben fpl*
output, outturn	*Ertrag m*
overhead absorption	*Übernahme f der Gemeinkosten*
overheads	*Gemeinkosten pl*
overspend	*zuviel ausgeben*
paper profit	*rechnerischer Gewinn m*
part payment	*Teilzahlung f*
pay *n*	*Gehälter ntpl*
pay *vb*	*zahlen*
payable at sight	*zahlbar bei Sicht f*
payable in advance	*im voraus zahlbar*
payable on demand	*zahlbar bei Sicht f*
payee	*Zahlungsempfänger(in) m(f)*
payment in full	*volle Zahlung f*
payment on invoice	*Zahlung f bei Rechnungsvorlage*
pay out	*ausgeben*
petty cash book	*Bargeldkassenbuch nt*
plant cost	*Betriebsunkosten pl*
pledge *n*	*Pfand nt*
positive cash flow	*Überhang m der Zahlungseingänge mpl*
profit	*Gewinn m*
profitable	*rentabel, gewinnbringend*
profit and loss account	*Gewinn-und-Verlustrechnung f*
profit centre	*Bilanzeinheit f*

payable at 90 days *or* **within 90 days of invoice** *zahlbar innerhalb von 90 Tagen nach Ausstellung der Rechnung*
they are slow payers *sie sind säumige Zahler*
payment to be made by *Zahlung fällig am*
we would appreciate immediate/prompt payment *wir möchten Sie um sofortige/prompte Zahlung bitten*
the department is showing an increased/a reduced profit *die Abteilung arbeitet mit größerem/geringerem Gewinn*

profit-making	*rentabel*
pro-forma invoice	*Pro-forma-Rechnung f*
pro rata *adj, adv*	*anteilmäßig*
provision	*Rückstellung f*
quarterly	*vierteljährlich*
quotation	*Kostenvoranschlag m*
quote *n*	*Kostenvoranschlag m*
quote *vb (price)*	*nennen*
rate of return	*Rendite f*
rationalization	*Rationalisierung f*
rationalize	*rationalisieren*
reallocation of resources	*Neuverteilung f der Ressourcen fpl*
receivable	*ausstehend*
replacement cost	*Wiederbeschaffungskosten pl*
reserves *npl*	*Rücklage f, Reserven fpl*
return on capital	*Kapitalverzinsung f*
revenue	*Einnahmen fpl*
revenue account	*Ertragskonto nt*
revenue expenditure	*Betriebsausgabe(n) f(pl)*
revolving credit	*Revolving-Kredit m*
running costs	*laufende Kosten pl*
salary	*Gehalt nt*
settle *(balance)*	*ausgleichen*
settle *(pay)*	*begleichen*
share capital	*Aktienkapital nt*
single-entry bookkeeping	*einfache Buchführung f*
sinking fund	*Tilgungsfonds m*
solvency	*Solvenz f*
solvent	*solvent*
standard cost	*Standardkosten pl*
statement (of account)	*Kontoauszug m*
stock *(in warehouse)*	*Lagerbestand m*
taxable	*steuerpflichtig*
tax year	*Steuerjahr nt*
terms of payment	*Zahlungsbedingungen fpl*
trade reference	*Kreditauskunft f*
trading account	*Betriebskonto nt*
treasury bill	*kurzfristiger Schatzwechsel m*
turnover	*Umsatz m*
undischarged debt	*unbeglichene Schuld f*

to be £1 million in the red *mit £1 Million in den roten Zahlen sein*
in round figures *aufgerundet or abgerundet*
what state are the company's finances in? *wie sieht es mit den Finanzen der Firma aus?*

unearned income	*Einkünfte fpl aus Kapitalvermögen nt*
unit cost	*Kosten pl pro Einheit f*
unit price	*Preis m pro Einheit f*
unpaid	*unbezahlt*
update *n*	*Aktualisierung f*
update *vb*	*aktualisieren, auf den neuesten Stand m bringen*
variance	*Abweichung f*
venture capital	*Risikokapital nt*
voucher	*Beleg m*
wage	*Lohn m*
waste of resources	*Wertminderung f der Ressourcen fpl*
working capital	*Betriebskapital nt*
work in progress	*im Gang befindliche Arbeit f*
write-off *n*	*Abschreibung f*
write off *vb*	*abschreiben*

See also **MARKETING AND PR**

above-the-line advertising expenditure	*Kosten* pl *der Herstellung von Werbung*
account *(client)*	*Kunde* m, *Kundin* f
account executive	*Kundenbetreuer(in)* m *(f)*
actor	*Schauspieler(in)* m *(f)*
ad	*Anzeige* f
adult audience	*Erwachsenenpublikum* nt
adult publishing	*auf Erwachsenenliteratur spezialisiertes Verlagswesen* nt
advertise	*werben*
advertisement	*Anzeige* f
advertiser	*Inserent(in)* m *(f)*
advertising	*Werbung* f
advertising agency	*Werbeagentur* f
advertising allowance	*Anzeigenrabatt* m
advertising brief	*Einsatzbesprechung* f
advertising budget	*Anzeigenetat* m
advertising campaign	*Werbekampagne* f
advertising manager	*Werbeleiter(in)* m *(f)*
advertising media	*Werbeträger* m inv
advertising rates	*Anzeigentarif* m
advertising space	*Anzeigenraum* m
advertising standards	*Grundsätze* mpl *ethischer Werbung*
advertising strategy	*Werbestrategie* f
agent *(literary)*	*(literarischer) Agent* m
agent *(theatrical)*	*Agent* m
article	*Artikel* m
artwork	*Design* nt
audience figures *(TV, radio)*	*Einschaltquote* f
audience figures *(magazine)*	*Leserzahlen* fpl
audience research	*Publikumsforschung* f
Audit Bureau of Circulation	*Organisation* f *zur Feststellung der Verbreitung von Werbeträgern*
author	*Autor(in)* m *(f)*
bestseller	*Bestseller* m

to advertise on TV/on the radio/in the press *im Fernsehen/im Radio/in der Presse werben*
what are your advertising rates? *wie ist Ihr Anzeigentarif?*
to increase the public's awareness of the product *die Aufmerksamkeit der Öffentlichkeit für das Produkt verstärken*

bestselling author	*Erfolgsautor(in) m (f)*
bi-annual, bi-annually	*zweimal jährlich*
billboard	*Reklametafel f*
billing	*Umsatz m einer Werbeagentur*
bi-monthly *adj (twice a month)*	*vierzehntäglich*
bi-monthly *adj (every two months)*	*zweimonatlich*
bi-monthly *adv (twice a month)*	*zweimal im Monat m*
bi-monthly *adv (every two months)*	*alle zwei Monate mpl*
blanket coverage	*Sättigungsreichweite f*
body copy	*Textteil m*
bold type	*Fettdruck m*
book rights	*Buchrechte ntpl*
brand awareness	*Markenbewußtsein nt*
brand image	*Markenimage nt*
broadcast *n*	*Sendung f*
broadcast *vb*	*senden*
broadcasting *(television)*	*Fernsehen nt*
broadcasting *(radio)*	*Rundfunk m*
broadsheet	*großformatige Zeitung f*
business section *(in newspaper)*	*Wirtschaftsteil m*
cable television	*Kabelfernsehen nt*
camera *(for photos)*	*Fotoapparat m*
camera *(cinema, TV)*	*Kamera f*
cameraman	*Kameramann m*
capital (letter)	*Großbuchstabe m*
caption	*Bildunterschrift f*
cassette	*Kassette f*
CD (compact disc)	*CD f (Compact-disc f)*
centre spread	*doppelseitige Anzeige f*
children's publishing	*auf Kinderbücher spezialisiertes Verlagswesen nt*
cinema	*Kino nt*
circulation	*Auflage(nhöhe) f*
classified advertisements	*Kleinanzeigen fpl*
comedy	*Komödie f*
commercial *n*	*Werbesendung f*
commercial *adj*	*kommerziell*
commercial break	*Programmunterbrechung f für Werbung*
copy *n (of book, magazine)*	*Exemplar nt*
copy *n (text)*	*Werbetext m*
copywriter	*Werbetexter(in) m (f)*
corporate advertising	*Firmenwerbung f*

cover price	*Einzelhandelspreis m*
creative department	*Kreativabteilung f*
customer profile	*Kundenprofil nt*
daily	*täglich*
daily (newspaper)	*Tageszeitung f*
designer	*Designer(in) m(f)*
desktop publishing (DTP)	*Desktop-Publishing nt (DTP nt)*
direct-mail advertising	*Postwurfwerbung f*
display advertising	*Großanzeigenwerbung f*
docudrama	*Dokumentarspiel nt*
documentary	*Dokumentarbericht m*
double-page spread	*doppelseitige Anzeige f*
down-market	*für den Massenmarkt m*
draft *n*	*Entwurf m*
drama series	*Spielfilmserie f*
edit *(newspaper, magazine)*	*herausgeben*
edit *(text)*	*überarbeiten*
edit *(film)*	*cutten*
euro-ad	*europaweiter Werbespot m*
exclusive (story)	*Exklusivbericht m*
feature film	*Spielfilm m*
feature-length	*mit Spielfilmlänge f*
film *n*	*Film m*
film *vb*	*filmen*
film crew	*Film Crew f*
film industry	*Filmindustrie f*
film rights	*Filmrechte ntpl*
freesheet	*Anzeigenblatt nt*
glossy magazine	*Hochglanzmagazin nt*
hard-hitting	*aggressiv*
hoarding	*Reklamewand f*
independent TV company	*unabhängige Fernsehanstalt f*
insert *n*	*Beilage f*
insert *vb*	*einlegen*
ISBN (international standard book number)	*ISBN f*
italic	*kursiv*
jingle *(with words)*	*gesungener Werbeslogan m*
jingle *(without words)*	*Werbemelodie f*
journalist	*Journalist(in) m(f)*
leaflet	*Prospekt m*

to endorse a product *ein Produkt unterstützen*
she is handling the Smith account *sie betreut die Firma Smith*
to launch a new publication *eine neue Zeitschrift herausbringen*

logo	*Logo nt*
magazine	*Zeitschrift f*
manufacturing costs	*Herstellungskosten pl*
mass-market *adj*	*für den Massenmarkt m, für die Massen fpl*
mass media	*Massenmedien ntpl*
media	*Medien ntpl*
media analysis	*Medienanalyse f*
media buyer	*Streuplaner(in) m(f)*
media coverage	*Berichterstattung f in den Medien*
media interest	*Medieninteresse nt*
media planner	*Medienplaner(in) m(f)*
media research	*Medienforschung f*
microphone	*Mikrofon nt*
mid-market	*mittelmäßig*
monthly	*monatlich*
monthly (magazine)	*Monatszeitschrift f*
music industry	*Musikindustrie f*
national press	*überregionale Presse f*
newspaper	*Zeitung f*
niche publishing	*auf Marktlücken spezialisiertes Verlagswesen nt*
packaging	*Verpackung f*
paste-up *n*	*Klebeumbruch m*
periodical	*Zeitschrift f*
photo call	*Fototermin m*
photograph *n*	*Fotografie f*
photograph *vb*	*fotografieren*
photographer	*Fotograf(in) m(f)*
photo opportunity	*Fotogelegenheit f*

to get the media interested in something *das Interesse der Medien für etwas erwecken*

to increase media awareness of something *Medienbewußtsein für etwas verstärken*

our new product is getting good media coverage *über unser neues Produkt wird ausführlich in den Medien berichtet*

to attract media interest (in a product) *das Interesse der Medien (für ein Produkt) gewinnen*

he/she has a strong media presence *es wird viel über ihn/sie in den Medien berichtet*

to get a mention in a publication *in einer Zeitschrift erwähnt werden*

please listen to/look at this and give me your opinion *bitte hören Sie sich das an/schauen Sie sich das an und sagen Sie mir, was Sie davon halten*

point-of-sale advertising	*Werbung f am Verkaufsort m*
poster	*Plakat nt*
postproduction	*Arbeiten fpl nach Drehschluß m*
(the) press	*(die) Presse f*
press agent	*Presseagent(in) m(f)*
press call	*Pressetermin m*
press conference	*Pressekonferenz f*
press officer	*Pressesprecher(in) m(f)*
press release	*Presseverlautbarung f*
preview *n*	*Vorschau f*
prime time	*Hauptsendezeit f*
produce *vb*	*produzieren*
producer	*Produzent(in) m(f)*
production company	*Produktionsgesellschaft f*
programme *(TV, radio)*	*Sendung f*
prospectus	*Prospekt m, Werbeschrift f*
public	*Öffentlichkeit f*
publication *(act of publishing)*	*Publizieren nt, Veröffentlichung f*
publication *(title)*	*Veröffentlichung f*
publication date	*Erscheinungsdatum nt*
publicity	*Publicity f*
publicize	*werben, bekanntmachen*
publish	*veröffentlichen*
publisher	*Verleger(in) m(f)*
publishing *(industry)*	*Verlagswesen nt*
publishing house	*Verlag m*
pulp fiction	*Schundliteratur f*
quality fiction	*anspruchsvolle Erzählliteratur f*
quarterly	*vierteljährlich*
quarterly *(magazine)*	*Vierteljahresschrift f*
radio	*Radio nt*
ratings	*Einschaltquote f*
reach *n*	*Reichweite f*
reach *vb*	*erreichen*
record *n (disc)*	*Schallplatte f, Platte f*
record *vb*	*aufnehmen*
recording studio	*Aufnahmestudio nt*
reference publishing	*auf Nachschlagewerke spezialisiertes Verlagswesen nt*

to place an advert in a publication *eine Anzeige in eine Zeitschrift setzen*
the ad is going out during prime time *der Werbespot wird während der Hauptsendezeit gesendet*
the public response was very promising *die Reaktion der Öffentlichkeit war äußerst vielversprechend*

review *n*	*Rezension f*
review *vb*	*besprechen, rezensieren*
review copy	*Rezensionsexemplar nt*
rights	*Rechte ntpl*
roman	*Antiqua f*
royalties	*Tantiemen fpl*
satellite	*Satellit m*
satellite TV	*Satellitenfernsehen nt*
sequel	*Fortsetzung f*
serial *(TV)*	*Fernsehserie f*
serialize	*in Fortsetzungen fpl veröffentlichen*
series	*Serie f*
short film	*Kurzfilm m*
single-column spread *(advert)*	*einspaltige Anzeige f*
slogan	*Slogan m*
sloped roman	*kursive Antiqua f*
sneak preview	*inoffizielle Premiere f, Sneak Preview m*
solus	*alleinstehende Anzeige f*
sound engineer	*Toningenieur(in) m(f)*
sponsor *n*	*Sponsor(in) m(f)*
sponsor *vb*	*sponsern*
spot	*Werbespot m*
subliminal advertising	*unterschwellige Werbung f*
Sunday newspaper	*Sonntagszeitung f*
Sunday supplement	*Sonntagsbeilage f*
synopsis	*Zusammenfassung f*
tabloid	*Boulevardblatt nt*
target *vb*	*abzielen auf*
target audience	*Zielgruppe f*
targeting	*Zielsetzung f*
target market	*Zielmarkt m*
teaser	*Neugier weckende Werbung f*
teenage publishing	*auf Jugendliteratur spezialisiertes Verlagswesen nt*
teletext	*Videotext m*
television	*Fernsehen nt*
television company	*Fernsehgesellschaft f*

they want the UK rights for ... *sie wollen die UK-Rechte für ...*
they are running the ad all this week *die Anzeige erscheint die ganze Woche über*
to sponsor a sporting event *eine Sportveranstaltung sponsern*
we are targeting young people *wir zielen auf junge Leute ab*

television film	*Fernsehfilm m*
television rights	*Übertragungsrechte ntpl*
testimonial	*Empfehlung f*
time slot	*Sendezeit f*
title	*Titel m*
trade press	*Fachpresse f*
typeface	*Schrift f*
up-market	*anspruchsvoll*
video *(film)*	*Video nt*
video *(cassette)*	*Videokassette f*
video camera	*Videokamera f*
viewing figures	*Einschaltquote f*
weekly	*wöchentlich*
weekly **(magazine/newspaper)**	*Wochenzeitschrift f*
young audience	*junges Publikum nt*

the central theme of a campaign *das Leitmotiv einer Kampagne*

Banking hours in Austria, Germany, Luxembourg and Switzerland
are generally as follows (Monday to Friday):-

Austria	08.00–12.30/13.30–15.00
	Thursdays till 17.30
Germany	09.00–12.00/13.30–15.30
	Thursdays till 17.30
Luxembourg	09.00–17.00
	Some banks are also open all day on Saturday
Switzerland	08.00–12.30/13.30–16.30
	Fridays till 18.00 or 18.30

If you simply want to cash traveller's cheques or change money, a
bureau de change or your hotel will probably be more convenient
and the commission may not be much higher. Before using your
credit card in a hotel or restaurant it is wide to check that it will be
accepted. Credit cards and Eurocheque cards are not as widely
used in Germany and Austria as in the UK and it is best not to let
your reserve of cash run too low. It is advisable to carry your
passport as well as your Eurocheque card for all banking opera-
tions as you may be asked to show it as proof of identity.

For a vocabulary list of banking terms, see **BANKING AND FINANCE**

PHRASES USED BY THE CUSTOMER

Where's the nearest bank/cash dispenser? *wo ist die nächste
Bank/der nächste Geldautomat?*
The account is in the name of Chalmers *das Konto läuft unter
dem Namen Chalmers*
I have an account with ... *ich habe ein Konto bei ...*
Do you have an agreement with ...? *haben Sie ein Abkommen mit
...?*
What is the charge for that service? *was kostet dieser Service?*
Do you cash traveller's cheques? *lösen Sie Reiseschecks ein?*
Do you change money? *wechseln Sie Geld?*
Can I cash a cheque/make a deposit here? *kann ich hier einen
Scheck einlösen/Geld einzahlen?*
To withdraw money from an account *Geld von einem Konto ab-
heben*
To deposit money in/pay money into an account *Geld auf ein
Konto einzahlen*
Can I withdraw cash on my credit card? *kann ich mit meiner Kre-
ditkarte Geld abheben?*
How much can I withdraw per day? *wieviel kann ich pro Tag ab-*

heben?

How long will the cheque take to clear? *wielange dauert das Verrechnen des Schecks?*

Who should I make the cheque out to? *auf welchen Namen soll ich den Scheck ausstellen?*

I'd like to open an account *ich möchte ein Konto eröffnen*

I'd like to close my account *ich möchte mein Konto auflösen*

What is the interest rate on that account? *wie hoch sind die Zinsen bei diesem Konto?*

Your cash dispenser isn't working *Ihr Geldautomat funktioniert nicht*

Your cash dispenser has swallowed my card *Ihr Geldautomat hat meine Karte geschluckt*

PHRASES USED BY THE BANK

Wir haben ein Abkommen mit ... *we have an agreement with ...*

Ihre Kunden können unsere Dienste kostenlos/gegen eine Gebühr von ... in Ansprach nehmen *their customers can use our services free of charge/for a charge of ...*

Für diesen Service wird eine Gebühr berechnet *there is a charge for that service*

Wir können diesen Scheck leider nicht einlösen *I'm sorry, we can't cash this cheque*

Diese Karte nehmen wir leider nicht an *I'm sorry, we don't accept those cards*

Die Verrechnung dieses Schecks dauert fünf Tage *the cheque will take five working days to clear*

Rechnen Sie fünf Tage für die Verrechnung des Schecks ein *allow five days for the cheque to clear*

Der Betrag wird Ihrem Konto nächsten Montag/am 1. Juli gutgeschrieben *your account will be credited next Monday/on 1 July*

Tut mir leid, aber der Scheck ist geplatzt *I'm sorry, but the cheque bounced*

Stellen Sie den Scheck auf den Namen ... aus *make the cheque out to ...*

Haben Sie irgendeinen anderen Ausweis? *do you have any other form of identity?*

Der Zinssatz für dieses Konto ist 11.5% netto/brutto *the interest rate on that account is 11.5% net/gross*

See also **ACCOUNTS AND PAYMENTS, AT THE BANK, ECONOMICS** and **INVESTMENTS**

acceptance	*Akzept nt*
accommodate	*eine Übergangsfinanzierung f gewähren*
accommodation	*Übergangsfinanzierung f*
accommodation bill	*Gefälligkeitswechsel m*
accommodation party	*Gefälligkeitszeichner(in) m (f)*
account	*Konto nt*
account number	*Kontonummer f*
accrual	*Anfall m*
accrued charges	*aufgelaufene Kosten pl*
accrued interest	*aufgelaufene Zinsen mpl*
act of bankruptcy	*Konkurshandlung f*
allocation of overheads	*Geschäftskostenaufteilung f*
amortization	*Amortisation f*
annual percentage rate (APR)	*Jahreszinssatz m*
annual return *(report)*	*Jahresbericht m*
anticipated profit	*erwarteter Gewinn m*
appreciate	*eine Wertsteigerung f erfahren*
appreciation	*Wertsteigerung f*
arrears	*Rückstände mpl*
arrestment	*Sperren nt*
assets	*Vermögenswerte mpl*
asset-stripping	*Aufkauf m eines Unternehmens und anschließender Verkauf einzelner Teile*
authorized capital	*autorisiertes Aktienkapital nt*
automated telling machine (ATM)	*Geldautomat m*
backer	*Geldgeber(in) m (f)*
backing	*Unterstützung f*
back-to-back loan	*Gegenakkreditiv nt*
bad debt	*uneinbringliche Forderung f*
balance *n*	*Kontostand m*
balance *vb*	*ausgleichen*
bank *n*	*Bank f*
bank *vb (money)*	*einzahlen*
bank with ...	*ein Konto bei ... haben*
bank account	*Bankkonto nt*
bankbook	*Sparbuch nt*

to look for/obtain backing for something *finanzielle Unterstützung für etwas suchen/erhalten*

bank charges	*Bankgebühren fpl*
bank deposit	*Bankeinlage f*
bank(er's) draft	*Banktratte f*
banker	*Bankier m*
banker's card	*Scheckkarte f*
banker's reference	*Bankauskunft f*
Bank for International Settlements (BIS)	*Bank f für Internationalen Zahlungsausgleich (BIZ f)*
bank giro credit	*Überweisungsauftrag m*
bank holiday	*öffentlicher Feiertag m*
banking *(profession)*	*Bankwesen nt*
banking facilities/services	*Bankdienstleistungen fpl*
bank loan	*Bankkredit m*
bank manager	*Bankdirektor(in) m(f)*
banknote	*Banknote f, Geldschein m*
Bank of England	*Bank of England f*
bank rate	*Diskontsatz m*
bankrupt *adj*	*bankrott*
go bankrupt	*Bankrott machen*
bankruptcy	*Bankrott m*
bank statement	*Kontoauszug m*
base rate	*Eckzins m*
basket of currencies	*Währungskorb m*
bearer	*Inhaber(in) m(f)*
bearer bill	*Inhaberwechsel m*
benchmark	*Maßstab m*
bid *n*	*Angebot nt*
bid *vb*	*bieten*
bill-broker	*Wechselmakler(in) m(f)*
bill of exchange	*Wechsel m*
blacklist *n*	*schwarze Liste f*
blacklist *vb*	*auf die schwarze Liste setzen*
blue-chip investment	*sichere Wertpapieranlage f*
book value	*Buchwert m*
borrow	*sich (dat) leihen*
borrower	*Kreditnehmer(in) m(f)*
borrowing	*Kreditaufnahme f*
branch	*Zweigstelle f*
branch manager	*Zweigstellenleiter(in) m(f)*

to put in a bid for something *ein Angebot für etwas einreichen*
to go out of business *bankrott machen*
this company has capital of £20 million *diese Firma hat ein Kapital von £20 Million*

break even	*kostendeckend arbeiten*
break-even point	*Break-Even-Punkt m*
break-up value	*Liquidationswert m*
bridging loan	*Überbrückungskredit m*
building society	*Bausparkasse f*
buoyant	*steigend*
buy out	*aufkaufen*
capital	*Kapital nt*
capital account	*Kapitalverkehrsbilanz f*
capital allowance	*Anlagenabschreibung f*
capital assets	*Kapitalvermögen nt*
capital expenditure	*Kapitalaufwand m*
capital gains	*Kapitalgewinn m*
capital goods	*Kapitalgüter ntpl*
capital-intensive	*kapitalintensiv*
capital investment	*Kapitalanlage f*
cash n	*Bargeld nt*
cash vb (cheque)	*einlösen*
cash account	*Kassenkonto nt*
cash card	*Geldautomatenkarte f*
cash dispenser	*Geldautomat m*
cash flow	*Cash-flow m*
cashier	*Schalterbeamter m,*
	Schalterbeamtin f
cash-in-hand	*Barbestand m*
cash reserves	*Bargeldreserven fpl*
central bank	*Zentralbank f, Notenbank f*
cheap money	*billiges Geld nt*
cheque	*Scheck m*
cheque (guarantee) card	*Scheckkarte f*
circulating capital	*Umlaufkapital nt*
clearing bank	*Clearingbank f*
clearing house	*Clearingstelle f*
collateral	*Sicherheit f*
collecting bank	*Inkassobank f*
commercial bank	*Handelsbank f*
compound interest	*Zinseszins m*
contingent liabilities	*Eventualverbindlichkeiten fpl*
convertible currency	*konvertierbare Währung f*
convertible loan stock	*konvertierbarer Anleihestock m*
corporate planning	*Unternehmensplanung f*
cost control	*Kostenkontrolle f*
costing	*Kalkulation f*
countersign	*gegenzeichnen*
counter staff	*Bankangestellten m/fpl*

credit *n (loan, deferred payment)*	*Kredit m*
credit *n (in account)*	*Guthaben nt*
credit *vb*	*gutschreiben*
credit agency	*Kreditauskunftei f*
credit balance	*Kreditsaldo m*
credit card	*Kreditkarte f*
credit facilities	*Kreditmöglichkeiten fpl*
credit limit	*Kreditgrenze f*
creditor	*Gläubiger(in) m(f)*
credit rating	*Einschätzung f der Kreditwürdigkeit f*
credit transfer	*bargeldlose Überweisung f*
crossed cheque	*Verrechnungsscheck m*
current account	*Girokonto nt*
current assets	*Umlaufvermögen nt*
current liabilities	*kurzfristige Verbindlichkeiten fpl*
cut back *vb*	*kürzen*
cutback *n*	*Kürzung f*
dear money	*teures Geld nt*
debenture	*Obligation f*
debenture capital	*Anleihekapital nt*
debit	*Soll nt*
debit balance	*Debetsaldo m*
debit note	*Lastschriftanzeige f*
debt	*Schuld f*
debt collection agency	*Inkassobüro nt*
debtor	*Schuldner(in) m(f)*
deferred annuity	*Anwartschaftsrente f*
deferred creditor	*nicht bevorrechtigter Gläubiger m*
deficit	*Defizit nt*
denomination	*Nennwert m*
deposit *n*	*Einzahlung f*
deposit *vb*	*einzahlen*
deposit account	*Sparkonto nt*
deposit receipt	*Einzahlungsbestätigung f*
deposit slip	*Einzahlungsbeleg m*
devaluation	*Abwertung f*
direct debit	*Einzugsauftrag m*
discounted cash flow *(method)*	*Barwertrechnung f*
downward trend	*rückläufige Tendenz f*
drawee	*Bezogene(r) f(m)*
drawer	*Aussteller(in) m(f)*

to be in debt *verschuldet sein*

earnings	*Verdienst m, Einkommen nt*
earnings per share	*Gewinn m je Aktie f*
easy money	*billiges Geld nt*
electronic funds transfer (EFT)	*elektronischer Zahlungsverkehr m (EZV m)*
encash	*einlösen*
endorse	*indossieren*
endorsee	*Indossat m*
endorser	*Indossant m*
Eurocheque	*Eurocheque m*
Eurocheque card	*Eurocheque-Karte f*
exchange control	*Devisenkontrolle f*
exchange rate	*Wechselkurs m*
Exchange Rate Mechanism (ERM)	*Wechselkursmechanismus m*
expenditure	*Aufwand m*
factoring	*Factoring nt*
finance *(world of)*	*Finanzwelt f, Finanzwesen nt*
finance *(backing)*	*Unterstützung f*
finance company	*Finanz(ierungs)gesellschaft f*
financial management	*Finanzmanagement nt*
financial risk	*finanzielles Risiko nt*
financial statement	*Bilanz f*
financial year	*Geschäftsjahr nt*
financier	*Finanzier m*
financing	*Finanzierung f*
fiscal year	*Steuerjahr nt*
fixed assets	*feste Anlagen fpl*
fixed charge	*feststehende Belastung f*
floating capital	*Umlaufkapital nt*
floating charge	*schwebende Belastung f*
flotation	*Auflegung f*
foreclose	*Zwangsvollstreckung f betreiben*
foreclosure	*Zwangsvollstreckung f*
foreign exchange *(currency)*	*Devisen fpl*
foreign exchange *(system)*	*Devisenhandel m*
foreign exchange broker	*Devisenmakler(in) m(f)*
foreign exchange dealer	*Devisenhändler(in) m(f)*

to expand into new markets *in neue Märkte vorstoßen*
to finance a project *ein Projekt finanzieren*
to get the necessary finance for a project *die nötige finanzielle Unterstützung für ein Projekt bekommen*
to seek/obtain/provide financial assistance *finanzielle Unterstützung suchen/erhalten/geben*
financially sound/unsound *kapitalkräftig/kapitalschwach*

foreign exchange market	Devisenmarkt m
forward exchange	Termindevisen pl
forward integration	Aufkauf m der Kundenfirmen
forward rate	Devisenterminkurs m
free currency	frei konvertierbare Währung f
frozen account	Sperrkonto nt
frozen assets	eingefrorene Guthaben ntpl
going concern	Unternehmen nt in vollem Betrieb m
handling charge	Bearbeitungsgebühr f
hard currency	harte Währung f
high-interest account	Konto nt mit hohem Zinssatz m
holding company	Holdinggesellschaft f
horizontal integration	horizontale Integration f
idle money	brachliegendes Kapital nt
indemnity	Entschädigung f
insolvency	Insolvenz f, Zahlungsunfähigkeit f
insolvent	zahlungsunfähig
interest	Zinsen pl
interest-earning account	Zinsenkonto nt
interest-free credit	zinsloses Darlehen nt
interest-free loan	zinsloses Darlehen nt
interest rate	Zinssatz m
international division	internationale Abteilung f
investment	Investition f
investment bank	Investmentbank f
investment income	Erträge mpl aus Anlagen fpl
investment portfolio	Wertpapierportefeuille nt
invisible assets	unsichtbare Vermögenswerte mpl
issued capital	ausgegebenes Kapital nt
joint account	gemeinsames Konto nt
joint-stock bank	Aktienbank f
joint venture	Joint-venture nt
labour-intensive	arbeitsintensiv
lend	leihen
lending rate	Darlehenszinssatz m
letter of credit	Akkreditiv nt
letter of guarantee	Garantie f
letter of indemnity	Indemnitätsbrief m

you/we/they will get your/our/their money back from the project der
   Aufwand für das Projekt macht sich bezahlt
a solid or **safe investment** eine solide or sichere Investition

limited liability	*beschränkte Haftung f*
liquidate	*liquidieren*
liquidation	*Liquidation f*
liquidator	*Liquidator m*
liquidity ratio	*Liquidationsquote f*
loan *n*	*Darlehen nt*
loan *vb*	*leihen*
loan account	*Darlehenskonto nt*
loan capital	*Fremdkapital nt*
loss leader	*Lockangebot nt*
management buyout	*Kaufübernahme f durch das Management*
merchant bank	*Merchant Bank f*
merchant banker	*Merchant Banker m*
merger	*Fusion f*
money	*Geld nt*
money-making *adj*	*gewinnbringend*
money-making *n*	*Gelderwerb m*
money market	*Geldmarkt m*
moratorium	*Moratorium nt*
mortgage *n*	*Hypothek f*
mortgage *vb*	*hypothekarisch belasten*
mortgagee	*Hypothekengläubiger(in) m(f)*
mortgagor	*Hypothekenschuldner(in) m(f)*
near-money	*leicht liquidierbares Vermögen nt*
negative cash flow	*Überhang m der Zahlungsausgänge mpl*
negotiating bank	*negoziierende Bank f*
night safe	*Nachtsafe m*
non-convertible currency	*nicht-konvertierbare Währung f*
non-profit-making	*gemeinnützig*
non-taxable	*steuerfrei*
numbered account	*Nummernkonto nt*
offer document	*schriftliches Übernahmeangebot nt*
official receiver	*Konkursverwalter(in) m(f)*
open cheque	*Barscheck m*
operation	*Betrieb m*
overdraft	*Überziehungskredit m*

to go into liquidation *in Liquidation treten*
to grant/refuse somebody a loan *jemandem einen Kredit gewähren/ verweigern*
to lose/make money *Geld verlieren/machen*
to offset losses against tax *Verluste von der Steuer absetzen*

overdraft limit	Überziehungsgrenze *f*
overheads	Gemeinkosten *pl*
paper profit	rechnerischer Gewinn *m*
payable on demand	zahlbar bei Sicht *f*
payable to	zahlbar an
payee	Zahlungsempfänger(in) *m (f)*
pay in	einzahlen
pension fund	Rentenfonds *m*
personal loan	Personaldarlehen *nt*
petrodollar	Petrodollar *m*
pledge *n*	Pfand *nt*
positive cash flow	Überhang *m* der Zahlungseingänge *mpl*
post-dated cheque	vordatierter Scheck *m*
pre-tax	vor Steuern
privatize	privatisieren
profitability	Rentabilität *f*
profit-making	rentabel
profit margin	Gewinnspanne *f*
rate of return	Rendite *f*
rationalization	Rationalisierung *f*
rationalize	rationalisieren
receivership	Konkursverwaltung *f*
regulator	Aufsichtsbehörde *f*
reschedule *(debt)*	umschulden
rescheduling	Umschuldung *f*
reserve currency	Reservewährung *f*
reserves	Rücklage *f*, Reserven *fpl*
restricted currency	eingeschränkte Währung *f*
return on investments (ROI)	Anlageverzinsung *f*
revaluation	Aufwertung *f*
revolving credit	Revolving-Kredit *m*
risk capital	Risikokapital *nt*
savings	Ersparnisse *fpl*
savings account	Sparkonto *nt*
savings bank	Sparkasse *f*
secure *adj*	gesichert
secure *vb*	sichern

to plough back the profits into the business *die Profite wieder in die Firma investieren*
to go public *öffentliche Rechtsform annehmen*
to put money into a venture *(Geld) in ein Unternehmen investieren*
to put up 20% of the capital for ... *20% des Kapitals für ... bereitstellen*
to go into receivership *den Konkurs eröffnen*
a good/bad risk *ein gutes/schlechtes Risiko*

secured creditor	gesicherter Gläubiger *m*
security *(for loan)*	Sicherheit *f*
self-financing	Eigenfinanzierung *f*
share capital	Aktienkapital *nt*
silent partner, sleeping partner	stiller Teilhaber *m*, stille Teilhaberin *f*, stiller Gesellschafter *m*, stille Gesellschafterin *f*
solvency	Solvenz *f*
solvent	solvent
sort code	Bankleitzahl *f*
special drawing rights (SDR)	Sonderziehungsrechte *ntpl* (SZR *ntpl*)
specimen signature	Unterschriftsprobe *f*
standing order	Dauerauftrag *m*
statement (of account)	Kontoauszug *m*
stop payment	Zahlung *f* stoppen
takeover bid	Übernahmeangebot *nt*
taxable	steuerpflichtig
tax-free	steuerfrei
tax haven	Steuerparadies *nt*
tax year	Steuerjahr *nt*
teller	Schalterbeamter *m*, Schalterbeamtin *f*
trade reference	Kreditauskunft *f*
transaction	Transaktion *f*
transfer *n*	Überweisung *f*
transfer *vb*	überweisen
traveller's cheque	Travellers Cheque *m*, Reisescheck *m*
treasury bill	kurzfristiger Schatzwechsel *m*
trend	Tendenz *f*
uncrossed cheque	Barscheck *m*
undercapitalized	unterkapitalisiert
undischarged debt	unbeglichene Schuld *f*
unissued capital	noch nicht ausgegebenes Kapital *nt*
unsecured creditor	nicht gesicherter Gläubiger *m*
unsecured loan	Blankokredit *m*
upward trend	steigende Tendenz *f*

we have a 10% stake in the company *wir sind mit 10% an dieser Firma beteiligt*
what state are the company's finances in? *wie sieht es mit den Finanzen der Firma aus?*

venture	*Risiko nt*
venture capital	*Risikokapital nt*
vertical integration	*vertikale Integration f*
voluntary liquidation	*freiwillige Liquidation f*
wind up	*liquidieren*
winding up	*Liquidation f*
withdraw	*abheben*
withdrawal	*Abhebung f*
World Bank	*Weltbank f*

BUYING AND SELLING

See also **ACCOUNTS AND PAYMENTS, ADVERTISING AND MEDIA** *and* **MARKETING AND PR**

account	*Konto nt*
all-in price	*Inklusivpreis m*
allow *(discount)*	*geben*
asking price	*Angebotspreis m*
banded pack	*Mehrfachpackung f im Einführungsangebot nt*
bar code	*Strichcode m, Bar-Code m*
bar code reader	*Bar-Code-Leser m*
bargain	*Sonderangebot nt*
bargain price	*Sonderpreis m*
bonus pack	*Bonuspackung f*
break-even analysis	*Break-Even-Analyse f*
break-even chart	*Gewinnschwellen-Diagramm nt*
break-even point	*Break-Even-Punkt m*
broken lot	*Restposten m*
brown goods	*kleinere Haushalts- und Elektrogeräte ntpl*
bulk buying	*Mengeneinkauf m*
business trip	*Geschäftsreise f*
buy	*kaufen*
buyer	*Käufer(in) m(f)*
buyer's market	*Käufermarkt m*
call frequency	*Besuchshäufigkeit f*
calling cycle	*Besuchsrhythmus m*
call report	*Vertreterbericht m*
canvass	*werben*
canvasser	*Kundenwerber(in) m(f)*
canvassing	*Kundenwerbung f*
cash discount	*Skonto nt or m*
cash on delivery (COD) *n*	*Barzahlung f bei Lieferung*
cash on delivery (COD) *adv*	*per Nachnahme f*
cash price	*Preis m bei Barzahlung f*
cash with order (cwo)	*Bezahlung f bei Auftragserteilung*

to accept/send goods on approval *Waren zur Ansicht erhalten/verschicken*
to sell at pre-Budget prices *zu Preisen vor Verkündung des Haushalts verkaufen*
I will call again tomorrow *(visit) ich komme morgen noch mal vorbei; (phone) ich rufe morgen noch mal an*
I regret that we must cancel our order *wir müssen unsere Bestellung leider stornieren*
we reserve the right to cancel this order *wir behalten uns das Recht vor, diese Bestellung zu stornieren*

catalogue	*Katalog m*
chain store	*Kettenladen m*
check-out (desk)	*Kasse f*
circular	*Wurfsendung f*
classified advertisements	*Kleinanzeigen fpl*
clearance sale	*Räumungsverkauf m*
client	*Kunde m, Kundin f*
cold call *(visit)*	*unangemeldeter Vertreterbesuch m*
cold call *(phone)*	*unangefordeter Anruf m*
commando selling	*aggressive Verkaufsstrategie f*
commission	*Kommission f*
commodity	*Ware f*
competition	*Wettbewerb m, Konkurrenz f*
competitive advantage/edge	*Wettbewerbsvorteil m*
competitive price	*konkurrenzfähiger Preis m*
concessionaire	*Konzessionär(in) m(f)*
conditions of sale	*Verkaufsbedingungen fpl*
consumer	*Verbraucher m*
consumer credit	*Verbraucherkredit m*
consumer goods	*Verbrauchsgüter ntpl*
consumerism	*Konsumdenken nt*
consumer market	*Verbrauchermarkt m*
convenience goods	*Güter ntpl des täglichen Bedarfs m*
cooling-off period	*Überdenkungsperiode f*
credit	*Kredit m*
credit account	*Kreditkonto nt*
credit note	*Gutschrift f*
customer	*Kunde m, Kundin f*
customer credit	*Kundenkredit m*
cut-price	*Schleuderpreis m*
cut-throat competition	*existenzgefährdende Konkurrenz f*
dead account	*totes Konto nt*
deadline	*Stichtag m*
deal	*Geschäft nt*

to close *or* **conclude a sale** *einen Verkauf abschließen*
to do cold calls *(visit) unangemeldete Kundenbesuche machen; (phone) unangeforderte Anrufe tätigen*
"no cold calling" *"keine unangemeldeten Vertreterbesuche"*
we are regrettably unable to accept your conditions of payment/delivery *wir können Ihre Zahlungsbedingungen/Lieferbedingungen leider nicht annehmen*
to do a deal *ein Geschäft machen*

deal in	*handeln mit*
deal with	*verhandeln mit*
dealer	*Händler(in) m(f)*
demonstration	*Vorführung f*
demonstration model	*Vorführmodell nt*
deposit	*Anzahlung f*
direct-mail advertising	*Postwurfwerbung f*
discount n	*Rabatt m*
discount vb	*Rabatt m geben*
discount house	*Diskonthaus nt*
discount store	*Billigladen m*
dispenser	*Automat m*
display n	*Auslage f*
display vb	*ausstellen*
distributor	*Verteiler m*
distributor network	*Verteilernetz nt*
domestic sales	*Inlandsabsatz m*
door-to-door salesman/woman	*Hausierer(in) m(f)*
door-to-door selling	*Verkauf m an der Haustür f*
down-market	*für den Massenmarkt m*
down payment	*Anzahlung f*
drop shipment	*Direktlieferung f*
dump bin	*Wühltisch m*
Dutch auction	*Versteigung f mit stufenweise erniedrigtem Ausbietungspreis*
end user	*Endverbraucher(in) m(f)*
estimate	*Kostenvoranschlag m*
exclusive agency agreement	*Alleinvertretungsvertrag m*
exhibit	*ausstellen*
exhibitor	*Aussteller(in) m(f)*
expense account	*Spesenkonto nt*
expenses	*Spesen pl*
face-to-face selling	*vis-à-vis Verkauf m*
fair wear and tear	*allgemeine Abnutzung f*
fast-moving consumer goods (FMCG)	*schnell verkäufliche Konsumgüter ntpl*

please confirm that you can deliver within 30 days *bitte bestätigen Sie, daß Sie innerhalb von 30 Tagen liefern können*
we require delivery of the goods within 30 days *wir brauchen die Waren innerhalb von 30 Tagen*
to go down-market *an weniger anspruchsvolle Kunden wenden*
to make an estimate *veranschlagen*
we estimate *or* **forecast sales of ... units in the first year** *wir rechnen mit einem or prognostizieren einen Umsatz von ... Stück im ersten Jahr*
in good faith *in gutem Glauben*

feature	*Merkmal nt*
firm price	*Festpreis m*
flash pack	*augenfällige Werbepackung f*
fluctuate	*schwanken*
fluctuation	*Schwankung f*
follow up	*nachfassen*
follow-up call *(visit)*	*Nachfaßbesuch m*
follow-up call *(phone)*	*zweiter Kontaktversuch m*
foreign sales	*Auslandsabsatz m*
forward sales	*Terminverkauf m*
franchise *n*	*Konzession f, Franchise f*
franchise *vb*	*konzessionieren*
franchisee	*Franchisenehmer(in) m(f)*
franchiser	*Franchisegeber(in) m(f)*
freebie	*Werbegeschenk nt*
gift voucher	*Geschenkgutschein m*
gimmick	*Gag m*
give-away	*Probe(packung) f*
goods	*Güter ntpl*
goods on approval	*Waren fpl zur Ansicht*
goods on consignment	*Kommissionswaren fpl*
gross sales	*Bruttoumsatz m*
guarantee *n*	*Garantie f*
guarantee *vb*	*garantieren*
hard sell	*aggressive Verkaufstaktik f*
hire purchase	*Ratenkauf m*
hire-purchase agreement	*Teilzahlungs(kauf)vertrag m*
home sales	*Inlandsabsatz m*
hype *n*	*Ausloben nt*
hype *vb*	*ausloben*
incentive	*Anreiz m*
incentive scheme	*Anreizsystem nt*
indirect demand	*indirekte Nachfrage f*
instalment	*Rate f*
introductory offer	*Einführungsangebot nt*
lead time	*Lieferzeit f*
lease back	*rückvermieten*
leaseback	*Rückvermietung f*

the item has a two-year guarantee *auf dem Artikel gibt es zwei Jahre Garantie*
is the item still under guarantee? *ist auf dem Artikel noch Garantie?*
to pay in instalments *in Raten zahlen*
an introductory offer will attract more buyers *ein Einführungsangebot wird mehr Käufer anziehen*
the lead time for delivery is ... *die Lieferzeit ist ...*

licensed trade	konzessionierter Alkoholhandel m
line	Artikel mpl
list price	Listenpreis m
market n	Markt m
market vb	vermarkten
market leader	Marktführer m
market price	Marktpreis m
market value	Marktwert m
mark-up (profit margin)	Gewinnaufschlag m
mark-up (increase)	Preiserhöhung f
merchandise n	Handelsware f
merchandise vb	kaufen und verkaufen
merchandiser	Verkaufsexperte m, Verkaufsexpertin f
model	Modell nt
new	neu
offer n	Angebot nt
offer vb	anbieten
offer price	Angebotspreis m
order n	Bestellung f
order vb	bestellen
order book	Auftragsbuch nt
order form	Bestellformular nt
order number	Bestellnummer f
order processing	Auftragsbearbeitung f
outlet (shop)	Verkaufsstelle f
outlet (market)	Absatzmöglichkeit f
out of print	vergriffen
own brand	Hausmarke f
pack	Paket nt
packaging	Verpackung f
personal selling	persönlicher Verkauf m
point of sale (POS)	Verkaufsort m, Point of Sale m (P.O.S. m)
point-of-sale advertising	Werbung f am Verkaufsort m

we would like to place a regular order for ... wir möchten eine turnusmäßige Bestellung für ... aufgeben
we confirm receipt of your order of 25 November wir bestätigen den Erhalt Ihrer Bestellung vom 25. November
with reference to your order of 26 June bezüglich Ihrer Bestellung vom 26. Juni
please find enclosed our order no. 2511 for ... anbei unsere Bestellung Nr. 2511 über (+acc) ...
to perform well against the competition der Konkurrenz etwas voraus sein

point-of-sale material	*Werbematerial nt am Verkaufsort m*
potential customer	*potentieller Kunde m, potentielle Kundin f*
premium offer	*Zugabeangebot nt*
price *n*	*Preis m*
price-cutting	*Preissenkung f*
price list	*Preisliste f*
price range	*Preisklasse f*
price-sensitive	*preisempfindlich*
price tag	*Preisschild nt*
price war	*Preiskrieg m*
product	*Produkt nt*
product range	*Produktpalette f*
profitable	*rentabel, gewinnbringend*
profit-making	*rentabel*
profit margin	*Gewinnspanne f*
promote	*werben für*
promotion	*Werbung f*
proprietary brand	*Hausmarke f*
pro rata *adj, adv*	*anteilmäßig*
publicize	*werben, bekanntmachen*
purchase order	*Bestellung f*
purchase price	*Kaufpreis m*
quotation	*Kostenvoranschlag m*
quote *n*	*Kostenvoranschlag m*
quote *vb (price)*	*nennen*
range	*Auswahl f*
recommended retail price	*unverbindliche Preisempfehlung f*
repeat order	*Nachbestellung f*
resale price maintenance (RPM)	*Preisbindung f der zweiten Hand*
retail outlet	*Einzelhandelsverkaufstelle f*
retail price	*Einzelhandelspreis m*
returns	*Retouren fpl*
sale	*see phrases below*
sales	*Absatz m*
sales analysis	*Absatzanalyse f*

we are currently having problems with our supplier *wir haben momentan Schwierigkeiten mit unserem Lieferanten*
please find enclosed our quotation for the supply of ... *anbei unser Kostenvoranschlag für die Lieferung von ...*
to quote for a job *einen Kostenvoranschlag für einen Auftrag machen*
these retail at £75 *der Einzelhandelspreis (dieser Artikel) ist £75*
to pay a retainer *einen Gebührenvorschuß zahlen*

sales campaign	*Verkaufskampagne f*
sales conference	*Versammlung f des Verkaufsstabs m*
sales drive	*Verkaufskampagne f, Verkaufsvorstoß m*
sales figures	*Absatzziffern fpl, Verkaufsziffern fpl*
sales force	*Verkaufsstab m*
sales forecast	*Absatzprognose f*
sales literature	*Verkaufsprospekt m*
salesman *(sales rep)*	*Vertreter m*
salesman *(in shop)*	*Verkäufer m*
sales manager	*Verkaufsleiter(in) m(f)*
salesmanship	*Verkaufstüchtigkeit f*
sales meeting	*Handelsvertreterversammlung f*
sales planning	*Absatzplanung f*
sales representative	*Vertreter(in) m(f)*
sales report	*Absatzbericht m*
saleswoman *(sales rep)*	*Vertreterin f*
saleswoman *(in shop)*	*Verkäuferin f*
sample	*Muster nt, Probe f*
second-hand	*gebraucht*
sell-by date	*Haltbarkeitsdatum nt*
seller's market	*Verkäufermarkt m*
service charge	*Bedienung f*
showcard	*Schaufensterplakat nt*
showroom	*Ausstellungsraum m*
slack period	*tote Saison f*
soft sell	*dezente Verkaufsmethode f*
sole agent	*Alleinvertreter(in) m(f)*
sole trader	*Einzelkaufmann m, Einzelkauffrau f*
special offer	*Sonderangebot nt*
spot price	*Kassapreis m, Lokopreis m*

to make a sale *einen Verkauf tätigen*
the product will be on sale to the public next month *das Produkt kommt nächsten Monat auf den Markt*
they have a sale on *die haben Ausverkauf*
to accept/supply goods on a sale or return basis *Waren mit Rückgaberecht annehmen/liefern*
sales of ... are rising/falling/stable *der Absatz von ... steigt/fällt/ist stabil*
sales are up/down on last quarter *seit dem letzten Quartal sind die Umsätze gestiegen/gefallen*
I will be speaking about this at the sales conference *darüber werde ich auf der Vertreterversammlung sprechen*

stock *n*	*Bestand m*
stock *vb*	*führen*
in stock	*vorrätig*
out of stock	*nicht vorrätig*
subcontract	*Subunternehmervertrag m*
supplier	*Lieferant(in) m(f)*
telesales	*Telefonverkauf m*
tender	*Angebot nt*
tender for	*ein Angebot nt einreichen für (+acc)*
testimonial	*Empfehlung f*
trade discount	*Händlerrabatt m*
trade fair	*Messe f*
trade-in price	*Eintauschwert m*
trade mission	*Handelsdelegation f*
trade price	*Großhandelspreis m*
travelling salesman	*Vertreter m*
undersell	*unter Wert m verkaufen*
unique selling point (USP)	*einmaliges Verkaufsargument nt (USP m)*
unit cost	*Kosten pl pro Einheit f*
unit price	*Preis m pro Einheit f*
up-market	*anspruchsvoll*
vending machine	*Automat m*
volume discount	*Mengenrabatt m*
warranty	*Garantie f*
white goods	*weiße Waren fpl*

this item is out of stock *dieser Artikel ist nicht auf Lager*
to put something out to tender *etwas ausschreiben*
we regret that the following items are unavailable at the moment *leider sind folgende Artikel momentan nicht erhältlich*
to go up-market *sich an anspruchsvollere Kunden wenden*

COMPANY STRUCTURES

See also **CONFERENCES AND PUBLIC SPEAKING, PERSONNEL** and **PROJECT MANAGEMENT**

accountant	*Bilanzbuchhalter(in) m(f)*
accounts (department)	*Buchhaltung f*
acting manager	*stellvertretender Manager m, stellvertretende Managerin f*
administrator	*Verwalter(in) m(f)*
affiliated company	*Schwestergesellschaft f*
apprentice	*Auszubildende(r) f(m) (Azubi m/f)*
apprenticeship	*Lehre f*
architect	*Architekt(in) m(f)*
area manager	*Bezirksleiter(in) m(f)*
assistant	*Assistent(in) m(f)*
assistant manager	*stellvertretender Geschäftsführer m, stellvertretende Geschäftsführerin f*
associate director	*stellvertretender Direktor m, stellvertretende Direktorin f*
board of directors	*Vorstand m*
boss	*Chef m, Chefin f*
branch	*Zweigstelle f*
branch manager	*Zweigstellenleiter(in) m(f)*
branch office	*Niederlassung f*
businessman	*Geschäftsmann m*
business people	*Geschäftsleute pl*
businesswoman	*Geschäftsfrau f*
cashier	*Kassierer(in) m(f)*
certified accountant	*öffentlich zugelassener Wirtschaftsprüfer m, öffentlich zugelassene Wirtschaftsprüferin f*
chairman	*Vorsitzender m*
chair(manship)	*Vorsitz m*
chair(person)	*Vorsitzende(r) f(m)*
chairwoman	*Vorsitzende f*
channels of communication	*Kommunikationskanäle mpl*

I am Sales Manager with Contax in London *ich bin Verkaufsleiter(in) bei Contax in London*
that department is based in London *diese Abteilung hat ihren Sitz in London*
I have been with the company for 3 years *ich bin seit 3 Jahren bei dieser Firma*
to be on the board of a company *im Aufsichtsrat einer Firma sein*
he is chairman of ... *er ist Vorsitzender (+gen) ...*

chargehand	*Vorarbeiter(in) m(f)*
chartered accountant (CA)	*Wirtschaftsprüfer(in) m(f)*
chief executive	*oberste Führungskraft f, Direktor(in) m(f)*
clerical staff	*Schreibkräfte fpl*
clerk	*Büroangestellte(r) f(m)*
company	*Firma f*
company director	*Direktor(in) m(f)*
company secretary	*Company Secretary m*
complaints department	*Abteilung f für Reklamationen*
computer programmer	*Programmierer(in) m(f)*
computing department	*Computerabteilung f*
conglomerate	*Konglomerat nt*
consultant	*Berater(in) m(f)*
co-ownership	*Miteigentum nt*
copy typist	*Schreibkraft f*
corporate image	*Firmenimage nt*
corporation	*juristische Person f*
cost accountant	*Kalkulator(in) m(f)*
customer services department	*Kundendienst m*
delegate *vb*	*delegieren*
department	*Abteilung f*
departmental	*Abteilungs-*
department manager	*Abteilungsleiter(in) m(f)*
deputy chief executive	*stellvertretender Direktor m, stellvertretende Direktorin f*
design department	*Design Abteilung f*
designer	*Designer(in) m(f)*
director	*Direktor(in) m(f)*
dispatch department	*Versandabteilung f*
estimator	*Schätzer(in) m(f)*
executive director	*leitender Direktor m, leitende Direktorin f*
export department	*Exportabteilung f*
export manager	*Exportmanager(in) m(f)*
factory worker	*Fabrikarbeiter(in) m(f)*
field sales manager	*Außendienstleiter(in) m(f)*
finance director	*Finanzdirektor(in) m(f)*
financial accountant	*Finanzbuchhalter(in) m(f)*
financial controller	*Leiter(in) m(f) der Finanzabteilung f*
foreman/woman	*Vorarbeiter(in) m(f)*

that is dealt with by our ... department *dafür ist unsere ...abteilung zuständig*

freelance worker	*freiberuflicher Mitarbeiter m,*
	freiberufliche Mitarbeiterin f
general manager	*Geschäftsführer(in) m(f)*
head of department	*Abteilungsleiter(in) m(f)*
head office	*Zentrale f*
homeworker	*Heimarbeiter(in) m(f)*
job evaluation	*Arbeitsplatzbewertung f*
job title	*Berufsbezeichnung f*
keyboarder	*Texterfasser(in) m(f)*
lawyer	*Rechtsanwalt m, Rechtsanwältin f*
legal department	*Rechtsabteilung f*
line manager	*leitender Angestellter m, leitende*
	Angestellte f
machinist	*Maschinist(in) m(f)*
mailroom	*Postabfertigungsraum m*
(the) management	*die (Unternehmens)leitung*
management consultant	*Unternehmensberater(in) m(f)*
manager(ess)	*Manager(in) m(f)*
manager(ess) (*of department*)	*Abteilungsleiter(in) m(f)*
managing director (MD)	*Geschäftsführer(in) m(f)*
market development manager	*Leiter(in) m(f) für*
	Marktentwicklung f
marketing (department)	*Marketing nt*
marketing director	*Marketing-Direktor(in) m(f)*
marketing manager	*Marketing-Manager(in) m(f)*
MD (managing director)	*Geschäftsführer(in) m(f)*
merger	*Fusion f*
middle management	*mittleres Management nt*
non-executive director	*Aufsichtsratsmitglied nt*
office junior	*Bürohilfe f*
office manager	*Büroleiter(in) m(f)*
office work	*Büroarbeit f*
organization chart	*Organisationsplan m*
parent company	*Muttergesellschaft f*
part-timer	*Teilzeitbeschäftigte(r) f(m)*
personal assistant (PA)	*persönlicher Assistent m,*
	persönliche Assistentin f
personnel department	*Personalabteilung f*
personnel management	*Personalführung f*
personnel manager	*Personalchef m*

I would like to meet your ... *ich würde gerne Ihre/Ihren ... kennenlernen*
I work in our Glasgow office *ich arbeite in unserem Glasgower Büro/ unserer Glasgower Niederlassung*

plant engineer	*Betriebsingenieur(in)* m*(f)*
president	*Präsident(in)* m*(f)*
press officer	*Pressesprecher(in)* m*(f)*
production control	*Produktionskontrolle* f
production manager	*Produktionsmanager(in)* m*(f)*
product manager	*Produktmanager(in)* m*(f)*
profit centre	*Bilanzeinheit* f
project manager	*Projektleiter(in)* m*(f)*
public relations (department)	*Public Relations* fpl
public relations officer	*Pressesprecher(in)* m*(f)*
quality controller	*Qualitätsingenieur(in)* m*(f)*
R & D (research and development)	*FuE* f *(Forschung* f *und Entwicklung* f*)*
rationalization	*Rationalisierung* f
receptionist	*Herr* m*/Dame* f *am Empfang*
records department	*Archiv* nt
registered office	*eingetragener Gesellschaftssitz* m
safety officer	*Sicherheitsbeamter* m, *Sicherheitsbeamtin* f
sales department	*Verkaufsabteilung* f
sales force	*Verkaufsstab* m
sales manager	*Verkaufsleiter(in)* m*(f)*
sales representative	*Vertreter(in)* m*(f)*
secretary	*Sekretär(in)* m*(f)*
security guard	*Wache* f
service department	*Kundendienstabteilung* f
shipping department	*Versandabteilung* f
sole agent	*Alleinvertreter(in)* m*(f)*
subsidiary (company)	*Tochtergesellschaft* f
switchboard operator	*Telefonist(in)* m*(f)*
temporary staff	*Aushilfspersonal* nt
think tank	*Planungsstab* m
trainee	*Auszubildende(r)* f*(m) (Azubi* m*/f)*
typing pool	*Schreibzentrale* f
typist	*Schreibkraft* f
undermanning	*Personalmangel* m
vice-chairman	*stellvertretender Vorsitzender* m
vice-chair(person)	*stellvertretender Vorsitz* m

he/she is their representative in Geneva *er/sie ist ihr Vertreter/ihre Vertreterin in Genf*
we are a subsidiary of ... *wir sind eine Tochtergesellschaft von/der ...*
the company has 3 subsidiaries, with 10,000 employees worldwide *die Firma hat 3 Tochtergesellschaften mit weltweit 10.000 Angestellten*

vice-chairwoman	*stellvertretende Vorsitzende f*
vice-president	*Vizepräsident(in) m(f)*
works council	*Betriebsrat m*

See also **MAKING CONTACT**

MAKING THEM

ON BEHALF OF YOUR COMPANY
We ordered it/them three weeks ago *wir haben es/sie vor drei Wochen bestellt*
Our order still hasn't arrived *unsere Bestellung ist immer noch nicht eingetroffen*
There must be some mistake *da muß ein Fehler vorliegen*
This is not what we ordered *das haben wir nicht bestellt*
Your service isn't fast enough *Ihr Service ist zu langsam*
It's too expensive *es ist zu teuer*
We need it/them sooner *wir brauchen es/sie eher*
The samples/goods you sent us were damaged/faulty *die Muster/Waren, die Sie uns geschickt haben, waren beschädigt/ fehlerhaft*
Your service department has let us down again *Ihre Kundendienstabteilung hat uns schon wieder im Stich gelassen*
If the parts don't arrive by Friday we'll have to cancel the order *wenn die Teile nicht bis Freitag eintreffen, müssen wir die Bestellung stornieren*
Part of the order is missing from the consignment *ein Teil der bestellten Ware fehlt*
This is the third time this has happened *das ist nun schon zum dritten Mal passiert*
What are you going to do about it? *was werden Sie unternehmen?*
You have not kept to the terms of our contract *Sie haben sich nicht an unsere Vertragsbedingungen gehalten*
Could you do something about it right away/as soon as possible/by tomorrow morning? *könnten Sie sofort/so bald wie möglich/bis (spätestens) morgen früh etwas unternehmen?*
I'm afraid this is not good enough *tut mir leid, aber das ist einfach nicht akzeptabel*
I need it by tomorrow at the latest *ich brauche es spätestens morgen*
We were expecting it last Tuesday *wir hatten es schon letzten Dienstag erwartet*
Your service engineer didn't turn up *Ihr Kundendienst ist nicht erschienen*
We are dissatisfied with your after-sales service *wir sind mit Ihrem Kundendienst nicht zufrieden*
We may be forced to take legal action *wir könnten uns gezwungen sehen, rechtliche Schritte einzuleiten*

IN A SHOP

I bought this here yesterday/last week *ich habe das gestern/letzte Woche hier gekauft*

This razor/calculator/lighter doesn't work *dieser Rasierapparat/ Rechner/dieses Feuerzeug funktioniert nicht*

It doesn't work properly *es funktioniert nicht richtig*

It's broken/faulty *er/sie/es ist kaputt/defekt*

It has a hole/tear in it *es hat ein Loch/einen Riß*

It doesn't do what it's supposed to *es erfüllt nicht seinen Zweck*

It's shop-soiled *es ist angeschmutzt*

It's the wrong model *es ist das falsche Modell*

It's not what I asked for *das hatte ich nicht bestellt*

Here's my receipt *hier ist meine Quittung*

I've lost my receipt *ich habe die Quittung verloren*

I'd like a refund *ich möchte mein Geld zurückhaben*

I'd like to exchange it for something else *ich möchte es umtauschen*

I'd like a replacement *ich möchte Ersatz*

I've been overcharged *man hat mir zu viel berechnet*

You've shortchanged me *Sie haben mir zu wenig herausgegeben*

HANDLING THEM

BY TELEPHONE

Can you tell me what the problem is? *können Sie mir sagen, wo das Problem liegt?*

When did you place your order? *wann haben Sie die Bestellung aufgegeben?*

When did this happen? *wann ist das passiert?*

Has this happened before? *ist das schon mal vorgekommen?*

Is the item still under guarantee? *ist auf dem Artikel noch Garantie?*

I see *ach so/aha*

I'm sorry (about that) *das tut mir leid*

Please accept our apologies *wir bitten Sie vielmals um Entschuldigung*

I'll see what I can do *ich will mal sehen, was sich da machen läßt*

Just leave it with me *überlassen Sie es mir*

I'll speak to the manager right away *ich werde sofort mit dem Geschäftsleiter/der Geschäftsleiterin sprechen*

I'm sure we'll be able to sort it out for you *wir werden das bestimmt regeln können*

I'll keep you informed *ich halte Sie auf dem laufenden*

I'll get back to you as soon as possible *ich benachrichtige Sie so bald wie möglich*

BY LETTER

Provided the item is still under guarantee, we will repair/replace it free of charge *wenn auf dem Artikel noch Garantie ist, reparieren/ersetzen wir ihn kostenlos*

We'll send you a replacement immediately/by return of post *wir schicken Ihnen sofort Ersatz/umgehend Ersatz*

You will not be charged for delivery/your order *die Zustellung/ Ihre Bestellung wird Ihnen nicht in Rechnung gestellt*

This was due to a clerical error *das ist aufgrund eines Schreibfehlers passiert*

I shall arrange for one of our service engineers to call on you *ich werde den Kundendienst vorbeischicken*

We shall be glad to give you a discount on your next order *wir geben Ihnen gerne bei Ihrer nächsten Bestellung einen Rabatt*

I am afraid we cannot help you with this particular problem *bei diesem speziellen Problem können wir Ihnen leider nicht helfen*

Our customer services department will be happy to help you *unser Kundendienst steht Ihnen gerne zur Verfügung*

Please contact your distributor *bitte setzen Sie sich mit dem Verteiler in Verbindung*

This is not really our responsibility *dafür sind wir eigentlich nicht verantwortlich*

Please send us details of your complaint in writing *bitte reichen Sie Ihre Beschwerde schriftlich ein*

IN PERSON

On the face of it, there appears to be nothing wrong with the item *auf den ersten Blick scheint der Artikel in Ordnung zu sein*

I doubt very much whether we shall be able to repair this *ich glaube nicht, daß wir das reparieren können*

If you could just bear with me for a moment, I'll fetch the manager *einen Augenblick bitte, ich hole den Manager*

I can see why this problem has caused you great distress *ich kann gut verstehen, daß Ihnen dieses Problem große Unannehmlichkeiten bereitet hat*

From what you've said, I suspect the cause of the fault is purely mechanical *aus dem, was Sie gesagt haben, geht hervor, daß die Ursache des Versagens rein mechanischer Art ist*

Would you mind leaving the item with us so that we can take a closer look at it? *würden Sie den Artikel bitte hierlassen, damit wir ihn uns mal genauer ansehen können?*

I think I see where the problem lies *ich glaube, ich weiß, wo das Problem liegt*

Robertson & Co
5 Montpelier Terrace
Alloway
Ayr KA5
Scotland, UK

Firma Ernst Gerhard
Präzisionsmaschinen
Gartenstr. 78-80
D-4000 Köln 1
Germany

9.10.91

Betr: Ihre Lieferung Rechnungsnr. 13567/91 vom 8.10.1991

Sehr geehrte Damen und Herren,

am 16.9 bestellten wir bei Ihrer Firma eine Präzisionsdünn-
schliffsäge vom Typ XLM 7172, die mit Rechnung vom 8.10.
geliefert wurde. Ihre Vertretung in Großbritannien hatte dieses
Gerät als besonders leise bezeichnet und bestätigt, daß es die
von uns gewünschte Qualität garantiert. Im Gegensatz zu dieser
Behauptung müssen wir allerdings feststellen, daß dieses Gerät
außergewöhnlich laut ist, und daß die Qualität unseren
Anforderungen nicht genügt.

Ihre Vertretung hat sich nunmehr geweigert, das Gerät zu ersetzen. Wir
fordern Sie auf, die Dünnschliffsäge sofort und auf Ihre
Kosten abholen zu lassen. Unseren Auftrag können Sie als
storniert betrachten.

Mit besten Empfehlungen

Cathryn Robertson

Cathryn Robertson

Dear Sirs,

Re: Yr order no. 13567/91 of 8 October 1991

The precision saw, model no. XLM7172, which we ordered from
your company on 16.9.91, was delivered and invoiced on 8
October 91. Your agents in Britain said this piece of
equipment had an exceptionally low noise level and they
further claimed that it would certainly meet our requirements
in terms of quality. However, we wish to point out that this
machine is exceptionally noisy and that its quality falls short
of our requirements.

Your agents have refused to replace the machine. We therefore
instruct you to have it collected at once at your expense.
You may consider our order cancelled.

Yours faithfully

Cathryn Robertson

Cathryn Robertson

abort	*abbrechen*
access *n*	*Zugriff m*
access *vb*	*zugreifen auf (+acc)*
access time	*Zugriffszeit f*
A/D converter	*Analog-Digital-Umsetzer m (ADU m)*
AI (artifical intelligence)	*KI f (künstliche Intelligenz f)*
alphanumeric	*alphanumerisch*
analog(ue)	*analog*
application	*Anwendung f*
application package	*Anwenderpaket nt*
application software	*Anwenderpaket nt*
archive *n*	*Archiv nt*
archive *vb*	*archivieren*
ASCII (file)	*ASCII(-Datei f)*
azerty keyboard	*Azerty-Tastatur f*
back up	*sichern*
back-up (copy)	*Sicherungskopie f*
back-up disk	*Sicherungsdiskette f*
bandwidth	*Bandbreite f*
baud rate	*Baudrate f*
benchmark test	*Vergleichstest m*
bespoke software	*kundenspezifische Software f*
binary code	*Binärcode m*
binary compatible	*binär-kompatibel*
bit	*Bit nt*
boot (up)	*laden*
bpi (bits per inch)	*bpi (Bits ntpl pro Inch m)*
bps (bits per second)	*bps (Bits ntpl pro Sekunde f)*
bubble memory	*Blasenspeicher m*
buffer	*Puffer m*
bug	*Programmierfehler m, Wanze f*
bulletin board	*Bulletin Board nt*
bundle	*Paket nt*
byte	*Byte nt*
CAD (computer-assisted design)	*CAD nt (rechnergestütztes Konstruieren f)*
CAD/CAM (computer-assisted design/manufacture)	*CAD/CAM nt (rechnergestütztes Konstruieren nt/ rechnergestützte Fertigungssteuerung f)*
CAL (computer-assisted learning)	*CAL nt (rechnergestütztes Lernen nt)*

to do a back-up *eine Sicherungskopie machen*

CAM (computer-assisted manufacture)	CAM nt (rechnergestützte Fertigungssteuerung f)
cartridge	Kassette f
CD-ROM	CD-ROM
centre	zentrieren
CGA (colour graphics adaptor)	Farbgrafikadapter m
character set	Zeichensatz m
chip	Chip m
CIM (computer input from microfilm)	CIM nt (computer input from microfilm)
CIM (computer-integrated manufacture)	CIM nt (rechnerintegrierte Fertigung f)
clipboard	Zwischenablage f
code	Code m
command	Befehl m
compatible	kompatibel
computer	Computer m
computer agency	Computerfirma f
computer game	Computerspiel nt
computer language	Computersprache f
computer literate	see phrases below
computer science	Informatik f
computer scientist	Informatiker(in) m(f)
computing	Computerwissenschaft f, Informatik f
computing department	Computerabteilung f
console	Konsole f
control key	Control-Taste f
control unit	Steuereinheit f
copy n	Kopie f
copy vb	kopieren
corrupt adj	korrupt
corrupt vb	korrumpieren
corruption	Korrumpierung f
cpi (characters per inch)	cpi (Zeichen ntpl pro Inch m)
CPM (critical path method)	CPM-Verfahren nt
CP/M (control program/ monitor)	CP/M nt
cps (characters per second)	cps (Zeichen ntpl pro Sekunde f)
cps (cycles per second)	cps (Zyklen mpl pro Sekunde f)

to do something by computer etwas auf dem Computer machen
the computer can handle the whole operation der Computer kann das Ganze machen
to be computer literate sich mit Computern auskennen

CPU (central processing unit)	CPU f (Zentraleinheit f)
crash	abstürzen
create (file)	anlegen
cursor	Cursor m
cut and paste	ausschneiden und einfügen
cybernetics	Kybernetik f
D/A converter	Digital-Analog-Umsetzer m (DAU m)
data	Daten ntpl
databank	Datenbank f
database	Datenbank f
database management	Datenbankverwaltung f
data capture	Datenerfassung f
data collection	Datensammlung f
data processing (DP)	Datenverarbeitung f (DV f)
data protection law	Datenschutzgesetz nt
data security	Datensicherheit f
debug	entwanzen
default adj	Vorgabe-, Standard-
default n	Vorgabe f
delete	löschen
delivery time	Lieferzeit f
deskside computer	Deskside-Computer m, Tower m
desktop computer	Desktop-Computer m, Tischcomputer m
device	Vorrichtung f
diagnostic program	Diagnoseprogramm nt
digit	Ziffer f
digital	Digital-
direct access	Direktzugriff m
directory	Inhaltsverzeichnis nt
disk	Diskette f
disk capacity	Plattenkapazität f
disk drive	Diskettenlaufwerk nt
diskette	Diskette f
document	Dokument nt
dongle	Kopierschutzstecker m
DOS	DOS nt
dot matrix printer	Matrixdrucker m
double-density diskette	Diskette f mit doppelter Schreibdichte
down	nicht verfügbar

you can do that using cut and paste das kann man mit "Ausschneiden und Einfügen" machen

download	*laden*
downtime	*Ausfallzeit f*
drive	*Laufwerk nt*
DTP (desktop publishing)	*DTP nt (Desktop-Publishing nt)*
dumb terminal	*dummes Terminal nt*
dump *n*	*Dump m, Speicherabzug m*
dump *vb*	*ausgeben*
edit	*editieren*
EGA (enhanced graphics adaptor)	*EGA m*
electronic mail	*elektronische Post f*
end user	*Endbenutzer m*
enter	*eingeben*
erase	*löschen*
error message	*Fehlermeldung f*
escape	*abbrechen*
expert system	*Expertensystem nt*
fault-tolerant	*fehlertolerant*
fibre-optic	*faseroptisch*
fibre-optic cable	*faseroptisches Kabel nt*
fibre-optic link	*faseroptische Verbindung f*
fibre optics	*Faseroptik f*
file *n*	*Datei f*
file *vb*	*ablegen*
filename	*Dateiname m*
floppy disk	*Floppy-Disk f*
font	*Schriftart f*
format *vb (disk)*	*formatieren*
formatting	*Formatieren nt*
form feeder	*Papiervorschub m*
function key	*Funktionstaste f*
garbage	*Garbage m*
gigabyte	*Gigabyte nt*
gigaflops	*Gigaflops pl*
GIGO (garbage in garbage out)	*GIGO*
(global) search and replace	*Suchen nt und Ersetzen nt*
graphics	*graphische Darstellung f*
hacking	*Hacken nt*
hard disk	*Festplatte f*
hardware	*Hardware f*
help menu	*Hilfe-Menü nt*
high-density diskette	*Diskette f mit hoher Schreibdichte*
high resolution *adj*	*hochauflösend*
high resolution *n*	*hohe Auflösung f*

hot key	*Funktionstaste f*
housekeeping	*Organisation f*
hybrid system	*Hybridsystem nt*
icon	*Ikon nt*
idle time	*Leerlaufzeit f*
incompatible	*nicht kompatibel*
indent	*einrücken*
information retrieval	*Informationsabruf m*
information technology	*Informationstechnik f*
ink jet printer	*Tintenstrahldrucker m*
input *n (process)*	*Input nt, Eingabe f*
input *n (data)*	*Eingabedaten ntpl*
input *vb*	*eingeben*
insert *vb*	*einfügen*
install	*installieren*
integrated accounting package	*integriertes Buchführungspaket nt*
intelligent terminal	*intelligentes Terminal nt*
interface	*Schnittstelle f*
interrupt	*unterbrechen*
I/O (input/output)	*E/A m (Eingabe/Ausgabe)*
IT (information technology)	*Informationstechnik f*
joystick	*Joystick m*
justify left/right	*linksbündig/rechtsbündig ausrichten*
key *n*	*Taste f*
keyboard	*Tastatur f*
key in	*eingeben*
keypad	*Tastenfeld nt*
keystroke	*Anschlag m*
kilobyte	*Kilobyte nt*
LAN (local area network)	*LAN nt*
language	*Sprache f*
laptop	*Laptop m*
laser disk	*Laserplatte f*
laser printer	*Laserdrucker m*
LCD (liquid crystal display)	*LCD nt*
letter quality	*Korrespondenzqualität f*
light pen	*Lichtstift m*
line feed	*Zeilenvorschub m*
line spacing	*Zeilenabstand m*
load *vb*	*laden*
log	*protokollieren*
logic	*Logik f*
log in/on	*anmelden*

log off/out	*abmelden*
machine-readable	*maschinenlesbar*
magnetic disk	*Magnetplatte f*
magnetic tape	*Magnetband nt*
mailbox	*Mailbox f*
mainframe	*Großrechner m*
main memory	*Hauptspeicher m*
margin	*Rand m*
MAT (machine-assisted translation)	*maschinenunterstützte Übersetzung f*
megabyte (Mb)	*Megabyte nt (MB nt)*
memory	*Speicher m*
menu	*Menü nt*
merge *n*	*Mischen nt*
merge *vb*	*mischen*
microchip	*Mikrochip m*
microcomputer	*Mikrocomputer m*
microdrive	*Feinfahrantrieb m*
microprocessor	*Mikroprozessor m (MP m)*
microsecond	*Mikrosekunde f*
millisecond	*Millisekunde f*
mips (millions of instructions per second)	*mips (Millionen Anweisungen fpl pro Sekunde f)*
MIS (management information system)	*MIS nt (Management-Informationssystem nt)*
mobile data system	*mobiles Datensystem nt*
model *(of hardware)*	*Modell nt*
modem	*Modem nt*
module	*Modul nt*
monitor	*Monitor m*
mouse	*Maus f*
multi-tasking	*Multitasking nt*
multi-user system	*Mehrbenutzersystem nt*
nanosecond	*Nanosekunde f*
network *n*	*Netzwerk nt*
network *vb*	*vernetzen*
off-line	*offline*
on-line	*online*
operating system	*Betriebssystem nt*
optical character reader (OCR)	*optischer Klarschriftleser m*
optical character recognition (OCR)	*optische Zeichenerkennung f*
output *n (process)*	*Output nt, Ausgabe f*
output *n (data)*	*Ausgabedaten ntpl*
output *vb*	*ausgeben*

overwrite	*überschreiben*
package	*Paket nt*
pagination	*Seitenformatierung f*
paperless office	*papierloses Büro nt*
password	*Paßwort nt*
PC (personal computer)	*PC m (Personalcomputer m)*
peripheral	*Peripheriegerät nt*
pirate	*eine Raubkopie f herstellen*
pirate copy	*Raubkopie f*
pixel	*Pixel nt*
plotter	*Plotter m*
port	*Anschluß m*
portable (computer)	*Portable nt*
printer	*Drucker m*
print-out	*Ausdruck m*
processor	*Prozessor m*
program *n*	*Programm nt*
program *vb*	*programmieren*
programmer	*Programmierer(in) m(f)*
programming	*Programmieren nt*
programming language	*Programmiersprache f*
prompt	*Prompt m, Eingabeaufforderung f*
protect	*sichern*
protocol	*Protokoll nt*
qwerty keyboard	*Qwerty-Tastatur f*
rack-mounted unit	*Einschubgerät nt*
RAM (random access memory)	*RAM nt*
random access	*wahlfreier Zugriff m*
real time	*Echtzeit f*
reboot	*rebooten, neu laden*
record	*Datensatz m*
reformat	*umformatieren*
response time	*Ansprechzeit f*
retrieve	*abrufen*
RISC (reduced instruction set computer)	*RISC m*
ROM (read-only memory)	*ROM nt*

the package includes hardware, software and consultancy *das Paket schließt Hardware, Software und Beratung ein*
the package is designed for all levels of users *das Paket ist für alle Anwendergruppen geeignet*
now press "return"/any key *drücken Sie jetzt "Return"/eine beliebige Taste*

run time	*Laufzeit f*
scratch file	*ungeschützte Datei f*
screen	*Bildschirm m*
SCSI (small computer systems interface)	*SCSI f*
search and replace	*Suchen nt und Ersetzen nt*
shared facility	*gemeinsam genutzte Systemeinrichtung f*
shareware	*Shareware f*
simulation	*Simulation f*
soak test	*Intensivtest m*
soft copy	*Softcopy f*
software	*Software f*
software engineer	*Software-Ingenieur(in) m (f)*
software engineering	*Softwareentwicklung f*
software house	*Softwarehaus nt*
software package	*Softwarepaket nt*
sort	*sortieren*
space bar	*Leertaste f*
speech generation	*Spracherzeugung f*
speech recognition	*Spracherkennung f*
speech synthesis	*Sprachsynthese f*
spellchecker	*Rechtschreibprüfung f*
spreadsheet	*Kalkulationstabelle f*
stand-alone	*Stand-alone-Gerät nt*
storage	*Speicher m*
string	*Zeichenfolge f*
style sheet	*Formatvorlage f*
syntax error	*Syntaxfehler m*
system	*System nt*
system operator	*Systembediener(in) m (f)*
systems analysis	*Systemanalyse f*
systems analyst	*Systemanalytiker(in) m (f)*
teletext	*Videotext m*
template	*Schablone f*
terminal	*Terminal nt*
test data	*Testdaten ntpl*
text editor	*Texteditor m*
time-sharing	*Time-sharing nt*
toolkit	*Werkzeug nt*

you can scroll up or down using the arrow keys *mit den Richtungstasten können Sie den Bildschirminhalt verschieben*
we need a software package which ... *wir brauchen ein Softwarepaket, das ...*

touch-sensitive	*berührungsempfindlich*
tpi (tracks per inch)	*tpi (Spuren fpl pro Inch m)*
update *n*	*Aktualisieren nt*
update *vb*	*aktualisieren*
upgrade	*ausbauen, verbessern*
upgradeable	*ausbaufähig*
user	*Benutzer(in) m(f)*
user-friendly	*benutzerfreundlich*
user-name	*Benutzername m*
utility software	*Hilfsprogramme ntpl*
validate	*validieren*
VDU (visual display unit)	*Bildschirmgerät nt*
VGA (video gate array)	*VGA nt*
videodisc	*Bildplatte f*
video game	*Videospiel nt*
Viewdata ®	*Bildschirmtext m*
virus	*Virus m*
WAN (wide area network)	*WAN nt (Weitverkehrsnetz nt)*
wildcard	*Platzhalter m*
window	*Fenster nt*
wordcount	*Wortzählung f*
word processing	*Textverarbeitung f*
word processor	*Textverarbeitungsanlage f*
wordwrap	*Zeilenumbruch m*
working disk	*Arbeitsdiskette f*
work station	*Arbeitsplatz m*
worm drive	*Laufwerk nt für Worm*
write-protected	*schreibgeschützt*
WYSIWYG (what you see is what you get)	*WYSIWYG nt*

the system needs to be totally upgraded *das System muß total überholt werden*
to write to a disk *auf Diskette schreiben*

See also **MEETINGS AND NEGOTIATIONS**

PRACTICAL PREPARATIONS BEFORE GIVING THE TALK

What time will I be speaking? *um wieviel Uhr ist meine Rede?*
Could I have 25 copies of this please? *kann ich hiervon bitte 25 Kopien haben?*
Could I have 25 copies of each of these? *kann ich hiervon bitte je 25 Kopien haben?*
I need them by 9 o'clock *ich brauche sie bis 9 Uhr*
I'd like this typed up *könnte ich das bitte getippt haben?*
Everyone needs one copy of each of these *jeder braucht hiervon je ein Exemplar*
Please hand these round *bitte reichen Sie die herum*
Has the ... been set up? *ist der/die/das ... aufgebaut?*
Could you help me set up the ...? *können Sie mir bitte beim Aufbauen des/der ... helfen?*
Can you show me how to work the ...? *können Sie mir bitte zeigen, wie der/die/das ... funktioniert?*
There isn't/aren't any ... *es gibt keinen/keine/kein ...*
Who is dealing with the refreshments/the technical side of things? *wer kümmert sich um die Erfrischungen/technischen Angelegenheiten?*
I'd like to record/film the talk *ich würde die Rede gerne auf Kassette/auf Video aufnehmen*
The room seems rather small/warm/cold/stuffy *der Raum erscheint ziemlich klein/warm/kalt/stickig*

INTRODUCING YOURSELF

Good morning/afternoon/evening, Ladies and Gentlemen *guten Morgen/Tag/Abend, meine (verehrten) Damen und Herren*
Let me introduce myself *darf ich mich vorstellen*
My name is ... and I'm with Contax *mein Name ist ... und ich bin bei Contax*
Let me welcome you to ... *ich möchte Sie willkommen in/bei/zu ... heißen*
I'm very pleased to be here/to be in ... *es freut mich hier/hier in ... sein zu können*
Please make allowances for my German *bitte entschuldigen Sie mein Deutsch*
My German is rather rusty, but I will do my best *mein Deutsch ist nicht mehr sehr fließend, aber ich werde mein Bestes tun*
Please stop me if there is anything you don't understand *bitte unterbrechen Sie mich, wenn Sie irgend etwas nicht verstehen*

YOUR JOB

My official job title is ... *meine offizielle Berufsbezeichnung ist* ...

My role within the company/department is to ... *meine Aufgabe innerhalb der Firma/Abteilung ist es,* ... *zu* ...

I deal with all matters regarding ... *ich kümmere mich um alle Angelegenheiten, die mit* ... *zu tun haben*

I am responsible for ensuring that ... *ich bin dafür verantwortlich, daß* ...

It is my job to ensure that ... *es ist meine Aufgabe, sicherzustellen, daß* ...

I report directly to head office *ich bin direkt der Zentrale unterstellt*

These departments report directly to me/us *diese Abteilungen sind mir/uns direkt unterstellt*

I started the job in 1990 *ich bin seit 1990 in dieser Stelle*

I have been with the company since March/for eighteen months *ich bin seit März/seit 18 Monaten bie der Firma*

I am based at our offices/plant in ... *ich arbeite in unserem Büro/ unserer Fabrik in* ...

See also **COMPANY STRUCTURES**

INTRODUCING YOUR COMPANY OR DEPARTMENT

As you know, we are in the field of ... *wie Sie wissen, arbeiten wir in der ...branche*

We are a subsidiary of ... *wir sind eine Tochter von* ...

We are the parent company of a group comprising ... *wir sind die Muttergesellschaft einer Unternehmensgruppe, zu der* ... *gehören*

We are affiliated with ... *wir sind eine Schwestergesellschaft von* ...

We have 20 branches in the UK *wir haben 20 Niederlassungen im UK*

We operate in 30 countries/across 3 continents *wir haben Niederlassungen in 30 Ländern/auf 3 verschiedenen Kontinenten*

The company employs 3,000 people worldwide *weltweit beschäftigt die Firma 3.000 Arbeitskräfte*

There are 20 people in the department/company *die Abteilung/ Firma hat 20 Angestellte*

See also **COMPANY STRUCTURES** *and* **INDUSTRIES AND TYPES OF COMPANY**

YOUR COMPANY OR DEPARTMENT'S PERFORMANCE

Our turnover was over £1 million last year *im letzten Jahr hatten wir einen Umsatz von über £ 1 Million*
We sold 100,000 units worldwide/in the UK *wir habe 100.000 Stück weltweit/im UK verkauft*
Last year we produced over a million units *letztes Jahr haben wir über eine Million Stück produziert*
There was an increase/decrease in sales of 10% last year *im letzten Jahr hatten wir einen Verkaufsanstieg/Verkaufsrückgang von 10%*
Production is rising/falling fast *die Produktion steigt/fällt rapide*
We are reasonably satisfied with this performance *wir sind durchaus zufrieden mit dieser Leistung*
We are not very satisfied with this performance *wir sind nicht sehr zufrieden mit dieser Leistung*
We are currently enjoying a period of relative/fast growth *momentan erleben wir eine Periode relativen/rapiden Wachstums*
The whole sector is depressed at the moment *der ganze Wirtschaftsbereich hat momentan einen Tiefstand erreicht*
We are suffering the effects of a recession at the moment *wir leiden momentan unter den Folgen einer Rezession*
We intend to improve (still further) on this performance *wir wollen diese Leistung (weiterhin) verbessern*

See also **ACCOUNTS AND PAYMENTS, BANKING AND FINANCE, BUYING AND SELLING, ECONOMICS, MANUFACTURING** *and* **PROJECT MANAGEMENT** *for specific vocabulary*

THE STRUCTURE OF THE TALK

First(ly) *erstens*
Secondly *zweitens*
Thirdly *drittens*
Fourthly *viertens*
Finally *schließlich*

AN INITIAL SUMMARY

I'm going to be talking about ... *ich werde über ... sprechen*
I would like to talk about ... *ich möchte über ... sprechen*
I would like to analyse/present ... *ich möchte ... analysieren/ vorstellen*
I will begin with an introduction to the subject *ich werde mit einer Einführung zu diesem Thema beginnen*

CONFERENCES AND PUBLIC SPEAKING

I will begin by giving you an overview of the situation *ich werde mit einem Überblick über die Situation beginnen*

I will begin with a short historical note *ich werde mit einem kurzen historischen Überblick beginnen*

Then I will move on to ... *dann werde ich zu ... übergehen*

After that, I will deal with ... *danach werde ich ... behandeln*

I will conclude with ... *ich werde mit ... abschließen*

I will try to anticipate future developments *ich werde versuchen, weitere Entwicklungen vorherzusagen*

And I will be happy to answer your questions at the end *zum Schluß beantworte ich gerne Ihre Fragen*

MOVING ON TO THE BODY OF THE TALK

First, let us look at ... *lassen Sie uns zuerst ... anschauen*

This brings me to my next point *das bringt mich auch schon zum nächsten Punkt*

Next, I would like to examine ... *als nächstes möchte ich ... untersuchen*

Let me now move on to the question of ... *lassen Sie mich nun auf die Frage des/der ... eingehen*

At this point, we must consider ... *an dieser Stelle müssen wir ... bedenken*

To digress for a moment *um kurz abzuschweifen*

Let me just add a footnote to this *lassen Sie mich hier kurz eine Anmerkung machen*

To return to my earlier point *um auf meinen früheren Punkt zurückzukommen*

As I mentioned a moment ago *wie ich eben schon erwähnte*

MAKING A POINT

As we all know ... *wie wir alle wissen ...*

I must emphasize that ... *ich muß betonen, daß ...*

This is a very important point *das ist ein ganz wichtiger Punkt*

The question is ... *die Frage ist ...*

The problem is ... *das Problem ist ...*

Let us not forget that ... *vergessen wir nicht, daß ...*

It is all too easy to forget that ... *man vergißt nur zu leicht, daß ...*

These are the points to remember *diese Punkte sollten wir im Gedächtnis behalten*

The main argument against/in favour of this is ... *das Hauptargument dagegen/dafür ist ...*

These are the facts to date *das sind die aktuellen Fakten soweit*

EXPRESSING AN OPINION

In my opinion *meiner Meinung nach*
Personally *ich persönlich*
It seems to me that ... *es scheint mir, daß ...*
From my/our point of view *von meinem/unserem Standpunkt aus gesehen*
I/we believe that ... *ich glaube/wir glauben, daß ...*
I am/we are (almost) sure that ... *ich bin/wir sind (so gut wie) sicher, daß ...*
Things are likely to change soon *die Dinge werden sich wahrscheinlich bald ändern*

I/we entirely approve of this *ich bin/wir sind voll und ganz damit einverstanden*
We are all very enthusiastic about the proposals *wir sind von Ihren Vorschlägen alle ganz begeistert*
I am/we are very much in favour of going ahead with the plans *ich bin/wir sind sehr dafür, die Pläne durchzuführen*

I/we don't think that it would work *ich glaube/wir glauben nicht, daß es klappen würde*
I/we can't support this idea *ich kann/wir können diese Idee nicht unterstützen*
I am/we are not too happy about these developments *ich bin/wir sind über diese Entwicklungen nicht sehr erfreut*
We are not at all sure that ... *wir sind uns überhaupt nicht sicher, daß ...*

I am not in a position to comment on this matter *ich bin nicht in der Lage, dazu einen Kommentar abzugeben*
I wouldn't like to give an opinion on that *dazu möchte ich mich nicht äußern*
I really have nothing to add *dem habe ich wirklich nichts hinzuzufügen*

EXPRESSING INTENTIONS

I/we intend to take action on this immediately *ich werde/wir werden daraufhin sofort etwas unternehmen*
My/our intention is to ... *ich habe vor, ... zu .../wir haben vor, ... zu ...*
I am/we are thinking of implementing the decisions before the end of the year *ich erwäge/wir erwägen, diese Entscheidungen noch vor Ende des Jahres durchzuführen*

We really have to get things moving immediately *wir müssen die Dinge wirklich sofort in Gang bringen*
We don't intend to ... *wir haben nicht vor, ... zu ...*
We are not thinking of carrying out the changes yet *wir planen noch nicht, diese Änderungen durchzuführen*
It probably won't come to that *so weit wird es wahrscheinlich nicht kommen*

EXPLANATIONS

In view of ... *in Anbetracht dessen, daß ...*
In view of the fact that ... *in Anbetracht der Tatsache, daß ...*
As a result of ... *als Folge von (+dat) ...*
Thanks to ... *dank (+gen) ...*
For lack of ... *mangels (+gen) ...*
On the grounds that ... *aufgrund (+gen) ...*
This was caused by external factors *das wurde durch externe Faktoren verursacht*
It was therefore necessary to act fast *daher war es nötig, schnell zu handeln*
The problem goes back to the oil crisis *das Problem geht auf die Ölkrise zurück*
It was like this: *das war folgendermaßen:*

SUMMING UP

Let me summarize the main points again *lassen Sie mich die Hauptpunkte noch einmal zusammenfassen*
Finally, I would just like to say ... *zum Schluß möchte ich noch sagen ...*
Are there any questions? *gibt es Fragen?*
Well, if there are no more questions, I will stop there *nun, wenn niemand mehr Fragen hat, komme ich zum Schluß*
Thank you (all) for your attention *(Ihnen allen) vielen Dank für Ihre Aufmerksamkeit*

ASKING QUESTIONS

I'd like to ask a question *ich möchte etwas fragen*
How much/many ...? *wieviel/wieviele?*
How often ...? *wie oft ...?*
Who? *wer?*
When? *wann?*
Why? *warum?*
Could you give us a few more details about? *könnten Sie uns*

noch einige Einzelheiten über ... geben?

Can I just pick you up on something you said earlier? *kann ich auf etwas zurückkommen, was Sie vorhin gesagt haben?*

I'm not sure I understood your point about ... Could you clarify it please? *ich bin (mir) nicht sicher, ob ich Ihre Bemerkung über ... richtig verstanden habe. Könnten Sie das bitte näher erläutern?*

Where can I get more information about ...? *wo kann ich weitere Information über ... erhalten?*

Can you give any examples of that? *können Sie dafür ein paar Beispiele geben?*

ANSWERING QUESTIONS

Could you repeat that please? *könnten Sie das bitte wiederholen?*

I didn't quite hear that *ich habe das nicht richtig verstanden*

Would you mind speaking a little more slowly? *könnten Sie bitte etwas langsamer sprechen?*

Could you repeat that in English please? *könnten Sie das bitte auf Englisch wiederholen?*

Can I answer that question later? *kann ich diese Frage später beantworten?*

Good question *eine gute Frage*

That's a difficult question but I'll do my best to answer it *das ist eine schwierige Frage, aber ich werde mein Bestes tun, sie zu beantworten*

I think it's best if ... answers that for you *ich glaube, ... kann das besser für Sie beantworten*

I can't give you an exact answer, I'm afraid *da kann ich Ihnen leider keine genaue Antwort geben*

Can I get back to you on that one? *kann ich später darauf zurückkommen?*

Let me clarify that for you *lassen Sie mich das erläutern*

You're quite right *da haben Sie ganz recht*

I agree entirely *da stimme ich Ihnen vollkommen zu*

I'm not sure I can agree with you there *ich bin nicht sicher, ob ich Ihnen da zustimmen kann*

I take your point, but ... *ich akzeptiere, was Sie sagen, aber ...*

USING VISUAL AIDS

Could we have the lights off please? *könnte bitte jemand das Licht ausschalten?*

Here you can see ... *hier sehen Sie ...*

Please look at figure two/three *schauen Sie sich bitte Abbildung zwei/drei an*

This chart illustrates ... *dieses Diagramm illustriert ...*
These are the figures for ... *das sind die Ziffern für ...*
This gives you a clear picture of ... *das gibt Ihnen einen klaren Überblick über ...*
The handouts in front of you will give you a better idea of this *die Kopien, die vor Ihnen liegen, geben Ihnen eine bessere Vorstellung davon*
As you can see in this diagram/photograph *wie Sie auf diesem Diagramm/Foto sehen können ...*
I have brought a short film/a few slides with me to illustrate this *ich habe einen kurzen Film/ein paar Dias mitgebracht, um das zu illustrieren*

PROBLEMS WITH EQUIPMENT AND MATERIALS

The ... isn't working *der/die/das ... funktioniert nicht*
Can you hear me all right? *können Sie mich verstehen?*
I am sorry about the quality of these photocopies *tut mir leid, die Fotokopien sind leider nicht so gut*
Please bear with me *einen Moment bitte*
As you would have seen if the projector/TV had been working *wenn der Projektor/Fernseher funktioniert hätte, hätten Sie das gesehen*

ADDITIONAL VOCABULARY

abstract	*Zusammenfassung f*
afternoon session	*Nachmittagssitzung f*
agenda	*Tagesordnung f*
audience	*Zuhörer pl, Publikum nt*
audio-visual aids	*audio-visuelle Hilfsmittel ntpl*
bar chart	*Balkendiagramm nt*
(black)board	*Tafel f*
case study	*Fallstudie f*
cassette	*Kassette f*
cassette player	*Kassettenrecorder m*
chart	*Diagramm nt*
conference	*Konferenz f*
conference centre	*Konferenzzentrum nt*
conference hall	*Konferenzsaal m*
conference room	*Konferenzzimmer nt*
convention	*Tagung f*
data	*Daten pl*
debate *n*	*Debatte f*
delegate	*Delegierter m, Delegierte f*

CONFERENCES AND PUBLIC SPEAKING

diagram	*Diagramm* nt
discussion	*Diskussion* f
eraser *(for board)*	*Schwamm* m
evening session	*Abendsitzung* f
exhibition hall	*Ausstellungshalle* f
felt pen	*Filzstift* m
figure two/three	*Abbildung* f *zwei/drei*
flipchart	*Flip-Chart* f
flowchart	*Flußdiagramm* nt
graph	*Schaubild* nt
hall	*Halle* f, *Saal* m
handout	*fotokopierte Notizen* fpl
illustration	*Illustration* f
keynote speaker	*Hauptredner(in)* m(f)
keynote speech	*Hauptrede* f
lectern	*Pult* nt
light	*Licht* nt
meeting	*Besprechung* f
meeting room	*Besprechungsraum* m
microphone	*Mikrofon* nt
morning session	*Morgensitzung* f
notepaper	*Schreibpapier* nt
notes	*Aufzeichnungen* fpl
overhead projector	*Overheadprojektor* m
PA system	*Lautsprecheranlage* f
photocopy *n*	*Fotokopie* f
photograph	*Fotografie* f
pie chart	*Kreisdiagramm* nt
podium	*Podest* nt
pointer	*Zeiger* m
presentation	*Präsentation* f
press conference	*Pressekonferenz* f
progress report	*Tätigkeitsbericht* m
projector	*Projektor* m
refreshments	*Erfrischungen* fpl
screen	*Leinwand* f
seminar	*Seminar* nt
slide	*Dia(positiv)* nt
slide projector	*Diaprojektor* m
speak	*reden*
speaker	*Redner(in)* m(f)
speech	*Rede* f
talk	*reden*
teleconferencing	*Telekonferenzschaltung* f
time limit	*zeitliche Begrenzung* f

trade fair	*Handelsmesse f*
transparency	*Dia(positiv) nt*
TV monitor	*Fernsehmonitor m*
video (film) *n*	*Video nt*
video camera	*Videokamera f*
video (cassettte)	*Videokassette f*
video conferencing	*Video-Konferenzschaltung f*
video recorder	*Videorecorder m*
whiteboard	*weiße Tafel f*
working group	*Arbeitsgruppe f*
workshop	*Workshop m*

See also **BANKING AND FINANCE** *and* **THE EUROPEAN COMMUNITY**

absolute monopoly	*unbeschränktes Monopol nt*
absorption	*Absorption f*
acquisition	*Aufkauf m*
active partner	*tätiger Gesellschafter m, tätige Gesellschafterin f*
adverse trade balance	*passive Handelsbilanz f*
affiliated company	*Schwestergesellschaft f*
amalgamate	*fusionieren*
amalgamation	*Fusion f*
anti-dumping duty	*Antidumpingzoll m*
anti-trust legislation	*Kartellgesetzgebung f*
asset-stripping	*Aufkauf m eines Unternehmens und anschließender Verkauf einzelner Teile*
associated company	*Beteiligungsgesellschaft f*
balance of payments	*Zahlungsbilanz f*
balance of trade	*Handelsbilanz f*
bankrupt *adj*	*bankrott*
go bankrupt	*Bankrott machen*
barter *n*	*Tauschhandel m*
barter *vb*	*tauschen*
bilateral trade	*bilateraler Handel m*
black economy	*Schattenwirtschaft f*
black market	*Schwarzmarkt m*
boom	*Hochkonjunktur f*
borrow	*Kredit m aufnehmen*
borrowing	*Kreditaufnahme f*
break-up value	*Liquidationswert m*
capital	*Kapital nt*
capital allowance	*Anlagenabschreibung f*
capital expenditure	*Kapitalaufwand m*
capital goods	*Kapitalgüter ntpl*
capital-intensive	*kapitalintensiv*
capital investment	*Kapitalanlage f*
capital movement	*Kapitalverkehr m*
capital structure	*Kapitalstruktur f*
cartel	*Kartell nt*
cash reserves	*Bargeldreserven fpl*
centralized economy	*zentral gesteuerte Wirtschaft f*

to absorb a loss *einen Verlust auffangen*
a favourable/unfavourable Budget *ein günstiger/ungünstiger Haushalt*

collateral	Sicherheit f
collective ownership	Gemeinschaftsbesitz m
conglomerate	Konglomerat nt
consortium	Konsortium nt
consume	verbrauchen
consumer	Verbraucher m
controlled economy	gelenkte Wirtschaft f
cooperative	Genossenschaft f
co-ownership	Miteigentum nt
cost of living index	Lebenshaltungskostenindex m
cost-push inflation	kostentreibende Inflation f
countertrading	zwischenstaatlicher Tauschhandel m
credit squeeze	Kreditbeschränkung f
cut back vb	kürzen
cutback n	Kürzung f
deficit	Defizit nt
deflation	Deflation f
deflationary	deflationistisch
demand-pull inflation	Nachfrageinflation f
denationalization	Reprivatisierung f
denationalize	reprivatisieren
depression	Wirtschaftskrise f
devaluation	Abwertung f
devalue	abwerten
development area	Fördergebiet nt
diseconomies of scale	Ertragsverringerung f bei steigender Unternehmensgröße
disinflation	Desinflation f
disinvest	desinvestieren
disinvestment	Desinvestition f
disposable personal income	verfügbares Einkommen nt
dollar area	Dollarraum m
dump	verschleudern
dumping	Dumping nt
earned income	Arbeitseinkommen nt
earnings	Verdienst m, Einkommen nt
economic climate	Wirtschaftsklima nt
economic growth	Wirtschaftswachstum nt
economics	Wirtschaftswissenschaften fpl

the economic development of a region/country *die wirtschaftliche Entwicklung einer Region/eines Landes*
a downturn in the economy *ein Abflauen der Wirtschaft*

economic trend	Wirtschaftsentwicklung f
economic warfare	Wirtschaftskrieg m
economies of scale	Größenvorteile mpl
economist	Wirtschaftswissenschaftler(in) m(f)
economize	sparen
economy	Wirtschaft f
embargo	Embargo nt
excess capacity	Überkapazität f
excess supply	Überangebot nt
exchange control	Devisenkontrolle f
Exchange Rate Mechanism (ERM)	Wechselkursmechanismus m
excise duty	Verbrauchssteuer f
fiscal measures	Steuermaßnahmen fpl
fiscal policy	Fiskalpolitik f
foreign investment	Auslandsinvestition f
free enterprise	freie Marktwirtschaft f
free trade	Freihandel m
full employment	Vollbeschäftigung f
galloping inflation	galoppierende Inflation f
gold reserves	Goldreserven fpl
gold standard	Goldstandard m
government intervention	staatlicher Eingriff m
government stock	Staatsanleihe f
gross domestic product (GDP)	Bruttoinlandsprodukt nt (BIP nt)
gross national product (GNP)	Bruttosozialprodukt nt (BSP nt)
growth rate	Wachstumsrate f
horizontal integration	horizontale Integration f
hyperinflation	galoppierende Inflation f
incomes policy	Einkommenspolitik f
income tax	Einkommenssteuer f
inflation	Inflation f
infrastructure	Infrastruktur f
Inland Revenue (IR)	britisches Finanzamt nt

there has been a sharp/gradual fall in ... *ein plötzlicher/allmählicher Rückgang (+gen) ... hat stattgefunden*

to float EC currencies against the dollar *EG-Währungen gegen den Dollar in Umlauf setzen*

to allow the exchange rate of sterling to float *den Wechselkurs des Pfundes freigeben*

a healthy/unhealthy economy *eine gesunde/angeschlagene Wirtschaft*

the economy is being held back by ... *die Konjunktur wird durch ... gedrosselt*

interest rate	Zinssatz m
invest (in)	investieren (in +acc)
investment	Investition f
investment grant	Investitionszuschuß m
invisible exports	unsichtbare Ausfuhren fpl
invisible imports	unsichtbare Einfuhren fpl
labour costs	Lohnkosten pl
labour-intensive	arbeitsintensiv
labour market	Arbeitsmarkt m
laissez-faire policy	Politik f eines wirtschaftlichen Liberalismus m
macroeconomics	Makroökonomie f
market economy	Marktwirtschaft f
market forces	Marktkräfte fpl
merge	fusionieren
merger	Fusion f
microeconomics	Mikroökonomie f
mixed economy	gemischte Wirtschaftsform f
mobility of labour	Mobilität f der Arbeitskräfte fpl
monetarism	Monetarismus m
monetarist	Monetarist(in) m(f)
monetary policy	Währungspolitik f
money supply	Geldvolumen nt
monopoly	Monopol nt
monopsony	Nachfragemonopol nt
nationalization	Verstaatlichung f
nationalize	verstaatlichen
nationalized industry	verstaatlichter Industriezweig m
natural resources	natürliche Ressourcen fpl
non-profit-making	gemeinnützig
oligopoly	Oligopol nt
overcapitalized	überkapitalisiert
overheated economy	überhitzte Konjunktur f
overproduction	Überproduktion f
overspend	zuviel ausgeben
paper money	Papiergeld nt
petrodollar	Petrodollar m
planned economy	Planwirtschaft f
price control	Preiskontrolle f

interest rates are falling/rising der Zinssatz fällt/steigt
to go into liquidation in Liquidation treten
to let market forces take effect die marktwirtschaftlichen Kräfte wirken lassen
the outlook is bright/gloomy die Perspektiven sind gut/schlecht

price-fixing	Preisbindung f
prices and incomes policy	Preis- und Einkommenspolitik f
price war	Preiskrieg m
private limited company	Gesellschaft f mit beschränkter Haftung (GmbH f)
privately-owned	in Privatbesitz m
private sector	privater Sektor m
privatization	Privatisierung f
privatize	privatisieren
productivity	Produktivität f
protectionism	Protektionismus m
public ownership	Staatseigentum nt
public sector	öffentlicher Sektor m
public utility	Versorgungsunternehmen nt
public works	öffentliche Arbeiten fpl
recession	Rezession f
redevelop	sanieren
redevelopment	Sanierung f
reflation	Reflation f
regional development grant	Regionalentwicklungszuschuß m
resale price maintenance (RPM)	Preisbindung f der zweiten Hand
reserve currency	Reservewährung f
retail price index	Einzelhandelspreisindex m
revaluation	Aufwertung f
sanctions	Sanktionen fpl
seasonally-adjusted figures	saisonbereinigte Zahlen fpl
shift in demand	Nachfrageverlagerung f
silent partner	stiller Teilhaber m, stille Teilhaberin f, stiller Gesellschafter m, stille Gesellschafterin f
sinking fund	Tilgungsfonds m
sleeping partner	stiller Teilhaber m, stille Teilhaberin f, stiller Gesellschafter m, stille Gesellschafterin f
sluggish	flau
slump n	starker Konjunkturrückgang m
socio-economic	sozialwirtschaftlich

to call in the receivers die Konkursverwalter bestellen
to go into receivership den Konkurs eröffnen
there has been a sharp/gradual rise in ... ein plötzlicher/allmählicher Anstieg (+gen) ... hat stattgefunden

special development area (SDA)	besonderes Entwicklungsgebiet nt
stabilization	Stabilisierung f
stagflation	Stagflation f
stagnation	Stagnation f
standard of living	Lebensstandard m
state-owned	staatseigen
subsidize	subventionieren
subsidy	Subvention f
supply and demand	Angebot nt und Nachfrage f
support buying	Stützungskäufe mpl
take over	übernehmen
takeover	Übernahme f
takeover bid	Übernahmeangebot nt
threshold agreement	Lohnschwellenvereinbarung f
trade barrier	Handelsschranke f
undercapitalized	unterkapitalisiert
under-employment	Unterbeschäftigung f
unemployment	Arbeitslosigkeit f
unit cost	Kosten pl pro Einheit f
unit price	Preis m pro Einheit f
venture capital	Risikokapital nt
vertical integration	vertikale Integration f
visible exports	sichtbare Ausfuhren fpl
visible imports	sichtbare Einfuhren fpl
wage-price spiral	Lohn-Preis-Spirale f
wage restraint	Niederhaltung f von Löhnen mpl

trade in goods and services Waren- und Dienstleistungsverkehr m
an upturn in the economy ein Wirtschaftsaufschwung m

See also **GERMAN ABBREVIATIONS AND INSTITUTIONS**

This is a general abbreviations list. Individual topics contain abbreviations specific to that topics.

When citing company names, it is not usual to translate the abbreviations in the names, e.g. Co, Corp, Inc, Ltd, plc. The translations given here are the equivalents in German.

The use of capital letters and full stops in abbreviations and acronyms may vary.

A/A *(articles of association)*	*Gesellschaftsvertrag m*
AAR *(against all risks)*	*gegen alle Gefahren*
a/c *(account)*	*Kto. (Konto nt)*
a/c *(account current)*	*GK (Girokonto nt)*
acv *(actual cash value)*	*Zeitwert m*
a/d *(after date)*	*a.d. (nach Ausstellungsdatum)*
ADC *(Advice of Duration and Charge)*	*Dauer- und Kostenanzeige f*
ad val *(ad valorem)*	*ad val. (ad valorem)*
af *(advance freight)*	*Frachtvorauszahlung f*
AGM *(annual general meeting)*	*JHV f (Jahreshauptversammlung f)*
AI *(artificial intelligence)*	*KI f (künstliche Intelligenz f)*
AIDA *(Attention, Interest, Desire, Action)*	*AIDA (Aufmerksamkeit, Interesse, Wunsch, Handeln)*
aka *(also known as)*	*alias*
am *(ante meridiem)*	*vorm. (vormittags)*
AO(C)B *(any other (competent) business)*	*Sonstiges*
approx *(approximately)*	*ca. (circa)*
APR *(annual(ized) percentage rate)*	*Jahreszinssatz m*
AR *(account rendered)*	*vorgelegte Rechnung f*
AR *(annual return)*	*Jahresrendite f*
A/R *(all risks (insurance))*	*Gesamtversicherung f*
A/s *(account sales)*	*Verkaufsrechnung f*
a/s *(after sight)*	*n.S. (nach Sicht)*
asap *(as soon as possible)*	*baldmögl. (baldmöglichst)*
ASR *(automatic send and receive)*	*automatischer Sende- und Empfangsmodus m*
asst *(assistant)*	*Assistent(in) m(f)*
av *(average)*	*Durchschn. (Durchschnitt m)*
B/D *(bank draft)*	*Bankanweisung f*
B/E *(bill of entry)*	*Zolldeklaration f*

B/E *(bill of exchange)*	*Wechsel m*
B/L *(bill of lading)*	*Konnossement nt*
BO *(branch office)*	*Filiale f*
B/P *(bills payable)*	*Wechselverbindlichkeiten fpl*
B/R *(bills receivable)*	*Wechselforderungen fpl*
Bros *(brothers)*	*Gebr. (Gebrüder pl)*
B/S *(balance sheet)*	*Bilanz f*
B/S *(bill of sale)*	*Übereignungsurkunde f*
BST *(British Summer Time)*	*britische Sommerzeit f*
© *(copyright)*	*© (Copyright nt)*
c *(circa)*	*ca. (circa)*
CA *(chartered accountant)*	*Wirtschaftsprüfer(in) m(f)*
c.a. *(current assets)*	*UV (Umlaufvermögen nt)*
C/A *(current account)*	*GK (Girokonto nt)*
C & F *(cost and freight)*	*Kosten und Fracht*
carr *(carriage)*	*Transport m*
cat *(catalogue)*	*Kat. (Katalog m)*
CB *(cash book)*	*Kassenbuch nt*
cc *(carbon copy)*	*Kopie f an*
CD *(cash discount)*	*Skonto nt*
c.d. *(cum dividend)*	*c.d. (cum dividendo; mit Dividende(n))*
CET *(Central European Time)*	*MEZ (Mitteleuropäische Zeit f)*
cf *(compare)*	*vgl. (vergleiche)*
CH *(customs house)*	*Zollamt nt*
CIA *(cash in advance)*	*Vorauszahlung f*
CIF *(cost, insurance and freight)*	*cif (Kosten, Versicherung und Fracht inkl.)*
CIF & C *(cost, insurance, freight and commission)*	*cif & c (Kosten, Versicherung, Fracht und Provision inkl.)*
CIF & I *(cost, insurance, freight and interest)*	*cif & i (Kosten, Versicherung, Fracht und Bankzinsen inkl.)*
CN *(credit note)*	*Gutschrift f*
Co *(company)*	*KG f (Kommanditgesellschaft f)*
c/o *(care of)*	*c/o (bei)*
COD *(cash on delivery, collect on delivery)*	*Nachn. (per Nachnahme)*
contd *(continued)*	*Forts. (Fortsetzung f)*
Corp *(corporation)*	*Ges. (Gesellschaft f)*
Coy *(company)*	*KG f (Kommanditgesellschaft f)*
C/P *(charter-party)*	*Chartergesellschaft f*
cwo *(cash with order)*	*Bezahlung f bei Auftragserteilung*
D/A *(deed of arrangement)*	*schriftliche Vergleichsvereinbarung f*
D/A *(deposit account)*	*Sparkonto nt*

D/A *(documents against acceptance)*	*Dokumente ntpl gegen Akzept nt*
DAP *(documents against payment)*	*Dokumente ntpl gegen Zahlung f*
DBA *(doing business as)*	*Firmenname m*
DCF *(discounted cash flow)*	*Barwertrechnung f*
DD *(demand draft)*	*Sichtwechsel m*
dept *(department)*	*Abt. (Abteilung f)*
dis *(discount)*	*Rab. (Rabatt m)*
ditto	*dto. (dito)*
D/N *(debit note)*	*Lastz. (Lastschriftzettel m)*
doz *(dozen)*	*Dtzd. (Dutzend nt)*
D/P *(deferred payment)*	*Ratenzahlung f*
D/R *(deposit receipt)*	*Einzahlungsbestätigung f*
ea *(each)*	*je*
E&OE *(errors and omissions excepted)*	*Irrtum vorbehalten*
e.g.	*z.B. (zum Beispiel)*
EGM *(extraordinary general meeting)*	*a.o.HV f (außerordentliche Hauptversammlung f)*
enc, encl *(enclosure)*	*Anl. (Anlage f)*
esp *(especially)*	*bes. (besonders)*
est *(estimate)*	*Kostenvoranschlag m*
est *(estimated)*	*gesch. (geschätzt)*
est, estd *(established)*	*gegr. (gegründet)*
et al	*et al.*
etc	*etc.*
et seq	*ff. (und folgende)*
excl *(excluding)*	*ausgen. (ausgenommen)*
excl *(exclusive)*	*exkl. (exklusive)*
ext(n) *(extension)*	*App. (Apparat m)*
FAQ *(free alongside quay)*	*f.a.q. (frei längsseite Kai)*
FAS *(free alongside ship)*	*f.a.s. (frei Längsseite Schiff)*
FD *(free delivered at dock)*	*f.D. (frei Dock)*
FIFO *(first in first out)*	*zuerst eingekauft - zuerst verbraucht*
fig *(figure)*	*Abb. (Abbildung f)*
FO *(firm offer)*	*festes Angebot nt*
FOB *(free on board)*	*f.o.b. (frei Schiff)*
FOC *(free of charge)*	*kostenlos*
FOT *(free of income tax)*	*einkommenssteuerfrei*
FP *(fully paid)*	*voll bezahlt*
FT index	*FT-Index m (Financial-Times-Index m)*
GA *(general average)*	*große Havarie f*

GDP *(gross domestic product)*	*BIP nt (Bruttoinlandsprodukt nt)*
GM *(general manager)*	*Hauptgeschäftsführer(in) m(f)*
GNP *(gross national product)*	*BSP nt (Bruttosozialprodukt nt)*
gov(t) *(government)*	*Reg. (Regierung f)*
gr wt *(gross weight)*	*Br.-G. (Bruttogewicht nt)*
gtd, guar *(guaranteed)*	*gar. (garantiert)*
h *(hour(s))*	*Std. (Stunde(n) f(pl))*
HO *(Head Office)*	*Z (Zentrale f)*
hon *(honorary)*	*ehrenamtlich*
HP *(hire purchase)*	*Ratenkauf m*
HP *(horsepower)*	*PS (Pferdestärke f)*
HQ *(headquarters)*	*Z (Zentrale f)*
hr *(hour(s))*	*Std. (Stunde(n) f(pl))*
ib, ibid *(ibidem)*	*ib., ibd. (ibidem; ebenda)*
i/c *(in charge (of))*	*v.D. (vom Dienst)*
i.e.	*d.h. (das heißt)*
Inc *(Incorporated)*	*e.G. (eingetragene Gesellschaft f)*
incl *(including, inclusive)*	*inkl. (inklusive)*
inst *(instant)*	*d.M. (dieses Monats)*
int *(interest)*	*Zinsen pl*
inv *(invoice)*	*Rechn., Rechng. (Rechnung f)*
IOU *(an I owe you)*	*Schuldschein m*
IT *(income tax)*	*LSt. (Lohnsteuer f)*
IT *(Information Technology)*	*IT f (Informationstechnik f)*
J/A *(joint account)*	*gemeinsames Konto nt*
Jr, jun *(junior)*	*jr., jun. (Junior m)*
k *(thousand)*	*K, Tsd. (Tausend nt)*
L/C *(letter of credit)*	*Akkreditiv nt*
LIFO *(last in first out)*	*zuletzt eingekauft - zuerst verbraucht*
loc cit	*l.c.; a.a.O. (loco citato; am angeführten Ort)*
lpm *(lines per minute)*	*Zeilen/min (Zeilen fpl pro Minute f)*
Ltd *(limited)*	*GmbH (Gesellschaft f mit beschränkter Haftung)*
M *(million)*	*Mio, Mill (Million(en) f(pl))*
max *(maximum)*	*Max.; max. (Maximum nt; maximal adj)*
MD *(managing director)*	*Gschf. (Geschäftsführer m)*
Messrs *(Messieurs)*	*Messrs. (Messieurs)*
min *(minimum)*	*Min.; min. (Minimum nt; minimal adj)*
min *(minute)*	*Min. (Minute f)*
misc *(miscellaneous)*	*versch. (verschieden)*

MO *(mail order)*	*Bestellung f durch die Post*
MO *(money order)*	*PA (Postanweisung f)*
mo *(month)*	*Mon. (Monat m)*
mon *(monetary)*	*monetär*
Mr	*Hr. (Herr m)*
MRP *(maker's recommended price)*	*empf. Preis (empfohlener Preis m)*
Mrs	*Fr. (Frau f)*
Ms	*Fr. (Frau f)*
N/A *(not applicable)*	*entf. (entfällt)*
no *(number)*	*Nr. (Nummer f)*
nr *(near)*	*b. (bei)*
NS *(not specified)*	*nicht spezifiziert*
nt wt *(net weight)*	*Nettogewicht nt*
O & M *(organization and methods)*	*Organisation und Methoden*
o/d *(on demand)*	*auf Verlangen*
OE *(omissions excepted)*	*Auslassungen vorbehalten*
ono *(or near(est) offer)*	*VHB (Verhandlungsbasis f)*
op cit	*op. cit.; im ausgegebenen Werk*
OR *(operational research)*	*Unternehmensforschung f*
OR *(owner's risk)*	*Gefahrtragung f des Eigentümers*
o/s *(out of stock)*	*nicht vorrätig*
PA *(personal assistant)*	*persönliche Assistentin f, persönlicher Assistent m*
pa *(per annum)*	*p.a. (per annum; pro Jahr)*
P & L A/C *(profit and loss account)*	*GuV f (Gewinn- und Verlustrechnung f)*
p & p *(postage and packing)*	*Porto und Verpackung*
pat *(patent)*	*Pat. (Patent nt)*
patd *(patented)*	*pat. (patentiert)*
pat pend *(patent pending)*	*Patent angemeldet*
PAYE *(pay as you earn)*	*Quellenabzugsverfahren nt*
pc *(per cent)*	*Pr. (Prozent nt)*
pd *(paid)*	*bez. (bezahlt)*
PERT *(programme evaluation and review technique)*	*Programmbewertung f und Revisionstechnik f*
ph *(per hour)*	*pro Stunde*
plc *(public limited company)*	*AG f (Aktiengesellschaft f)*
pls *(please)*	*bitte*
pm *(post meridiem)*	*nachm. (nachmittags)*
PN *(promissory note)*	*Schuldschein m*
PO *(postal order)*	*Postanweisung f*
PO *(post office)*	*PA nt (Postamt nt)*
PO Box	*Postf. (Postfach nt)*

POS *(point of sale)*	*P.O.S. (Point of Sale m)*
pp *(pages)*	*S. (Seiten fpl)*
pp *(per procurationem)*	*pp., ppa. (per procurationem; in Vollmacht)*
PR *(personal representative)*	*Verwalter(in) m(f)*
PR *(public relations)*	*PR f (Public Relations fpl)*
PRO *(public relations officer)*	*Pressesprecher(in) m(f)*
pro tem *(pro tempore)*	*z.Zt. (zur Zeit)*
prox *(proximo)*	*n.M. ((des) nächsten Monats)*
PS *(postscript)*	*PS (Postskriptum nt)*
PS *(private secretary)*	*Privatsekretär(in) m(f)*
PTO *(please turn over)*	*b.w. (bitte wenden)*
Pty *(proprietary (company))*	*Dachgesellschaft f*
pw *(per week)*	*pro Woche*
qv *(quod vide)*	*s.d. (siehe dies; siehe dort)*
® *(registered trademark)*	*eingetr. Wz (eingetragenes Warenzeichen nt)*
re *(regarding)*	*betr. (betreffs)*
ref *(reference)*	*Az. (Aktenzeichen nt)*
RO *(receiving order)*	*Konkurseröffnungsbeschluß m*
RP *(reply paid)*	*mit Rückantwort*
RPM *(resale price maintenance)*	*vertikale Preisbindung f*
RRP *(recommended retail price)*	*unverbindliche Preisempfehlung f*
RSVP *(répondez s'il vous plaît)*	*u.A.w.g. (um Antwort wird gebeten)*
sae *(stamped, addressed envelope)*	*frankierter Rückumschlag m*
SD *(sine die)*	*s.d. (sine die; ohne Tagesangabe)*
SDR *(special drawing rights)*	*SZR ntpl (Sonderziehungsrechte ntpl)*
SE *(stock exchange)*	*Börse f*
Sen, Sr *(senior)*	*sen., Sr. (Senior m)*
SI *(Système International (d'Unités))*	*S.I. (Internationales Einheitensystem nt)*
sic	*sic*
SME *(small and medium-sized enterprises)*	*KMU ntpl (klein- und mittelständische Unternehmen ntpl)*
SN *(shipping note)*	*Schiffszettel m*
Soc *(society)*	*Ges. (Gesellschaft f)*
SOR, S/R *(sale or return)*	*Verkauf mit Rückgaberecht*
STD *(subscriber trunk dialling)*	*Selbstwählferndienst m*
ster, stg *(sterling)*	*Sterling m*
TB *(treasury bill)*	*kurzfristiger Schatzwechsel m*
tel	*Tel. (Telefon nt)*
TM *(Trademark)*	*Wz (Warenzeichen nt)*

ult *(ultimo)* — ult. *(ultimo; des letzten Monats)*
USP *(unique selling point)* — USP m *(einmaliges Verkaufsargument nt)*

v *(versus)* — v. *(versus; gegen)*
v *(vide)* — v. *(vide; siehe)*
VAT *(value added tax)* — MwSt. f *(Mehrwertsteuer f)*
VC *(vice chairman)* — stellvertretende Vorsitzende f, stellvertretender Vorsitzender m

viz — viz. *(nämlich)*
vv *(vice versa)* — v.v. *(vice versa; umgekehrt)*
WB *(waybill)* — Frbr. *(Frachtbrief m)*
WIP *(work-in-progress)* — im Gang befindliche Arbeit f
wk *(week)* — Wo. *(Woche f)*
WP *(word processor)* — Textverarbeitungsanlage f
wpm *(words per minute)* — WpM, wpm *(Wörter ntpl pro Minute f)*
wt *(weight)* — Gew. nt *(Gewicht nt)*
YAR *(York-Antwerp Rules)* — Y.A.R. *(York-Antwerpener Regeln fpl)*
yr *(year)* — J. *(Jahr nt)*

See also **AT THE HOTEL** and **TRAVEL**

MEETING PEOPLE

There are two forms of address in German: the formal *Sie* and the informal *du*. You are advised to stick to the formal *Sie* unless you know the person well or they themselves initiate the switch to *du*. This may happen over drinks, after successful negotiations or if you are invited to your host's home, when you might be asked *sollen wir uns nicht duzen?* (do you mind if we call each other by our first names?).

If you are on formal terms you address people by their surname, Herr Schmidt, Frau Schmidt etc. In the morning you would use *guten Morgen*, after lunch *guten Tag* and in the evening *guten Abend*. The use of Fräulein is restricted to girls under 18. It is not customary to ask *how are you?* when being introduced. This is a greeting for someone you already know. Handshaking is customary when greeting and saying goodbye, not just when meeting someone for the first time. It is discourteous not to shake hands.

GREETINGS
Hello *hallo*
Good morning *guten Morgen*
Good afternoon *guten Tag*
Good evening *guten Abend*
Goodnight *gute Nacht*
Goodbye *auf Wiedersehen*

IF YOU'VE NEVER MET
What's your name? *wie ist Ihr Name?*
How do you do? *angenehm*
Pleased to meet you, Mr/Ms ... *angenehm (the person's name is not used in German)*
Here's my (business) card *bitte, meine Visitenkarte*
Do you have a (business) card? *haben Sie eine Visitenkarte?*
I'd like to/May I introduce you to ... *ich möchte Ihnen/darf ich Ihnen ... vorstellen?*
I don't think we've met. I'm ... *ich glaube, wir haben uns noch nicht kennengelernt. Ich bin ...*
This is Mr/Ms ... *das ist Herr/Frau ...*

IF YOU'VE MET BEFORE
It's nice to see you again! *wie schön, Sie wiederzusehen*
How are you? *wie geht es Ihnen?*

(I'm) fine, thank you *gut, danke*
I'm/we're pleased you were able to come *ich freue mich/wir freuen uns, daß Sie kommen konnten*

MAKING YOURSELF UNDERSTOOD
I do not speak much German *ich spreche nicht gut Deutsch*
I learned German at school *ich habe Deutsch in der Schule gelernt*
Do you speak English? *sprechen Sie Englisch?*
Would you mind speaking a bit more slowly? *könnten Sie bitte etwas langsamer sprechen?*
Sorry/pardon? *wie bitte?*
Could you speak up, please? *könnten Sie bitte etwas lauter sprechen?*
I don't understand *ich verstehe (Sie) nicht*
It doesn't matter *das macht nichts*
Can you follow me? *können Sie mir folgen?*
I understand you quite well *ich verstehe Sie recht gut*

MAKING GENERAL CONVERSATION

AS HOST
How was your journey/flight? *wie war die Reise/der Flug?*
Did your flight leave on time? *ist Ihr Flugzeug pünktlich gestartet?*
Is this your first visit to London/Scotland *sind Sie das erste Mal in London/Schottland?*
You look well *Sie sehen gut aus*
How is Mr/Ms ...? *wie geht es Herrn/Frau ...?*
How is your family? *wie geht es Ihrer Familie?*
How long do you plan to stay in Britain? *wie lange wollen Sie in Großbritannien bleiben?*
I have been practising my German since we last met *seit wir uns das letzte Mal gesehen haben, habe ich viel Deutsch geübt*
Your English is excellent *Ihr Englisch ist ausgezeichnet*
Did you have trouble finding us? *hatten Sie Schwierigkeiten, uns zu finden?*
Would you like something to drink/a cup of coffee? *möchten Sie etwas zu trinken/eine Tasse Kaffee?*
Where are you staying? *wo sind Sie untergebracht?*
How is business? *was macht das Geschäft?*

AS GUEST
My flight was delayed 2 hours *mein Flug hatte 2 Stunden Verspätung*
Thank you for coming to meet me (at the airport/station) *vielen Dank, daß Sie mich (am Flughafen/Bahnhof) abgeholt haben*

This is my first visit to your country/town/city *ich bin das erste Mal in Ihrem Land/Ihrer Stadt*
I'm planning to stay a few days *ich habe vor, einige Tage zu bleiben*
I'm flying back next week/tomorrow afternoon *ich fliege nächste Woche/morgen nachmittag zurück*
The weather is so much more pleasant here *das Wetter ist so viel angenehmer hier*
I am staying in the ... (hotel) *ich bin im ... (Hotel) untergebracht*

IN THE PUB/HOTEL

DRINKS AND DRINKING TERMS

alchohol-free	*alkoholfrei*
apéritif	*Aperitif m*
beer	*Bier nt*
bitter	*Altbier nt*
bitter lemon	*Bitter Lemon nt*
brandy	*Brandy m*
champagne	*Sekt m, Champagner m*
cider	*Apfelwein m*
cocktail	*Cocktail m*
Coke®	*Coke® nt*
crisps	*Chips mpl*
dry	*trocken*
fresh orange	*Orangensaft m*
gin	*Gin m*
gin and tonic	*Gin Tonic m*
grapefruit juice	*Grapefruitsaft m*
with ice	*mit Eis*
lager	*Pils nt*
lemon	*Zitrone f*
lemonade	*Limonade f*
lime	*Limone f*
liqueur	*Likör m*
low-alcohol	*alkoholarm*
malt whisky	*Malt Whisky m*
medium dry	*halbtrocken*
mineral water	*Mineralwasser nt*
neat	*pur*
orange	*Orange f*
peanuts	*Erdnüsse fpl*
pineapple juice	*Ananassaft m*
red wine	*Rotwein m*
rosé wine	*Rosé m*

rum	*Rum m*
shandy	*Bier nt mit Limonade*
sherry	*Sherry m*
soda	*Soda nt*
soft drink	*alkoholfreies Getränk nt*
stout	*Starkbier nt*
straight	*pur*
sweet	*süß*
tonic water	*Tonicwater nt*
vermouth	*Wermut m*
vodka	*Wodka m*
white wine	*Weißwein m*
whisky	*Whisky m*

OFFERING DRINKS

Can I buy you a drink? *möchten Sie etwas trinken?*
What would you like to drink? *was möchten Sie trinken?*
Would you like an apéritif? *möchten Sie einen Aperitif?*
Do you drink your whisky neat? *trinken Sie Ihren Whisky pur?*
Would you like ice/lemon in it? *mit Eis/Zitrone?*
Would you like something to eat? *möchten Sie etwas zu essen?*

BUYING DRINKS

I'll have a ..., please *ich hätte gerne einen/eine/ein ..., bitte*
Make mine a double/treble ..., please *für mich einen doppelten/ dreifachen ..., bitte*
I don't drink alcohol *ich trinke keinen Alkohol*
Nothing for me, thanks, I'm driving *nichts für mich, danke, ich muß noch Auto fahren*
No ice, thanks *ohne Eis, bitte*
Do you have any ice? *haben Sie Eis?*
Can I have a chilled/a unchilled bottle, please? *kann ich bitte eine gekühlte/ungekühlte Flasche haben?*

SMOKING

Do you smoke? *rauchen Sie?*
Would you like a cigarette? *möchten Sie eine Zigarette?*
Do you mind if I smoke? *stört es Sie, wenn ich rauche?*
Have you got a light? *haben Sie Feuer?*
What brand do you smoke? *welche Marke rauchen Sie?*
Can I offer you a light? *möchten Sie Feuer?*
It's very smoky in here *es ist sehr verraucht hier*
No thanks, I don't smoke *nein danke, ich bin Nichtraucher(in)*

EATING OUT

IN THE RESTAURANT
Lunch is traditionally the main meal of the day in Germany, although many professional prople tend to have a short lunch at or near their place of work.

ARRIVING AT THE RESTAURANT
A table for two/three, please *einen Tisch für zwei/drei Personen, bitte*
I (don't) have a reservation *ich habe (k)einen Tisch bestellt*
I have reserved a table for three *ich habe einen Tisch für drei bestellt*
Could we have a menu, please? *können wir bitte die Speisekarte haben?*

ORDERING
Do you have a set menu? *haben Sie ein Tagesmenü?*
I'll take the menu at 20 DM *ich hätte gerne das Menü zu 20 DM*
I'd like (the) "..." *ich hätte gerne "..."*
And "..." to follow *und dann "..."*
What do you recommend? *was können Sie empfehlen?*
May I see the wine list? *kann ich bitte die Weinkarte haben?*
Which wine would you recommend with ...? *welchen Wein würden Sie zum/zur ... empfehlen?*
What is the dish of the day? *was ist das Tagesgericht?*
What is (the) "..."? *was ist "..."?*
How is the dish cooked? *wie ist dieses Gericht zubereitet?*
Are there any vegetarian dishes on the menu? *haben Sie auch vegetarische Gerichte auf der Speisekarte?*
Can I have the "..." but without the "..."? *kann ich den/die/das ... haben, aber ohne den/die/das ...?*
Is this dish very spicy? *ist diseses Gericht sehr scharf?*
Does this have ... in it? *ist dieses Gericht mit ...?*
Are vegetables included? *ist da Gemüse dabei?*
Could you bring some (more) water/bread/butter, please? *könnten Sie uns bitte (noch) etwas Wasser/Brot/Butter bringen?*
What types of cheese do you have? *welche Käsesorten haben Sie?*
Nothing else, thank you *danke, nichts mehr*

PROBLEMS
This is not what I ordered *das habe ich nicht bestellt*
I ordered ... *ich habe ... bestellt*
My food is cold *mein Essen ist kalt*

This if off *das ist schlecht*
My steak/fish is burnt *mein Steak/Fisch ist angebrannt*
You haven't brought me my salad/dessert yet *Sie haben mir den Salat/den Nachtisch noch nicht gebracht*

PAYING
Could I have the bill, please? *ich möchte zahlen, bitte*
The meal was delicious *das Essen war ausgezeichnet*
Is service included? *ist das inklusive Bedienung?*
There seems to be a mistake here *da scheint etwas nicht zu stimmen*
What is this sum for? *wofür ist dieser Betrag?*

TIPPING

In Austria, service is normally included in the bill, so you would be expected simply to round up the sum to the nearest 10 Schillings. If service is not included, you should give 10% of the bill as a tip.

A small gratuity for friendly service is normally all that is required in Germany, where bills are usually marked *mit Bedienung* (service included).

In Luxembourg, give an extra tip if the service is outstanding, otherwise service charges are nearly always included in the bill.

A tip is not expected in Switzerland, where service is always included in the bill.

See also **THE EUROPEAN COMMUNITY**

additive	Zusatzstoff m
aerosol spray	Aerosolspray nt
air pollution	Luftverschmutzung f
anti-pollution measure	Umweltschutzmaßnahme f
atmosphere	Atmosphäre f
baseline study	Studie f vor Ort
biodegradable	biologisch abbaubar
biosphere	Biosphäre f
breakdown (of matter)	Abbau m
CFC (chlorofluorocarbon)	FCKW m (Fluorochlorkohlenwasserstoff m)
clean air	saubere Luft f
clean technology	saubere Technologie f
clean up vb	säubern
clean-up campaign	Säuberungskampagne f
colouring	Farbstoff m
compliance audit	Prüfen nt der Einhaltung von Vorschriften
conservation	Umweltschutz m
conserve	erhalten
contaminate	verunreinigen
contamination	Verschmutzung f
damage	Schaden m
damaging	schädlich
decontaminate	entgiften
decontamination	Entgiftung f
degradation	Degradierung f
Department of the Environment (DOE)	britisches Umweltministerium nt
detergent	Waschmittel nt
development area	Fördergebiet nt
directive	Direktive f
dump n	Mülldeponie f
dump vb	ablagern
dumping	Schuttabladen nt
ecological	ökologisch
ecologist	Ökologe m, Ökologin f
ecology	Ökologie f

to clean up one's act auf umweltfreundliche Produktionsweise umstellen
to have a high/low lead/carbon monoxide content einen hohen/niedrigen Gehalt an Blei/Kohlenmonoxyd haben

emission	*Emission f*
energy conservation	*Energiesparen nt*
energy-saving device	*energiesparende Vorrichtung f*
energy-saving policy	*energiebewußte Politik f*
environment	*Umwelt f*
environmental assessment *or* audit	*Umweltverträglichkeitsprüfung f*
environmental damage	*Umweltschaden m*
environmental impact	*Umwelteinfluß m*
environmentalist	*Umweltschützer(in) m(f)*
environmental lobby	*Umwelt-Lobby f*
environmentally friendly	*umweltfreundlich*
environmental management	*Umwelt-Management nt*
environmental statement	*Umweltschutzerklärung f*
filter	*Filter m*
fossil fuels	*fossile Brennstoffe mpl*
global warming	*Erwärmung f der Erdatmosphäre f*
green	*grün*
greenfield site	*unerschlossenes Bauland nt*
greenhouse effect	*Treibhauseffekt m*
greenhouse gas	*Treibhausgas nt*
greening	*zunehmendes Umweltbewußtsein nt*
green issues	*Umweltfragen fpl*
guideline	*Richtlinie f*
health hazard	*Gesundheitsrisiko nt*
herbicide	*Herbizid nt*
impact *n*	*Auswirkung f*
impact (on) *vb*	*Auswirkung f haben (auf +acc)*
insecticide	*Insektizid nt*
Integrated Pollution Control (IPC)	*Integrierte Verschmutzungskontrolle f*
landfill site	*Mülldeponie f*
leakage	*Leck nt*
legislation	*Gesetzgebung f*
minimize	*minimieren*

the effect of this on the environment *die Folgen, die das für die Umwelt hat*

to stress the environmental advantages of a product *die Umweltfreundlichkeit eines Produktes betonen*

this product is "greener" than its competitors *dieses Produkt ist umweltfreundlicher als Konkurrenzprodukte*

the greening of industry *das zunehmende Umweltbewußtsein innerhalb der Industrie*

natural resources	*natürliche Ressourcen fpl*
noise pollution	*Lärmbelästigung f*
noxious substance	*Schadstoff m*
nuclear waste	*Atommüll m*
optimum	*Optimum nt*
outflow	*Abfluß m*
ozone-friendly	*ozonfreundlich*
ozone-safe	*ozonsicher*
parameter	*Parameter m*
pesticide	*Pestizid nt*
phosphate	*Phosphat nt*
pollutant	*Schadstoff m*
pollute	*verschmutzen*
polluted	*verschmutzt*
pollution	*Verschmutzung f*
pollution-free *(product, process)*	*umweltfreundlich*
preservation	*Erhaltung f*
preserve	*erhalten*
propellant	*Treibgas nt*
protect	*schützen*
radioactivity	*Radioaktivität f*
recyclable	*wiederverwertbar*
recycle	*recyceln*
recycled paper	*Recyclingpapier nt*
recycling plant	*Recycling-Anlage f*
regulator	*Aufsichtsbehörde f*
residue	*Rückstand m*
resource utilization	*Ausbeutung f der Ressourcen fpl*
reusable	*wiederverwendbar*
smoke	*Rauch m*
spoil *n*	*Abraum m*
spoil *vb*	*zerstören*
standards	*Standards mpl*
sustainable development	*tragbare Entwicklung f*
toxic	*giftig*

this product helps to protect the environment *dieses Produkt ist umweltfreundlich*
this packaging contains 90% recycled material *diese Verpackung besteht zu 90% aus recyceltem Material*
it is our aim to reduce emissions by 25% (by next year) *wir planen, (bis nächstes Jahr) unsere Emissionen um 25% zu reduzieren*
to respect all the regulations governing pollution levels *alle Vorschriften über Verschmutzungsgrade beachten*
this chemical has a very high/low toxicity level *diese Chemikalie hat eine sehr hohe/niedrige Toxizität*

toxicity	*Giftigkeit f*
toxin	*Toxin nt*
treat	*behandeln*
waste	*Abfall m*
waste disposal	*Müllbeseitigung f*
waste management	*Abfallentsorgung f*
waste minimization	*Abfallminimierung f*
waste product	*Abfallprodukt nt*
water pollution	*Wasserverschmutzung f*

See also THE ENVIRONMENT, INSTITUTIONS AND ORGANIZA-TIONS *and* GERMAN ABBREVIATIONS AND INSTITUTIONS

associated states	*assoziierte Mitgliedstaaten* mpl
CERN (Conseil Européen pour la Recherche Nucléaire)	*CERN*
Channel Tunnel	*Kanaltunnel* m
collaborative project	*kollaboratives Projekt* nt
Common Agricultural Policy (CAP)	*gemeinsame Agrarpolitik* f *(GAP f)*
Common Budget	*Gemeinschaftshaushalt* m
Common External Tariff (CET)	*Gemeinsamer Außenzoll* m
Common Market	*Gemeinsamer Markt* m
community law	*Gemeinschaftsrecht* nt
Continent	*Kontinent* m
continental	*kontinental*
Council of Europe	*Europarat* m
Council of Ministers	*Ministerrat* m
directive	*Direktive* f
directorate	*Verwaltungsrat* m
Directorate General (DG)	*Generaldirektion* f
ECU (European Currency Unit)	*ECU* m *(Europäische Währungseinheit* f*)*
EEC national	*Staatsangehörige(r)* f(m) *eines EG-Mitgliedstaates* m
EEC passport	*Europapaß* m
EEC passport-holder	*Inhaber(in)* m(f) *eines Europapasses*
EEC regulations	*EG-Verordnungen* fpl
EEC subsidy	*EG-Subvention* f
ESPRIT (European Strategic Programme for R & D in Information Technology)	*ESPRIT*
EURATOM	*EURATOM* f
EUREKA (European Research Coordination Agency)	*EUREKA (Europäische Behörde* pl *für Koordinierung in der Forschung)*
euro-ad	*europaweiter Werbespot* m

better access to European markets *besseren Zugang zu europäischen Märkten*
with the opening of the Channel Tunnel *mit der Öffnung des Kanaltunnels*
external value of the ECU *externer Wert des ECU*
weights of currencies in the ECU *relativer Wert der Währungen im ECU*
we will accept payment in ECUs *wir akzeptieren Zahlung in ECU*
to enter the EC *der EG beitreten*

Eurobeach	*Eurostrand m*
Eurobond	*Eurobond m*
Eurobond issue	*Eurobond Emission f*
Eurocheque	*Eurocheque m*
Eurocheque card	*Eurocheque-Karte f*
Eurocrat	*Eurokrat(in) m(f)*
Eurocurrency	*Eurowährung f*
Eurocurrency credit	*Eurowährungskredit m*
Eurocurrency market	*Euro(geld)markt m*
Eurodeposit	*Euroeinlage f*
eurodollar	*Eurodollar m*
EUROENVIRON	*EUROENVIRON, Europäisches Umweltbüro nt*
Euromarket	*Euromarkt m*
Euro MP	*Europaabgeordnete(r) f(m)*
Europe	*Europa nt*
European *adj*	*europäisch*
European *n*	*Europäer(in) m(f)*
European Bank for Reconstruction and Development (EBRD)	*Europäische Bank f für Wiederaufbau und Entwicklung*
European Broadcasting Union (EBU)	*EBU f*
European Coal and Steel Community (ECSC)	*Europäische Gemeinschaft f für Kohle und Stahl (EGKS f)*
European Commission	*Europäische Kommission f*
European Community (EC)	*Europäische Gemeinschaft f (EG f)*
European Court of Auditors	*Europäischer Steuergerichtshof m*
European Court of Justice (ECJ)	*Europäischer Gerichtshof m*
European Development Fund (EDF)	*Europäischer Entwicklungsfonds m (EEF m)*
European directive	*Europäische Richtlinie f*
European Economic Community (EEC)	*Europäische Wirtschaftsgemeinschaft f (EWG f)*
European Free Trade Area (EFTA)	*Europäische Freihandelszone f (EFTA f)*
European Free Trade Association (EFTA)	*Europäische Freihandelsassoziation f (EFTA f)*

to take out a eurodollar loan *einen Eurodollar-Kredit aufnehmen*
we are a very European company *unsere Firma ist stark nach Europa hin orientiert*

European Investment Bank (EIB)	Europäische Investitionsbank f (EIB f)
Europeanize	europäisieren
European Monetary Cooperation Fund (EMCF)	Europäischer Fonds m für währungspolitische Zusammenarbeit (EFWZ m)
European Monetary System (EMS)	Europäisches Währungssystem nt (EWS nt)
European Monetary Union (EMU)	Europäische Währungsunion f (EWU f)
European Parliament (EP)	Europäisches Parlament nt
European Regional Development Fund (ERDF)	Europäischer Fonds m für regionale Entwicklung (EFRE m)
European Social Fund	Europäischer Sozialfonds m (ESF m)
European Space Agency (ESA)	Europäische Weltraumorganisation f (EWO f)
European Union	Europäische Union f
European Unit of Account (EUA)	Europäische Rechnungseinheit f
europhile	europhil
Europort	Europort m
Eurosterling	Europfund nt
Eurotunnel	Eurotunnel m
Exchange Rate Mechanism (ERM)	Wechselkursmechanismus m
federal	föderalistisch
federalism	Föderalismus m
federation	Föderation f
free trade	Freihandel m
green pound	grünes Pfund nt
guideline	Richtlinie f
hard ECU	harter ECU m
intra-community trade	innergemeinschaftlicher Handel m

we are hoping to expand our business with continental Europe wir hoffen auf eine Geschäftsausweitung nach Europa

free movement of labour and capital throughout Europe freie Bewegung von Arbeitskräften und Kapital innerhalb Europas

this product/measure respects all the EC guidelines on ... dieses Produkt/ diese Maßnahme entspricht allen EG-Richtlinien über (+acc) ...

to look towards Europe for business sich in Europa nach Geschäftsbeziehungen umschauen

THE EUROPEAN COMMUNITY

Member States	Mitgliedstaaten *mpl*
MEP (Member of the European Parliament)	MdEP *nt* (Mitglied *nt* des Europäischen Parlaments)
Organization for Economic Cooperation and Development (OECD)	Organisation *f* für wirtschaftliche Zusammenarbeit und Entwicklung (OECD *f*)
pan-European	pan-europäisch
single (European) market	(Europäischer) Binnenmarkt *m*
subsidize	subventionieren
subsidy	Subvention *f*
trade barrier	Handelsschranke *f*

within the single market *innerhalb des europäischen Binnenmarkts*
to take advantage of the abolition of trade barriers *die Beseitigung der Handelsbarrieren ausnutzen*

See also **THE EUROPEAN COMMUNITY**

When citing company names, it is not usual to translate the abbreviations in the names, such as AG, GmbH. The translations for these given here are the equivalents in English.

The use of capital letters and full stops in abbreviations and acronyms may vary.

For a guide to pronouncing the letters of the alphabet in German, see page viii.

AA *nt (Auswärtiges Amt nt)*	*German Foreign Office*
a.A. *(auf Anordnung)*	*by order*
a.a.O. *(am angegebenen Ort)*	*loc cit (loco citato)*
Abb. *(Abbildung f)*	*ill(us); fig (illustration; figure)*
Abf. *(Abfahrt f)*	*dep (departure)*
ABM *fpl (Arbeitsbeschaffungs- maßnahmen fpl)*	*job creation scheme*
Abo *nt (Abonnement nt)*	*sub (subscription)*
Abr. *(Abrechnung f)*	*bill*
Abs. *(Absatz m)*	*para (paragraph)*
Abs. *(Absender m)*	*sender*
Abt. *(Abteilung f)*	*dept (department)*
a.d. *(an der)*	*on the*
ADAC *m (Allgemeiner Deutscher Automobil-Club m)*	*German motoring organi- zation*
Adr. *(Adresse f)*	*address*
AG *f (Aktiengesellschaft f)*	*plc (public limited company)*
AGV *f (Arbeitsgemeinschaft f der Verbraucherverbände)*	*consumer groups' associa- tion*
AKW *nt (Atomkraftwerk nt)*	*nuclear power station*
Alu *nt (Aluminium nt)*	*aluminium*
Alu *f (Arbeitslosenunterstützung f)*	*unemployment benefit*
Angest. *(Angestellte(r) f(m))*	*employee*
Anh. *(Anhang m)*	*app (appendix)*
Ank. *(Ankunft f)*	*arr (arrival)*
Anl. *(Anlage f)*	*enc, encl (enclosed, enclosure)*
a.o.HV *f (außerordentliche Hauptversammlung f)*	*EGM (extraordinary general meeting)*
AOK *f (Allgemeine Ortskranken- kasse f)*	*medical insurance scheme*
APA *f (Austria Presse Agentur f)*	*Austrian Press Agency*
App. *(Apparat m)*	*ext(n) (extension)*

ARD f *(Arbeitsgemeinschaft f der öffentlich-rechtlichen Rundfunkanstalten der Bundesrepublik Deutschland)* — German broadcasting association

ASU f *(Abgassonderuntersuchung f)* — exhaust emissions check

ASU f *(Arbeitsgemeinschaft f Selbständiger Unternehmer)* — association of private traders

im Auftr. *(im Auftrag m)* — pp (per procurationem; on behalf of)

AUMA m *(Ausstellungs- und Messe-Ausschuß m der Deutschen Wirtschaft)* — German trade fair and exhibitions committee

Ausg. *(Ausgabe f)* — ed (edition)

ausgen. *(ausgenommen)* — excl (excluding)

av. *(arbeitsverwendungsfähig)* — operable

AVO f *(Allgemeine Vergütungsordnung f)* — general wage regulations

AZ, Az. *(Aktenzeichen nt)* — ref (reference)

BAG nt *(Bundesarbeitsgericht nt)* — German industrial tribunal

baldmögl. *(baldmöglichst)* — asap (as soon as possible)

BAT m *(Bundesangestelltentarif m)* — German salary scale

Bauj. *(Baujahr nt)* — year of construction or manufacture

b.a.w. *(bis auf weiteres)* — until further notice

BDA nt *(Besoldungsdienstalter nt)* — seniority, length of service

BDI m *(Bundesverband m der Deutschen Industrie)* — German CBI

Beitr. *(Beitrag m)* — fee; subscription; contribution

Ber. *(Bericht m)* — report

bes. *(besonders)* — esp (especially)

Best.-Nr. *(Bestellnummer f)* — order number

Betr.; betr. *(Betreff m; betreffend adj; betreffs prep)* — re (regarding)

Bez. *(Bezirk m)* — district

bez. *(bezahlt)* — pd (paid)

bez. *(bezüglich)* — concerning

Bf. *(Bahnhof m)* — (railway) station

BFM nt *(Bundesfinanzministerium nt)* — German ministry of finance

BG f *(Berufsgenossenschaft f)* — professional association with liability for industrial safety and insurance

BGB nt *(Bürgerliches Gesetzbuch nt)* — civil code

Bhf. *(Bahnhof m)* — (railway) station

BIP nt *(Bruttoinlandsprodukt nt)* — GDP (gross domestic product)

BIZ f *(Bank f für Internationalen Zahlungsausgleich)* — BIS (Bank for International Settlements)

BJ, Bj. *(Baujahr nt)* — year of construction or manufacture

BLZ *(Bankleitzahl f)* — bank sort code

BP *(Bundespost f)* — German Post Office

BPA nt *(Bundespresse- und Informationsamt nt)* — German press and information office

BR m *(Bayerischer Rundfunk m)* — Bavarian broadcasting company

BRD f *(Bundesrepublik f Deutschland)* — FRG (Federal Republic of Germany)

Br.-G *(Bruttogewicht nt)* — gr wt (gross weight)

BSP nt *(Bruttosozialprodukt nt)* — GNP (gross national product)

btto. *(brutto)* — gross

Btx m *(Bildschirmtext m)* — teletext

Bundesfinanzminister nt — German ministry of finance

Bundesrat m — upper house of German and Austrian Parliament; Swiss Parliament; member of Swiss or Austrian Bundesrat

Bundestag m — Bundestag (lower house of German Parliament)

BVG nt *(Betriebsverfassungsgesetz nt)* — German Industrial Relations Act

BVM nt *(Bundesverkehrsministerium nt)* — German department of transport

b.w. *(bitte wenden)* — PTO (please turn over)

BWM nt *(Bundeswirtschaftsministerium nt)* — German ministry of trade

BWR m *(Bundeswirtschaftsrat m)* — German economic development council

Bz. *(Bezirk m)* — district

bzgl. *(bezüglich)* — re (with reference to)

bzw. *(beziehungsweise)* — or; that is; respectively

ca. *(circa)* — c (circa)

cbm *(Kubikmeter m)* — m^3 (cubic metre)

ccm *(Kubikzentimeter m)* — cm^3 (cubic centimetre)

DAAD m *(Deutscher Akademischer Ausstauschdienst m)* — German academic exchange service

DAG f *(Deutsche Angestellten-Gewerkschaft f)* — German clerical and administrative workers' union

DAK f *(Deutsche Angestellten-Krankenkasse f)* — German clerical and administrative workers' health insurance company

DAS m *(Deutscher Automobilschutz m)* — German motoring organization

DB f *(Deutsche Bundesbahn f)* — German railways

DBP nt *(Deutsches Bundespatent nt)* — German patent

DBP f *(Deutsche Bundespost f)* — German Post Office

DDR f *(Deutsche Demokratische Republik f)* — GDR ((former) German Democratic Republic)

desgl. *(desgleichen)* — the same

Dez. *(Dezember m)* — Dec (December)

DFF m *(Deutscher Fernsehfunk m)* — East German TV channel

DFG f *(Deutsche Forschungsgemeinschaft f)* — German Research Council

DGB m *(Deutscher Gewerkschaftsbund m)* — German TUC

dgl. *(dergleichen, desgleichen)* — the same

d.h. *(das heißt)* — i.e. (id est, that is)

DIN f *(Deutsche Industrie-Norm f)* — German industrial standard

Dipl.-Ing. *(Diplomingenieur m)* — qualified engineer

d.J. *(dieses Jahres)* — of this year

DM f *(Deutsche Mark f)* — DM (Deutschmark)

d.M *(dieses Monats)* — inst (of this month)

dpa f *(Deutsche Presse-Agentur f)* — German Press Agency

dt. *(deutsch)* — German

Dtzd. *(Dutzend nt)* — doz (dozen)

DV f *(Datenverarbeitung f)* — DP (data processing)

DVA f *(Datenverarbeitungsanlage f)* — data processing equipment or system

dz *(Doppelzentner m)* — 100 kilograms

dz. *(derzeit)* — at present

EDV f *(elektronische Datenverarbeitung f)* — EDP (electronic data processing)

EEF m *(Europäischer Entwicklungsfonds m)* — EDF (European Development Fund)

EFRE m *(Europäischer Fonds m für regionale Entwicklung)* — ERDF (European Regional Development Fund)

EFWZ m *(Europäischer Fonds m für währungspolitische Zusammenarbeit)* — EMCF (European Monetary Cooperation Fund)

EG f *(Europäische Gemeinschaft f)* — EC (European Community)

e.G. *(eingetragene Gesellschaft f)*	*Inc (Incorporated)*
EGKS *f (Europäische Gemeinschaft f für Kohle und Stahl)*	*ECSC (European Coal and Steel Community)*
EIB *f (Europäische Investitionsbank f)*	*EIB (European Investment Bank)*
Einf. *(Einführung f)*	*introduction*
eingetr. Wz. *(eingetragenes Warenzeichen nt)*	® *(registered trademark)*
Einl. *(Einleitung f)*	*introduction; induction*
einschl. *(einschließlich)*	*inc, incl (including)*
EMNID *m (Erforschung, Meinung, Nachrichten, Informationsdienst m)*	*German market and opinion research service*
Empf. *(Empfänger m)*	*addressee, consignee, receiver*
empf. *(empfohlen)*	*recommended*
engl. *(englisch)*	*English*
entf. *(entfällt)*	*N/A (not applicable)*
entspr. *(entsprechend)*	*appropriate; accordingly*
Erdg. *(Erdgeschoß nt)*	*ground floor*
ESF *m (Europäischer Sozialfonds m)*	*ESF (European Social Fund)*
evtl. *(eventuell)*	*possible; possibly*
EWG *f (Europäische Wirtschaftsgemeinschaft f)*	*EEC (European Economic Community)*
EWO *f (Europäische Weltraumorganisation f)*	*ESA (European Space Agency)*
EWS *nt (Europäisches Währungssystem nt)* ·	*EMS (European Monetary System)*
EWU *f (Europäische Währungsunion f)*	*EMU (European Monetary Union)*
exkl. *(exklusive)*	*exclusive of*
EZV *m (elektronischer Zahlungsverkehr m)*	*EFT (electronic funds transfer)*
FA *nt (Finanzamt nt)*	*tax office*
Fa *(Firma f)*	*Co (company)*
FAZ *f (Frankfurter Allgemeine Zeitung f)*	*German newspaper*
FB *m (Fachbereich m)*	*(specialist) field*
FFF *(Film, Funk, Fernsehen)*	*film, radio and television*
FH *(Fachhochschule f)*	*technical college; art college*
Fil. *(Filiale f)*	*br (branch)*
Finanzamt *nt*	*tax office*
Forts. *(Fortsetzung f)*	*instalment; continuation*
Fr. *(Frau f)*	*Mrs, Ms*
franz. *(französisch)*	*French*

Frbr. *(Frachtbrief m)*	*WB (waybill)*
Frl. *(Fräulein nt)*	*Miss*
frz. *(französisch)*	*French*
FuE *f (Forschung f und Entwicklung f)*	*R & D (research and development)*
GAA *nt (Gewerbeaufsichtsamt nt)*	*factory inspectorate*
GAP *f (gemeinsame Agrarpolitik f)*	*CAP (Common Agricultural Policy)*
gar. *(garantiert)*	*gtd, guar (guaranteed)*
Gbf *(Güterbahnhof m)*	*goods station*
Gebr. *(Gebrüder mpl)*	*Bros (Brothers)*
gedr. *(gedruckt)*	*printed*
gegr. *(gegründet)*	*est, estd (established)*
geh. *(geheim; geheftet)*	*secret; stapled*
Gem. *(Gemeinde f)*	*district*
Gen. *(Genossenschaft f)*	*cooperative*
gen. *(genannt)*	*named, called*
Gen.-Dir. *(Generaldirektor m)*	*chairman*
gepr. *(geprüft)*	*tested*
Gerätesicherheitsgesetz *nt*	*technical equipment safety law*
Ges. *(Gesellschaft f)*	*Co (company)*
gesch. *(geschätzt)*	*est (estimated)*
ges. gesch. *(gesetzlich geschützt)*	*protected by law*
Gew. *(Gewerkschaft f)*	*trade union*
Gew. *nt (Gewicht nt)*	*wt (weight)*
gez. *(gezeichnet)*	*signed*
ggf. *(gegebenenfalls)*	*if need be*
GK *(Girokonto nt)*	*a/c (account current)*
GmbH *f (Gesellschaft f mit beschränkter Haftung)*	*Ltd (Limited)*
GO *f (Gebührenordnung f)*	*tariff, scale of charges*
GS *(geprüfte Sicherheit f)*	*tested for safety*
Gschf. *(Geschäftsführer m)*	*MD (managing director)*
GuV *f (Gewinn- und Verlustrechnung f)*	*P & L A/C (profit and loss acount)*
Hbf. *(Hauptbahnhof m)*	*central station*
HG *f (Handelsgesellschaft f)*	*commercial company*
Hg. *(Herausgeber m)*	*ed (editor; publisher)*
hg. *(herausgegeben)*	*edited; published*
HGB *nt (Handelsgesetzbuch nt)*	*statutes of commercial law*
Höchstgew. *(Höchstgewicht nt)*	*max wt (maximum weight)*
HR *m (Hessischer Rundfunk m)*	*Hessen Radio*
Hr. *(Herr m)*	*Mr*
Hrsg. *(Herausgeber m)*	*ed (editor; publisher)*
hrsg. *(herausgegeben)*	*ed (edited; published)*

i.A. *(im Auftrag)* — *pp (per procurationem; on behalf of)*

IAEO *f (Internationale Atomenergie-Organisation f)* — *IAEA (International Atomic Energy Agency)*

IAO *f (Internationale Arbeitsorganisation f)* — *ILO (International Labour Organization)*

IFO *nt (Institut nt für Wirtschaftsforschung)* — *German institute for economic research*

IG *f (Industriegewerkschaft f)* — *industrial trade union*

IGB *m (Internationaler Gewerkschaftsbund m)* — *International Trades Union Congress*

IGH *m (Internationaler Gerichtshof m)* — *ICJ (International Court of Justice)*

IHK *f (Industrie- und Handelskammer f)* — *CC (Chamber of Commerce)*

IHK *f (Internationale Handelskammer f)* — *ICC (International Chamber of Commerce)*

Ing. *(Ingenieur m)* — *engineer*

Inh. *(Inhaber(in) m(f))* — *prop (proprietor)*

Inh. *(Inhalt m)* — *cont (content(s))*

inkl. *(inklusive)* — *inclusive of*

i.Sa. *(in Sachen)* — *in re*

I.V. *(in Vertretung)* — *on behalf of*

I.v. *(Irrtum vorbehalten)* — *subject to correction*

i.V. *(in Vertretung)* — *on behalf of*

i.V. *(in Vollmacht)* — *by proxy*

i.V. *(in Vorbereitung)* — *in preparation*

IWF *m (Internationaler Währungsfonds m)* — *IMF (International Monetary Fund)*

J. *(Jahr nt)* — *yr (year)*

Jg. *(Jahrgang m)* — *year*

JHV *f (Jahreshauptversammlung f)* — *AGM (annual general meeting)*

jur. *(juristisch)* — *legal*

Kant. *(Kanton m)* — *canton*

Kap. *(Kapitel nt)* — *chap (chapter)*

Kat. *(Katalog m)* — *cat (catalogue)*

Kf. *(Kraftfahrer m)* — *driver*

Kfm. *(Kaufmann m)* — *businessman*

kfm. *(kaufmännisch)* — *commercial*

Kfz *nt (Kraftfahrzeug nt)* — *motor vehicle*

KG *f (Kommanditgesellschaft f)* — *limited partnership*

kh., k.H. *(kurzerhand)* — *immediately*

KI *f (künstliche Intelligenz f)* — *AI (artificial intelligence)*

Kj. *(Kalenderjahr nt)* — *calendar year*

k.J. *(künftigen Jahres)* — next year
KK *f (Krankenkasse f)* — health insurance (company)
KKW *nt (Kernkraftwerk nt)* — nuclear power station
km/st *(Kilometer pro Stunde)* — kph (kilometres per hour)
KMU *ntpl (klein- und mittelständische Unternehmen ntpl)* — SME (small and medium-sized enterprises)
Komm. *(Kommission f)* — commission
Kt. *(Kanton m)* — canton
Kto. *(Konto nt)* — a/c (account)
Landtag *m* — provincial Parliament
landw. *(landwirtschaftlich)* — agric (agricultural)
Lastz. *(Lastschriftszettel m)* — D/N (debit note)
Ld. *(Land nt)* — German "Land"
Ldkrs. *(Landkreis m)* — administrative district
lfd. *(laufend)* — current
l.J. *(laufenden Jahres)* — current year
LKW, Lkw *m (Lastkraftwagen m)* — HGV (heavy goods vehicle)
l.M. *(laufenden Monats)* — inst (current month)
LSt. *(Lohnsteuer f)* — IT (income tax)
LVA *f (Landesversicherungsanstalt f)* — social security organization for one German "Land"
M. *(Mitglied nt)* — member
M. *(Monat m)* — m (month)
m.a.W. *(mit anderen Worten)* — in other words
Max.; max. *(Maximum nt; maximal adj)* — max (maximum)
Md. *(Milliarde(n) f(pl))* — billion (1000 million)
m.d.W.d.G.b. *(mit der Wahrnehmung der Geschäfte beauftragt)* — entrusted with the care of somebody's business
m.E. *(meines Erachtens)* — in my opinion
MEZ *(Mitteleuropäische Zeit f)* — CET (central European time)
Mill. *(Million(en) f(pl))* — M (million)
Min. *(Minute f)* — min (minute)
Min.; min. *(Minimum nt; minimal adj)* — min (minimum)
Min.-Dir. *(Ministerialdirektor m)* — permanent secretary in the German Civil Service
Min.-Rat *(Ministerialrat m)* — assistant secretary in the German Civil Service
Mio *(Million(en) f(pl))* — M (million)
Mitgl. *(Mitglied nt)* — member
Mon. *(Monat m)* — mo (month)
Mrd. *(Milliarde(n) f(pl))* — billion (1000 million)
MSchr. *(Monatsschrift f)* — monthly (magazine)
mtl. *(monatlich)* — monthly; per month

MV *f (Mitgliederversammlung f)*   *general meeting*
MVA *f (Müllverbrennungsanlage*   *rubbish incinerator*
f)
m.W. *(meines Wissens)*   *to my knowledge*
MWST, MwSt *f (Mehrwertsteuer*   *VAT (value-added tax)*
f)
Nachdr. *(Nachdruck m)*   *reprint; reproduction*
Nachf. *(Nachfolger(in) m(f))*   *successor*
nachm. *(nachmittags)*   *pm (in the afternoon)*
(per) Nachn. *((per) Nachnahme*   *COD (cash on delivery)*
f)
Nchf. *(Nachfolger(in) m(f))*   *successor*
NDR *m (Norddeutscher Rundfunk*   *North German Radio*
m)
Ndrh. *(Niederrhein m)*   *Lower Rhine*
Neudr. *(Neudruck m)*   *reprint*
n.J. *((des) nächsten Jahres)*   *next year*
n.M. *((des) nächsten Monats)*   *next month*
NO *(Nordost)*   *NE (north east)*
no. *(netto)*   *net*
nordd. *(norddeutsch)*   *North German*
Nr. *(Nummer f)*   *no (number)*
NRW *(Nordrhein-Westfalen)*   *North Rhine-Westphalia*
NS *(Nachschrift f)*   *PS (post scriptum)*
n.S. *(nach Sicht)*   *a/s (after sight)*
ntto *(netto)*   *net*
NWDR *m (Nordwestdeutscher*   *North West German Radio*
Rundfunk m)
O *(Osten m)*   *E (east)*
ÖBB *fpl (Österreichische Bundes-*   *Austrian railways*
bahnen fpl)
öff. *(öffentlich)*   *public(ly)*
o.G. *(ohne Gewähr)*   *subject to change; without liability*
OHG *f (offene Handelsge-*   *general partnership*
sellschaft f)
Okt. *(Oktober m)*   *Oct (October)*
ÖPD *m (Österreichischer Presse-*   *Austrian Press Service*
dienst m)
ORF *m (Österreichischer Rund-*   *Austrian broadcasting company*
funk m)
öS. *(österreichischer Schilling m)*   *Austrian schilling*
öst *(österreichisch)*   *Austrian*
ÖTV *f (Gewerkschaft öffentliche*   *transport union*
Dienste, Transport und Verkehr
f)

PA *nt (Postamt nt)* — *PO (post office)*
PA *(Postanweisung f)* — *MO (money order)*
p.A. *(per Adresse)* — *c/o (care of)*
PC *m (Personal-Computer m)* — *PC (personal computer)*
Pf *(Pfennig m)* — *pfennig*
Pfd. *(Pfund nt)* — *lb (pound(s))*
PKW, Pkw *m (Personenkraftwagen m)* — *car*
PLZ *(Postleitzahl f)* — *post code*
poln. *(polnisch)* — *Polish*
Postf. *(Postfach nt)* — *PO Box*
pp., ppa. *(per procura)* — *pp (per procurationem)*
Pr., Proz. *(Prozent nt)* — *%, pc (per cent)*
PS *(Pferdestärke f)* — *HP (horsepower)*
PSchA *nt (Postscheckamt nt)* — *national Giro office*
PTT *(Post, Telefon, Telegraph)* — *Swiss postal, telephone and telegraph service*

qcm *(Quadratzentimeter m)* — *cm² (square centimetre(s))*
qkm *(Quadratkilometer m)* — *km² (square kilometre(s))*
qm *(Quadratmeter m)* — *m² (square metre(s))*
Rab. *(Rabatt m)* — *dis (discount)*
Rdsch. *(Rundschau f)* — *magazine programme*
Rdschr. *(Rundschreiben nt)* — *circular*
Rechn., Rechng. *(Rechnung f)* — *bill, invoice*
Red. *(Redakteur(in) m(f))* — *ed (editor)*
Red. *(Redaktion f)* — *editor; editorial staff; editorial office*
Reg. *(Regierung f)* — *gov(t) (government)*
Rhld. *(Rheinland nt)* — *Rhineland*
Rj. *(Rechnungsjahr nt)* — *financial year*
R.-Nr. *(Rechnungsnummer f)* — *invoice number*
s *(siehe)* — *v, vid (see)*
S. *(Seite f)* — *p (page)*
s.a. *(siehe auch)* — *see also*
SB *(Selbstbedienung f)* — *self service*
SBB *fpl (Schweizerische Bundesbahnen fpl)* — *Swiss railways*
schwäb. *(schwäbisch)* — *Swabian*
schweiz. *(schweizerisch)* — *Swiss*
s.d. *(siehe dies; siehe dort)* — *qv (quod vide)*
SDR *m (Süddeutscher Rundfunk m)* — *South German radio*
sfr *(Schweizer Franken m)* — *SF, FS (Swiss francs)*
SO *(Südost)* — *SE (south east)*
s.o. *(siehe oben)* — *see above*

sog. *(sogenannt)*	*so-called*
sowj(et). *(sowjetisch)*	*Soviet*
Sped. *(Spediteur m; Spedition f)*	*carrier, forwarding agent; transport, shipping*
s.S. *(siehe Seite)*	*see page*
SSV *(Sommerschlußverkauf m)*	*summer sale*
St. *(Stock m)*	*floor, storey*
St. *(Stück nt)*	*unit; piece*
St., st *(Stunde f)*	*h, hr (hour)*
StA *(Stammaktie(n) f(pl))*	*ordinary share(s)*
staatl. *(staatlich)*	*state(-run)*
Std., Stde. *(Stunde f)*	*h, hr (hour)*
stdl. *(stündlich)*	*hourly; per hour*
stellv. *(stellvertretend)*	*acting*
StV, Stv. *(Stellvertreter m)*	*deputy; representative*
s.u. *(siehe unten)*	*see below*
südd. *(süddeutsch)*	*South German*
SWF *m (Südwestfunk m)*	*South West German broadcasting company*
s.w.u. *(siehe weiter unten)*	*see (further) below*
SZ *f (Süddeutsche Zeitung f)*	*South German newspaper*
s.Z. *(seinerzeit)*	*at that time*
SZR *ntpl (Sonderziehungsrechte ntpl)*	*SDR (special drawing rights)*
t *(Tonne(n) f(pl))*	*tonne(s)*
tägl. *(täglich)*	*daily; per day*
Tel.Adr. *(Telegramm-Adresse f)*	*telegram address*
TO *f (Tarifordnung f)*	*salary scale*
Tsd. *(Tausend nt)*	*k (thousand)*
u. *(und)*	*and*
u.a. *(und andere(s))*	*et al (and others)*
u.a. *(unter anderem)*	*amongst other things*
u.ä. *(und ähnliche(s))*	*and similar*
u.A.w.g. *(um Antwort wird gebeten)*	*RSVP (répondez s'il vous plaît)*
u. desgl. (m) *(und desgleichen (mehr))*	*and the like*
u. dgl. (m) *(und dergleichen (mehr))*	*and the like*
u.E. *(unseres Erachtens)*	*in our opinion*
u.ff. *(und folgende (Seiten))*	*ff, et seq (and following (pages))*
unbest. *(unbestimmt)*	*indefinite, uncertain*
usf. *(und so fort)*	*and so on*
USt *f (Umsatzsteuer f)*	*turnover tax; sales tax*
usw *(und so weiter)*	*etc (et cetera)*

u.U. *(unter Umständen)* — possibly

u.v.a.(m.) *(und viele(s) andere (mehr))* — and much or many more

u.W. *(unseres Wissens)* — to our knowledge

u.zw. *(und zwar)* — viz; i.e. (namely; that is)

V.a.G. *(Verein m auf Gegenseitigkeit)* — mutual company

v.D. *(vom Dienst)* — i/c (in charge (of))

VDE m *(Verband m Deutscher Elektrotechniker)* — Association of German Electrical Engineers (responsible for electrical safety standards)

VDI m *(Verein m Deutscher Ingenieure)* — Association of German Mechanical Engineers (responsible for mechanical safety standards)

VDP m *(Verband m Deutscher Presse)* — German press association

VE *(Verrechnungseinheiten fpl)* — clearing or accounting units

VEB m *(volkseigener Betrieb m)* — former East German state-owned company

Ver. *(Verein m)* — Soc (society)

Verb. *(Verband m)* — Assoc (association)

Verf. *(Verfasser m)* — author

Verl. *(Verlag m, Verleger m)* — publ (publisher)

versch. *(verschieden)* — misc (miscellaneous)

Verw. *(Verwaltung f)* — management; administration

Verz. *(Verzeichnis nt)* — catalogue; index

vgl. *(vergleiche)* — cf (compare)

v.g.u. *(vorgelesen, genehmigt, unterschrieben)* — read, approved, signed

v.H. *(vom Hundert)* — %, pc (per cent)

VHB *(Verhandlungsbasis f)* — ono (or near(est) offer)

Vj. *(Vierteljahr nt)* — quarter

v.J. *(vorigen Jahres)* — of last year

vm. *(vormittags)* — am (in the morning)

v.M. *(vorigen Monats)* — ult (of last month)

V-Mann m *(Verbindungsmann m, Vertrauensmann m)* — intermediary

vorm. *(vormittags)* — am (in the morning)

Vors. *(Vorsitzende(r) f(m))* — chairwoman, chairman

Vorst. *(Vorstand m)* — board of directors; director

v.R.w. *(von Rechts wegen)* — legally

v.T. *(vom Tausend)* — per thousand

v.v. *(vice versa)* — v.v. (vice versa)

w. *(wenden)* — PTO (please turn over)

w. *(werktags)* — (on) working days

WAA f *(Wiederaufbereitungs-* *reprocessing plant*
anlage f)
WDR m *(Westdeutscher Rundfunk* *West German radio*
m)
Westf. *(Westfalen)* *Westphalia*
WEZ *(westeuropäische Zeit f)* *GMT (Greenwich mean time)*
WHK f *(Welthandelskammer f)* *UNIDO (UN Industrial Develop-*
ment Organization)
wirtsch. *(wirtschaftlich)* *economic*
WiWi m *(f)* *(Wirtschaftswis-* *economist*
senschaftler(in) m(f))
w.o. *(wie oben)* *as above*
WSV *(Winterschlußverkauf m)* *winter sale*
Wttbg. *(Württemberg nt)* *Württemberg*
Wz *(Warenzeichen nt)* ® *(registered trademark)*
Z *(Zentrale f)* *HO; HQ (head office; headquar-*
ters)
ZAV f *(Zentralstelle f für Arbeits-* *Job Centre*
vermittlung)
z.B. *(zum Beispiel)* *e.g. (for example)*
z.b.V. *(zur besonderen Verwen-* *for particular application or use*
dung)
z.d.A. *(zu den Akten)* *for our files; for filing*
ZDF nt *(Zweites Deutsches Fern-* *German TV channel*
sehen nt)
z.H., z.Hd. *(zu Händen)* *attn (for the attention of)*
z.R. *(zur Rücksprache)* *for consultation*
Zs. *(Zeitschrift f)* *periodical*
z.T. *(zum Teil)* *partly*
Ztg. *(Zeitung f)* *newspaper*
Ztschr. *(Zeitschrift f)* *periodical*
zus. *(zusammen)* *together*
zus. *(zusätzlich)* *additional; in addition*
zuz. *(zuzüglich)* *plus*
zw. *(zwischen)* *bet (between)*
z.w.V. *(zur weiteren Veranlas-* *for appropriate action*
sung)
z.Z. *(zur Zeit)* *at present*
zzgl. *(zuzüglich)* *plus*
z.Zt. *(zur Zeit)* *at present*

See also **ENTERTAINING, MAKING CONTACT** *and* **TRAVEL**

Austrian hotels are graded A1 (5 star), A (4 star), B (3 star), C (2 star) and D (1 star). For more details about hotels and rates, you should contact the Austrian National Tourist Office, 30 George Street, London W1R OAL. Tel: 071 629 0461. Fax: 071 499 6038. There is no official classification system for hotels in Germany although some guidebooks offer their own star ratings. There is a central room reservation service run by the German National Tourist Board, the DZT (Deutsche Zentrale für Tourismus). Contact DZT-Serviceabteilung ADZ (Allgemeine Deutsche Zimmerreservierung), Corneliusstraße 34, D-6000 Frankfurt/Main 1. Tel: (069) 740767. Fax: (069) 751056. In the UK, the German National Tourist Office may be contacted for details of hotels and rates at Nightingale House, 65 Curzon Street, London SW1P 2AG. Tel: 071 495 3990. Fax: 071 495 6129.

Hotels in Luxembourg may request classification and will be graded on an official scale of 1 to 5 stars. Not all hotels are classified. The Luxembourg Tourist Office, 36 Piccadilly, London W1V 9PA will supply details of hotels and rates. Tel: 071 434 2800. Fax: 071 734 1205.

For details about hotels and rates in Switzerland, you should contact the Swiss National Tourist Office, Swiss Centre, Swiss Court, London W1V 8EE. Tel: 071 734 1921. Fax: 071 437 4577.

MAKING A RESERVATION

I'd like to make a reservation *ich möchte ein Zimmer reservieren*
What are your room rates? *was sind Ihre Preise?*
How much is a room per night, with breakfast? *was kostet eine Übernachtung mit Frühstück?*
I'd like a single room with bath/shower for two nights *ich hätte gern(e) ein Einzelzimmer mit Bad/Dusche für zwei Nächte*
If possible, I would like a room with a view of ... *ich hätte gern(e) ein Zimmer mit Blick auf ..., wenn möglich*
I would like a room which isn't too noisy, please *ich hätte gern(e) ein ruhiges Zimmer*
Please make sure a hairdryer is provided in my room *ich brauche auf jeden Fall auf meinem Zimmer einen Fön*
Please send me a brochure about your hotel *können Sie mir bitte ein Prospekt von Ihrem Hotel schicken?*
Which credit cards do you accept? *welche Kreditkarten nehmen Sie?*
Can you suggest another hotel that might have a vacancy? *können Sie mir vielleicht ein anderes Hotel empfehlen, das even-*

tuell noch Zimmer frei hat?

CHECKING IN/OUT

I have a reservation in the name of ... *ich habe eine Buchung auf den Namen ...*

I confirmed my booking by phone/fax/letter *ich habe meine Buchung telefonisch/per Fax/brieflich bestätigt*

Can I see the room please? *kann ich das Zimmer bitte sehen?*

Which floor is my room on? *auf welchem Stock ist mein Zimmer?*

When will my room be ready? *wann kann ich in mein Zimmer?*

Please have my luggage taken up/brought down *bitte lassen Sie mein Gepäck nach oben/nach unten bringen*

Has anyone else from Smith & Co. checked in yet? *ist schon jemand anderes von der Firma Smith & Co. eingetroffen?*

I'll be staying for 3 days *ich bleibe drei Tage*

I'd like to stay an extra night/two extra nights *ich möchte noch eine Nacht/noch zwei Nächte bleiben*

I shall be leaving tomorrow at 9 o'clock *ich reise morgen früh um 9 Uhr ab*

What time must I vacate the room? *um wieviel Uhr muß ich das Zimmer räumen?*

I'd like to pay my bill *ich möchte meine Rechnung bezahlen*

I'd like an itemized bill please *können Sie auf der Rechnung bitte alle Posten einzeln aufführen?*

Can I pay by credit card/with traveller's cheques? *kann ich mit Kreditkarte/Reiseschecks bezahlen?*

Please send the bill to ... *bitte schicken Sie die Rechnung an ...*

Has my bill been settled? *ist meine Rechnung schon bezahlt?*

HOTEL SERVICES

Do you have ... in the hotel? *haben Sie ... im Hotel?*

Where's the ...? *wo ist der/die/das ...?*

Do you provide transport to the airport/station/city centre? *fahren Sie Ihre Gäste zum Flughafen/zum Bahnhof/in die Stadt?*

(When) does the hotel close at night? *(wann) schließt das Hotel nachts?*

What is the voltage here? *wieviel Volt haben die Steckdosen?*

Put it on my bill *setzen Sie es auf meine Rechnung*

I'd like a six o'clock alarm call *ich hätte gern(e) einen Weckruf um sechs Uhr*

Can I leave this in the safe? *kann ich das im Safe lassen?*

Can I leave my luggage here and collect it later? *kann ich mein Gepäck hierlassen und später abholen?*

I'd like ... cleaned/washed/polished/ironed *ich möchte ... putzen lassen/waschen lassen/putzen lassen/bügeln lassen*
I'd like this letter typed up/photocopied *können Sie diesen Brief bitte tippen/fotokopieren lassen?*
May I have an extra ...? *kann ich noch einen/eine/ein ... haben?*
Please call a porter/taxi *bitte rufen Sie einen Portier/ein Taxi*

MEALS

When do you stop serving breakfast/lunch/dinner? *bis wann gibt es Frühstück/Mittagessen/Abendessen?*
Do you provide room service? *gibt es Zimmerservice?*
I'd like breakfast/lunch/dinner in my room *ich möchte das Frühstück/das Mittagessen/das Abendessen auf dem Zimmer*
May I see the breakfast/lunch/dinner/snack menu? *kann ich bitte die Speisekarte für das Frühstück/das Mittagessen/das Abendessen/für Snacks sehen?*
Do you serve English breakfasts? *gibt es bei Ihnen englisches Frühstück?*
I'm dining alone — can you recommend a good restaurant? *ich werde alleine essen — können Sie mir ein gutes Restaurant empfehlen?*

See also **ENTERTAINING**

MESSAGES/COMMUNICATIONS

What do I dial for outside/overseas calls? *was muß ich verwählen, um rauszutelefonieren/im Ausland anzurufen?*
Give me 34 72 16 please *verbinden Sie mich bitte mit 34 72 16 (vierunddreißig zwoundsiebzig sechzehn* or *drei-vier sieben-zwo eins-sechs)*
Where can I send a fax from? *wo kann ich ein Fax schicken?*
What is the hotel's fax/phone/telex number? *wie ist die Faxnummer/Telefonnummer/Telexnummer vom Hotel?*
I'd like this letter posted/faxed *können Sie diesen Brief bitte abschicken/faxen lassen?*
Are there any messages for ...? *haben Sie eine Nachricht für ...?*
Please forward any messages to ... *bitte schicken Sie mir alle Nachrichten nach ...*
I can be contacted at this number *ich bin unter dieser Nummer zu erreichen*
I'm expecting a Mr Cowan. Please call me when he arrives *ich erwarte einen Herrn Cowan. Bitte rufen Sie mich (an), wenn er eintrifft*

Please send him/her up *bitte schicken Sie ihn/sie auf mein Zimmer*

Please tell him/her I'll be down in a moment *bitte sagen Sie ihm/ ihr, daß ich gleich runterkomme*

See also **MAKING CONTACT**

PROBLEMS

My room is noisy/dirty/too cold/too hot *mein Zimmer ist laut/ schmutzig/zu kalt/zu warm*

I'd like a different room please *können Sie mir ein anderes Zimmer geben?*

There is no ... in my room *auf meinem Zimmer ist kein(e) ...*

The ... in my room is not working *der/die/das ... in meinem Zimmer funktioniert nicht*

The ... in my room is broken *der/die/das ... in meinem Zimmer ist kaputt*

I ordered ..., and it has not been brought up to my room *ich habe ... bestellt, aber es ist noch nicht auf mein Zimmer gebracht worden*

Please cancel my order *bitte streichen Sie meine Bestellung*

I've locked myself out of my room *ich habe mich aus meinem Zimmer ausgeschlossen*

I've lost my key *ich habe meinen Schlüssel vorloren*

ADDITIONAL VOCABULARY

adjacent rooms	*nebeneinanderliegende Zimmer npl*
air conditioned	*klimatisiert*
alarm call	*Weckruf m*
balcony	*Balkon m*
bank	*Bank f*
bar	*Bar f*
bath	*Bad nt*
bed	*Bett nt*
blanket	*Decke nt*
breakfast	*Frühstück nt*
business service centre	*Business Service Centre nt*
car park *(open-air)*	*Parkplatz m*
car park *(covered)*	*Parkhaus nt*
chambermaid	*Zimmermädchen nt*
check in *vb*	*sich anmelden*
check out *vb*	*abreisen*

check-out time	*Abreisezeit f*
coffee shop	*Cafeteria f*
conference facilities	*Konferenzräumlichkeiten fpl*
conference room	*Konferenzzimmer nt*
connecting rooms	*angrenzende Zimmer pl*
dining room	*Speisesaal m*
discotheque	*Diskothek f*
doorman	*Portier m*
double room	*Doppelzimmer nt*
emergency exit	*Notausgang m*
with en suite bathroom	*mit Bad nt*
envelope	*Briefumschlag m, Umschlag m*
fire exit	*Notausgang m*
foyer	*Empfangshalle f*
full board	*Vollpension f*
function suite	*Veranstaltungsräume mpl*
garage	*Garage f*
hairdresser	*Friseur m, Friseuse f*
hairdryer	*Fön ® m*
half board	*Halbpension f*
hot water	*heißes Wasser nt*
key	*Schlüssel m*
landing	*Flur m*
laundry service	*Wäscherei f*
lift	*Fahrstuhl m*
lobby	*Einggangshalle f*
lounge	*Gesellschaftsraum m*
manager(ess)	*Geschäftsführer(in) m(f)*
meeting room	*Besprechungsraum m*
mini-bar	*Minibar f*
motel	*Motel nt*
night porter	*Nachtportier m*
non-smoking room	*Nichtraucherzimmer nt*
notepaper	*Briefpapier nt*
operator *(person)*	*Telefonist(in) m(f)*
operator *(service)*	*Vermittlung f*
pillow	*(Kopf)kissen nt*
porter	*Portier m*
with private bathroom	*mit Bad nt*
quilt	*Steppdecke f*
receipt	*Quittung f*
reception	*Empfang m, Rezeption f*
receptionist	*Empfangschef m, Empfangsdame f, Herr m/Dame f am Empfang*
register *n*	*Gästebuch nt*

register *vb*	*sich anmelden*
restaurant	*Restaurant nt*
room	*Zimmer nt*
room rates	*Zimmerpreise mpl*
room service	*Zimmerservice m*
safe	*Safe m or nt*
sauna	*Sauna f*
secretarial services	*Schreibdienste mpl*
sheet (for bed)	*Bettlaken nt*
shower	*Dusche f*
single room	*Einzelzimmer nt*
soap	*Seife f*
suite	*Suite f*
swimming pool	*Schwimmbad nt*
switchboard	*Vermittlung f*
television	*Fernsehapparat m*
towel	*Handtuch nt*
twin beds	*zwei (gleiche) Einzelbetten ntpl*
valet service	*Reinigungsdienst m*
washbasin	*Waschbecken nt*
writing paper	*Schreibpapier nt*

See also **ACCOUNTS AND PAYMENTS** *and* **STOCK MANAGEMENT**

accredited agent	bevollmächtigter Vertreter(in) m(f)
advice note	Versandanzeige f
agency	Agentur f, Vertretung f
agent	Vertreter(in) m(f)
agent's commission	Vertreterprovision f
air cargo	Luftfracht f
air consignment note	Luftfrachtbrief m
air freight	Luftfracht f
air waybill	Luftfrachtbrief m
anti-dumping duty	Antidumpingzoll m
banker's reference	Bankauskunft f
bilateral trade	bilateraler Handel m
bill of entry	Zolldeklaration f
bill of exchange	Wechsel m
bill of lading	Konnossement nt
blocked currency	blockierte Währung f
bond	unter Zollverschluß m nehmen
in bond	unter Zollverschluß m
bonded goods	Waren fpl unter Zollverschluß m
bonded warehouse	Zollgutlager nt
breakage	Bruchschaden m
broken lot	Restposten m
bulk buying	Mengeneinkauf m
bulk cargo	Massenfrachtgut nt
c & f (cost and freight)	Kosten pl und Fracht f
cargo	Fracht f; Kargo m
carriage forward	Fracht f zahlt Empfänger
carriage free *or* paid	frachtfrei
carriage inwards	vom Käufer m getragene Frachtkosten pl
carriage outwards	vom Verkäufer m getragene Frachtkosten pl
carrier	Spediteur m
carton	Karton m
cartonned	in Kartons verpackt
cash on delivery (COD) n	Barzahlung f bei Lieferung
cash on delivery (COD) adv	per Nachnahme f

please contact our agent in Brussels *bitte setzen Sie sich mit unserer Vertretung in Brüssel in Verbindung*
goods held in bond *Waren unter Zollverschluß*
to take goods out of bond *Waren verzollen*

certificate of origin	*Ursprungszeugnis nt*
certificate of shipment	*Ladeschein m*
certificate of value	*Wertbescheinigung f*
channel of distribution	*Absatzweg m*
CIF (cost, insurance and freight)	*cif (Kosten, Versicherung und Fracht inkl.)*
CIF & C (cost, insurance, freight and commission)	*cif & c (Kosten, Versicherung, Fracht und Provision inkl.)*
CIF & I (cost, insurance, freight and interest)	*cif & i (Kosten, Versicherung, Fracht und Bankzinsen inkl.)*
clean bill of exchange	*reiner Wechsel m*
clean bill of lading	*reines Konnossement nt*
clearance	*Zollabfertigung f*
clearance certificate	*Zollbescheinigung f*
COD (cash on delivery)	*per Nachnahme*
collect	*abholen*
collection	*Abholung f*
community transit form	*Transitpapiere ntpl der EG*
confirmed irrevocable letter of credit	*unwiderrufliches bestätigtes Akkreditiv nt*
confirming house	*Vertretung f überseeischer Importfirmen fpl*
consign	*versenden*
consignee	*Empfänger m*
consignment	*Sendung f*
consignment note	*Frachtbrief m*
consignor	*Versender m*
consular invoice	*Konsulatsfaktur f*
container	*Container m*
containerization	*Containerisierung f*
containerize	*in Container mpl verpacken*
container ship	*Containerschiff nt*
countertrading	*zwischenstaatlicher Tauschhandel m*
country of origin	*Herkunftsland nt*
courier	*Kurier m*
crate	*Kiste f*
creditworthiness	*Kreditwürdigkeit f*

the goods will be collected/delivered on 31 May *die Waren werden am 31. Mai abgeholt/geliefert*
the goods are ready for collection *die Waren sind abholbereit*
the consignment consists of ... *die Warensendung besteht aus ...*
to send goods on consignment *Waren in Kommission geben*
in duplicate/triplicate/in 5 copies *in zweifacher/dreifacher/fünffacher Ausfertigung*

customs	*Zoll m*
customs broker	*Zollmakler m*
customs clearance	*Zollabfertigung f*
customs declaration	*Zollerklärung f*
customs duty	*Zoll(gebühr f) m*
customs entry	*Einfuhrerklärung f*
customs form	*Zollformular nt*
customs official	*Zollbeamter m, Zollbeamtin f*
customs receipt	*Zollquittung f*
customs registered number	*Zollregistriernummer f*
customs regulation	*Zollbestimmung f*
customs union	*Zollunion f*
damage	*Schaden m*
damaged	*beschädigt*
deck cargo	*Deckladung f*
delay	*Verzögerung f*
deliver	*liefern*
deliverable state	*lieferfähiger Zustand m*
delivered price	*Lieferpreis m*
delivery	*Lieferung f*
delivery note	*Lieferschein m*
delivery time	*Lieferzeit f*
demurrage *(paid to docks)*	*Liegegeld nt*
demurrage *(paid to shipowner)*	*Überliegegeld nt*

it will take 24 hours for the goods to clear customs *die Zollabfertigung der Waren wird 24 Stunden dauern*

to obtain customs clearance for a shipment *die Zollpapiere für eine Ladung bekommen*

we are still waiting for customs clearance *wir warten immer noch auf die Zollabfertigung*

we will take care of the customs formalities *wir kümmern uns um die Zollformalitäten*

we would be grateful if you could take care of the customs formalities *wir wären Ihnen dankbar, wenn Sie sich um die Zollformalitäten kümmern könnten*

please send us a customs receipt *bitte senden Sie uns eine Zollquittung*

the goods were damaged in transit *die Waren wurden beim Transport beschädigt*

what is the reason for the delay? *was ist der Grund für die Verzögerung?*

to deliver something on time/late *etwas rechtzeitig/verspätet liefern*

we can deliver the goods immediately *wir können die Waren sofort liefern*

I am afraid that we cannot accept goods delivered after ... *Waren, die nach dem ... geliefert werden, können wir leider nicht annehmen*

please allow ... days for delivery *Lieferung folgt innerhalb von ... Tagen*

we are still awaiting delivery of the goods *wir warten immer noch auf die Lieferung der Waren*

depository *(place)*	*Hinterlegungstelle f*
depot	*Depot nt*
destination	*Bestimmungsort m*
dispatch	*versenden*
dispatch department	*Versandabteilung f*
distribute	*verteilen*
distribution	*Vertrieb m*
distribution centre	*Verteilungszentrum nt*
distribution costs	*Vertriebskosten pl*
distribution network	*Vertriebsnetz nt*
distributor	*Verteiler m*
dock(s)	*Hafenanlagen fpl*
dock *vb*	*docken*
dock dues	*Dockgebühren fpl*
docket	*Inhaltsvermerk m*
documentary bill of exchange	*Dokumententratte f*
documents against acceptance (D/A)	*Dokumente ntpl gegen Akzept nt*
documents against payment (D/P)	*Dokumente ntpl gegen Zahlung f*
documents of title	*Eigentumsurkunde f*
driver	*Fahrer(in) m(f)*
drop shipment	*Direktlieferung f*
duty-free	*zollfrei*
duty-paid price	*Preis m einschließlich Zoll*
embargo	*Embargo nt*
estimated time of arrival (ETA)	*voraussichtliche Ankunft f*
Europallet	*Europalette f*
exceed	*überschreiten*
ex dock	*ab Kai m*
ex factory	*ab Werk nt*
export(s)	*Export(e) m(pl)*
export	*exportieren*

the goods were dispatched on 31 May *die Waren wurden am 31. Mai abgeschickt*

please advise us of the documentation required *bitte teilen Sie uns mit, welche Unterlagen erforderlich sind*

the duty will be paid by the purchaser/consignee *der Zoll wird vom Käufer/Empfänger bezahlt*

exports are 10% up/down on last year *Exporte sind gegenüber dem Vorjahr um 10% gestiegen/gefallen*

we hope to increase our exports by 30% *wir hoffen, unseren Export um 30% steigern zu können*

to export 1,000 units p.a. to Africa *jährlich 1.000 Stück nach Afrika exportieren*

export agent	*Exportvertreter(in) m(f)*
Export Credit Guarantee	*britische staatliche*
Department (ECGD)	*Exportkreditabteilung f*
export drive	*Exportkampagne f*
exporter	*Exporteur m*
export house	*Exporthaus nt*
export invoice	*Exportrechnung f*
export licence	*Ausfuhrgenehmigung f*
export manager	*Exportmanager(in) m(f)*
export trade	*Exporthandel m*
express delivery	*Eilzustellung f*
ex ship	*ab Schiff nt*
ex works	*ab Werk nt*
fair-trade agreement	*Preisbindungsabkommen nt*
FAQ (free alongside quay)	*f.a.q. (frei Längsseite Kai m)*
FAS (free alongside ship)	*f.a.s. (frei Längsseite Schiff nt)*
FD (free delivered at dock)	*f.D. (frei Dock nt)*
FOB (free on board)	*f.o.b. (frei an Bord m)*
FOR (free on rail)	*frei Schiene f*
foreign bill	*Fremdwährungswechsel m*
forwarding agent	*Spediteur m*
franco	*franko*
free currency	*frei konvertierbare Währung f*
free of tax	*steuerfrei*
free to receiving station	*frei Bestimmungsbahnhof*
freight *n*	*Fracht f*
freight *vb*	*verfrachten*
freight forward	*Fracht f gegen Nachnahme f*
freight forwarder	*Spediteur m*
freight forwarding	*Spedition f*
freight inward	*Eingangsfracht f*
freight train	*Güterzug m*
General Agreement on Tariffs	*Allgemeines Zoll- und*
and Trade (GATT)	*Handelsabkommen nt (GATT)*
goods	*Güter npl*
goods in transit	*Transitgüter ntpl*
goods received note	*Wareneingangsbescheinigung f*
goods train	*Güterzug m*
handling charge	*Bearbeitungsgebühr f*
harbour dues	*Hafengebühren fpl*

oil-exporting/grain-exporting countries *ölexportierende/getreide-
exportierende Länder*
30% of our production is for the export market *30% unserer Produktion
sind für den Export bestimmt*

haulage	*Transport m*
haulage contractor *(firm)*	*Transportunternehmen nt*
haulage (cost)	*Transportkosten pl*
HS number	*HS Nummer f*
import(s)	*Import(e) m(pl)*
import	*importieren*
import ban	*Einfuhrverbot nt*
import duty	*Einfuhrzoll m*
importer	*Importeur m*
import-export *(business)*	*Import-Export-Handel m*
importing	*Einführen nt*
import levy	*Einfuhrabgabe f*
import licence	*Einfuhrgenehmigung f*
import quota	*Einfuhrkontingent nt*
import surcharge	*Importabgabe f*
import tariff	*Einfahrzolltarif m*
impound	*beschlagnahmen*
in-bond price	*Preis m ausschließlich Zollgutlagerung f*
Incoterms	*Incoterms pl*
insurance certificate	*Versicherungsbescheinigung f*
joint venture	*Joint-venture nt*
late delivery	*Lieferverzögerung f*
lay days	*Liegezeit f*
lead time	*Lieferzeit f*
load *n*	*Ladung f*
load *vb*	*(be)laden*
loading bay	*Ladeplatz m*
loading dock	*Ladedock nt*
lorry	*Lastwagen m*
loss in transit	*Transportschaden m, Transportverlust m*
low-loader	*Tieflader m*
manifest	*Manifest nt*
maritime law	*Seerecht nt*

the goods have been held up at Customs *die Waren wurden beim Zoll aufgehalten*

the ship has been held up by the weather *das Schiff wurde durch ungünstige Wetterverhältnisse aufgehalten*

to import products into Britain *Produkte nach Großbritannien importieren*

I represent a British import-export company *ich vertrete eine britische Import-Export-Firma*

to apply for/get an import licence *eine Einfuhrlizenz beantragen/erhalten*

the import licence has been refused *die Einfuhrgenehmigung wurde verweigert*

merchantman	*Handelsschiff nt*
non-acceptance	*Nichtannahme f*
non-delivery	*Nichtlieferung f*
notification	*Benachrichtigung f*
packet tying machine	*Paketschnürmaschine f*
pallet	*Palette f*
palletization	*Palettisierung f*
palletize	*palettieren*
palletized cartons	*palettierte Kartons mpl*
parcel post	*Paketpost f*
payload	*Nutzlast f*
perishable goods	*verderbliche Waren fpl*
port of entry	*Zoll(abfertigungs)hafen m*
post free, post paid	*portofrei*
pro-forma invoice	*Pro-forma-Rechnung f*
Red Star International ®	*Red Star International ®*
re-export	*wiederausführen*
road haulage	*Güterkraftverkehr m*
rolling and wrapping machine	*Roll- und Verpackungsmaschine f*
sail	*abfahren*
sample	*Muster nt, Probe f*
scheduled flight	*Linienflug m*
ship *n*	*Schiff nt*
ship *vb*	*verladen*
shipment *(load)*	*Ladung f*
shipowner	*Schiffseigner m*
shipper	*Spediteur m*
shipping *(transportation)*	*Verschiffung f*
shipping agent	*Seehafenspediteur m*

the goods should be packed using ... *die Waren sollten mit ... verpackt werden*

how would you prefer the order to be packed/shipped? *wie möchten Sie die Bestellung verpackt/geliefert haben?*

there is a penalty of ... for late delivery *bei Lieferverzug ist eine Konventionalstrafe (in Höhe) von ... zu zahlen*

is that price FOB or CIF? *ist dieser Preis fob oder cif?*

please confirm receipt of the goods *bitte bestätigen Sie uns den Erhalt der Waren*

we received the consignment safely on 2 August *wir haben Ihre Lieferung einwandfrei am 2. August erhalten*

to send goods by air/post/rail/road/sea *Waren per Luftfracht/Post/ Schiene/Straße/Seefracht verschicken*

we make three shipments per month to Switzerland *wir liefern dreimal im Monat in die Schweiz*

shipping company	*Reederei f*
shipping department	*Versandabteilung f*
shipping documents	*Versanddokumente ntpl*
shipping note	*Schiffszettel m*
ship's manifest	*Ladeverzeichnis nt*
ship's report	*Schiffsmeldung f*
shockproof	*stoßfest*
shrink-wrap	*einschweißen*
sole agent	*Alleinvertreter(in) m(f)*
stamp duty	*Stempelgebühr f*
supercargo	*Superkargo m*
tachograph	*Tachograph m*
tariff barrier	*Zollschranke f*
tax exemption	*Steuerbefreiung f*
tax haven	*Steuerparadies nt*
trade barrier	*Handelsschranke f*
trade fair	*Messe f*
trade mission	*Handelsdelegation f*
trade reference	*Kreditauskunft f*
tranship	*umladen*
transhipment	*Umladung f*
in transit	*beim Transport*
truck	*Lastwagen m*
trucking company	*LKW-Transportunternehmen nt*
van	*Lieferwagen m*
VAT (value-added tax)	*MwSt f (Mehrwertsteuer f)*
vessel	*Schiff nt*
warehouse	*Lager(haus) nt*
warrant	*Lagerschein m*
waterproof	*wasserdicht*
weight limit	*zulässiges Gewicht nt*

aeronautical industry	*Luftfahrtindustrie f*
agribusiness	*Landwirtschaft f*
arms trade	*Waffenhandel m*
banking	*Bankwesen nt*
business	*Geschäft nt, Unternehmen nt*
car industry	*Automobilindustrie f*
caterer	*Caterer m*
catering (industry)	*Hotel- und Gaststättengewerbe nt*
chemical industry	*chemische Industrie f*
civil engineering	*Hoch- und Tiefbau m*
commerce	*Handel m*
computing	*Computerwissenschaft f, Informatik f*
construction industry	*Bauindustrie f*
consultancy	*Beratungsunternehmen nt*
copy shop	*Kopierladen m*
distillery	*Brennerei f*
diversification	*Diversifikation f*
electronics	*Elektronik f*
engineering	*Technik f*
entertainment industry	*Vergnügungsindustrie f*
fashion industry	*Modeindustrie f*
finance	*Finanzwesen nt*
food industry	*Nahrungsmittelindustrie f*
food processing	*Nahrungsmittelverarbeitung f*
growth industry	*Wachstumsindustrie f*
heavy industry	*Schwerindustrie f*
industrial capacity	*industrielle Kapazität f*
industrial estate	*Industriegebiet nt*
industrialist	*Industrielle(r) f(m)*
industry	*Industrie f*
information industry	*Informationsindustrie f*
iron and steel	*Eisen nt und Stahl m*
light industry	*Leichtindustrie f*
manufacturing	*Herstellung f*
manufacturing sector	*Herstellungssektor m*

what's your field? *in welcher Branche arbeiten Sie?*
the company is moving into the field of ... *die Firma verlegt sich auf (+acc) ...*
this sector of industry is growing/declining *dieser Industriesektor zeigt eine aufsteigende/fallende Tendenz*
I'm in ... *ich bin in der ...-Branche tätig*
to work in industry *in der Industrie arbeiten*
in Britain, this is a privatized/state-owned industry *in Großbritannien ist diese Industrie privatisiert/verstaatlicht*

metallurgy	*Metallurgie f*
mining	*Bergbau m*
music industry	*Musikindustrie f*
nationalize	*verstaatlichen*
nuclear industry	*Atomindustrie f*
oil industry	*Erdölindustrie f*
petroleum industry	*petrochemische Industrie f*
pharmaceutical industry, pharmaceuticals	*Pharmaindustrie f*
power industry	*Energieindustrie f*
printer's	*Druckerei f*
printing industry	*Druckereigewerbe nt*
private company	*Privatgesellschaft f*
private limited company	*Gesellschaft f mit beschränkter Haftung (GmbH f)*
privately-owned	*in Privatbesitz m*
private sector	*privater Sektor m*
privatize	*privatisieren*
processing industry	*Verarbeitungsindustrie f*
public company	*Aktiengesellschaft f (AG f)*
public limited company (plc)	*Aktiengesellschaft f (AG f)*
publishing	*Verlagswesen nt*
registered company	*eingetragene Gesellschaft f*
service industry	*Dienstleistungsindustrie f*
shipbuilding	*Schiffsbau m*
state-owned	*staatseigen*
state sector	*Staatssektor m*
steel industry	*Stahlindustrie f*
subsidiary (company)	*Tochtergesellschaft f*
telecommunications	*Fernmeldewesen nt*
tertiary industry	*Dienstleistungsindustrie f*
tertiary sector	*tertiärer Sektor m, Dienstleistungssektor m*
textile industry, textiles	*Textilindustrie f*
timber industry	*Holzindustrie f*
tobacco industry	*Tabakindustrie f*
tourist industry	*Fremdenverkehrsindustrie f*
translation agency	*Übersetzungsbüro nt*
travel agency	*Reisebüro nt*
travel industry	*Reiseindustrie f*
winemaking	*Weinherstellung f*

See also **THE EUROPEAN COMMUNITY**

International organizations or institutions usually have an official German version of their name. Wherever possible, we have given this German name as a translation. Where the English name of a British or American organization will be recognized by German speakers, we have given this English name as a translation. If the English name will not be recognized, and there is no German name, we have provided a German definition of the organization. When discussing such organizations, it is best to cite the English name, followed by the German definition.

American National Standards Institute (ANSI)	*amerikanischer Normenausschuß m*
American Standards Association (ASA)	*amerikanischer Normenausschuß m*
Association for Payment Clearing Services (APACS)	*Gesellschaft f für Zahlungsverrechnungsservices mpl*
Association of British Ports (ABP)	*Vereinigung f britischer Häfen*
Association of South-East Asian Nations (ASEAN)	*Vereinigung f südostasiatischer Nationen (ASEAN f)*
Bank for International Settlements (BIS)	*Bank f für Internationalen Zahlungsausgleich (BIZ f)*
Bank of England	*Bank of England f*
Bay Street	*Bay Street*
BBC (British Broadcasting Corporation)	*BBC f*
Big Eight *(accounting firms)*	*die führenden 8 Wirtschaftsprüfer mpl*
Big Four (Banks)	*die führenden 4 Londoner Großbanken fpl*
Board of Trade	*britisches Handelsministerium nt*
British Airports Authority (BAA)	*britische Flughafenbehörde f*
British Airways (BA)	*British Airways (BA)*
British Exporters' Association (BEXA)	*Vereinigung f britischer Exportunternehmen*
British Overseas Trade Board (BOTB)	*britische Außenhandelsbehörde f*

please send me details of your organization's activities *bitte senden Sie mir Informationen über die Aktivitäten Ihrer Organisation*

British Standards Institution (BSI)	*britischer Normenausschuß m*
Central Office of Information (COI)	*britische zentrale Informationsstelle f*
Chamber of Commerce	*Handelskammer f*
Civil Aviation Authority (CAA)	*britische Behörde f für Zivilluftfahrt*
COMEX	*Warenbörse f*
Common Fund for Commodities (CFC)	*Gemeinsamer Fonds m für Bedarfsgüter*
Confederation of British Industry (CBI)	*britischer Arbeitgeberverband m*
Consumers' Association	*Verbraucherverband m*
Department of Trade and Industry (DTI)	*britisches Ministerium nt für Handel und Industrie*
Export Credit Guarantee Department (ECGD)	*britische staatliche Exportkreditabteilung f*
Food and Agricultural Organization (FAO)	*UNO-Organisation f für Ernährung und Landwirtschaft (FAO f)*
Foreign Office (FO)	*britisches Außenministerium nt*
General Agreement on Tariffs and Trade (GATT)	*Allgemeines Zoll- und Handelsabkommen nt (GATT)*
Group of 3 (G3)	*die Dreiergruppe f (G3 f)*
Group of 5 (G5)	*die Fünfergruppe f (G5 f)*
Group of 7 (G7)	*die Siebenergruppe f (G7 f)*
Group of 10 (G10)	*die Zehnergruppe f (G10 f)*
HM Customs (HMC)	*britisches Zollamt nt*
Independent Broadcasting Authority (IBA)	*britisches Aufsichtsgremium nt der Fernseh- und Rundfunkanstalten*
Independent Television Commission (ITC)	*unabhängige britische Fernsehkommission f*
Inland Revenue (IR)	*britisches Finanzamt nt*
Internal Revenue Service (IRS)	*amerikanisches Steueramt nt*

it would be wiser to contact ... before going ahead *es wäre vernünftiger, erst mit ... in Verbindung zu treten, bevor weitere Schritte unternommen werden*
the organization that deals with this is the ... *die hierfür zuständige Organisation ist ...*
what is the equivalent organization in ...? *was ist die entsprechende Organisation in ...?*
there is no equivalent body in Britain *es gibt in Großbritannien keine entsprechende Behörde*

INSTITUTIONS AND ORGANIZATIONS

International Atomic Energy Agency (IAEA)	Internationale Atomenergie-Organisation f (IAEO f)
International Bank for Reconstruction and Development (IBRD)	Internationale Bank f für Wiederaufbau und Entwicklung (IBRD f)
International Chamber of Commerce (ICC)	Internationale Handelskammer f (IHK f)
International Court of Justice (ICJ)	Internationaler Gerichtshof m (IGH m)
International Development Association (IDA)	Internationale Entwicklungsorganisation f
International Finance Corporation (IFC)	Internationale Finanz-Corporation f (IFC f)
International Fund for Agricultural Development (IFAD)	Internationaler Fonds m für Agrarentwicklung
International Labour Organization (ILO)	Internationale Arbeitsorganisation f (IAO f)
International Monetary Fund (IMF)	Internationaler Währungsfonds m (IWF m)
International Standards Organization (ISO)	Internationaler Normenausschuß m
International Telecommunications Union (ITU)	Internationale Fernmelde-Union f (IFU f)
International Trade Organization (ITO)	Internationale Handelsorganisation f
Lloyd's of London	Lloyd's
Monopolies and Mergers Commission	britisches Kartellamt nt
Office of Fair Trading (OFT)	britische Behörde f gegen unlauteren Wettbewerb
Organization for Economic Cooperation and Development (OECD)	Organisation f für wirtschaftliche Zusammenarbeit und Entwicklung (OECD f)
Organization of Arab Petroleum Exporting Countries (OAPEC)	Organisation f der arabischen erdölexportierenden Länder (OAPEC f)

I am sure that the local Chamber of Commerce would be able to help *ich bin sicher, daß Ihnen die Handelskammer vor Ort behilflich sein kann*
is there an office of ... in London? *gibt es ein ...-Büro in London?*
this organization is roughly the same as your ... *diese Organisation entspricht in etwa Ihrem/Ihrer ...*

Organization of Petroleum Exporting Countries (OPEC)	*Organisation f der erdölexportierenden Länder (OPEC f)*
Trades Union Congress (TUC)	*britischer Gewerkschaftskongreß m*
UN Conference on Trade and Development (UNCTAD)	*Welthandels- und Entwicklungskonferenz f der Vereinten Nationen, Welthandelskonferenz f (WHK f)*
UN Industrial Development Organization (UNIDO)	*Organisation f für industrielle Entwicklung der Vereinten Nationen (UNIDO f)*
Wall Street	*Wall Street f*
World Bank	*Weltbank f*

accident	*Unfall m*
accidental	*unbeabsichtigt*
accident insurance	*Unfallversicherung f*
act of God	*höhere Gewalt f*
actuarial	*versicherungsmathematisch*
actuarial tables	*versicherungsmathematische Tabellen fpl*
actuary	*Aktuar(in) m(f), Versicherungsmathematiker(in) m(f)*
adjust	*regulieren*
adjuster	*Schadenssachverständige(r) f(m)*
adjustment	*Regulierung f*
airworthiness	*Flugtüchtigkeit f*
all-risks policy	*Allgefahrenpolice f*
annuity	*jährliche Zahlung f*
assess	*schätzen*
assessor	*Schadensabschätzer(in) m(f)*
assurance company	*Versicherungsgesellschaft f*
average (ship)	*Havarie f*
average clause	*Havarieklausel f*
award	*zuerkannter Schadensersatz m*
barratry	*Baratterie f*
beneficiary	*Begünstigte(r) f(m)*
blanket policy	*Pauschalpolice f*
broker	*Makler(in) m(f)*
buildings insurance	*Gebäudeversicherung f*
cancel	*annullieren*
car insurance	*Kraftfahrzeugversicherung f*
cash bonus	*Bardividende f*
cash surrender value	*Rückkaufswert m*
cessation of risk	*Erlöschen nt des Risikos*
claim n	*Anspruch m*
claim vb	*Ansprüche mpl geltend machen*
claimant	*Geschädigte(r) f(m)*
claims department	*Schadensabteilung f*
clause	*Klausel f*
commencement of risk	*Risikobeginn m*

I would like to cancel my policy, no. 315/M *ich möchte meine Police Nr. 315/M kündigen*

to put in a claim *einen Anspruch geltend machen*

to handle a claim *einen Schadensfall bearbeiten*

the company cannot settle your claim until you have answered the following queries *unsere Gesellschaft kann Ihre Forderung erst regulieren, wenn Sie folgende Fragen beantwortet haben*

compensation	*Entschädigung f*
comprehensive insurance	*Vollkaskoversicherung f*
comprehensive policy	*Globalpolice f*
contributory pension scheme	*beitragspflichtige Rentenversicherung f*
cover *n*	*Versicherung f*
cover *vb*	*versichern*
cover note	*Deckungszusage f*
damage *n*	*Schaden m*
damage *vb*	*beschädigen*
damage survey	*Schadensuntersuchung f*
double indemnity	*doppelte Leistung f*
endowment assurance	*gemischte Lebensversicherung f*
endowment policy	*Lebensversicherungspolice f*
estimator	*Schätzer(in) m(f)*
excess clause	*Schadenselbstbeteiligungsklausel f*
exemption clause	*Freistellungsklausel f*
extent of cover	*Versicherungshöhe f*
fidelity bond	*Kaution f*
fire and theft policy	*Feuer- und Diebstahlversicherungspolice f*
fire damage	*Feuerschaden m*
fire-damaged	*brandbeschädigt*
fire insurance	*Feuerversicherung f*
force majeure clause	*höhere-Gewalt-Klausel f*
fraudulent claim	*unredlicher Anspruch m*
free of particular average (FPA)	*frei von besonderer Havarie*
freight insurance	*Frachtversicherung f*
friendly society	*Versicherungsverein m auf Gegenseitigkeit*
general average loss	*Havarie-Grosse-Schaden m*
graduated pension	*gestaffelte Sozialrente f*
green card	*grüne Versicherungskarte f*
health insurance	*Krankenversicherung f*
(home) contents insurance	*Hausratversicherung f*

we require a policy that covers ... *wir brauchen eine Police, die ... mit einschließt*

what is covered by the policy? *was ist durch die Police versichert?*

this is not covered by the policy *das ist in der Police nicht abgedeckt*

I enclose a cover note *beiliegend übersende ich Ihnen eine Deckungszusage*

please send me a cover note and full details of the policy *bitte senden Sie mir eine Deckungszusage und genaue Informationen über die Police*

the policy comes into force as of ... *die Police tritt ab ... in Kraft*

house insurance	*Gebäudeversicherung f*
indemnity insurance	*Schadensversicherung f*
insurance	*Versicherung f*
insurance agent *or* broker	*Versicherungsmakler(in) m(f)*
insurance certificate	*Versicherungsbescheinigung f*
insurance claim	*Versicherungsanspruch m*
insurance company	*Versicherungsgesellschaft f*
insurance manager	*Versicherungsmanager(in) m(f)*
insurance premium	*Versicherungsprämie f*
insure	*versichern (lassen)*
insured *adj*	*versichert*
insured *n*	*Versicherte(r) f(m)*
insurer	*Versicherungsträger m*
knock-for-knock agreement	*Schadenteilungsabkommen nt*
liability	*Haftung f*
liability insurance	*Haftpflichtversicherung f*
liable	*haftbar*
life annuity	*Leibrente f*
life expectancy	*Lebenserwartung f*
life insurance	*Lebensversicherung f*
Lloyd's agent	*Lloyd's Agent m*
Lloyd's Certificate of Marine Insurance	*Lloyd's Seeversicherungszertifikat nt*
Lloyd's List	*Lloyd's Liste f*
Lloyd's of London	*Lloyd's*
loading	*Prämienzuschlag m*
lump sum settlement	*Pauschalregulierung f*
malicious damage	*mutwilliger Schaden m*
marine insurance	*Seeversicherung f*
marine survey	*Schiffsbesichtigung f*
medical insurance	*Krankenversicherung f*
motor insurance	*Kraftfahrzeugversicherung f*
mutual insurance company	*Versicherungsverein m auf Gegenseitigkeit*
negligence	*Fahrlässigkeit f*
negligent	*fahrlässig*
new for old	*neu für alt*

to insure something/someone against something *etwas/jemanden gegen etwas versichern*

you need to insure the goods against fire/theft/damage/loss *Sie müssen die Waren gegen Feuer/Diebstahl/Schaden/Verlust versichern*

your company car is not insured for personal use *der Firmenwagen ist nicht für privaten Gebrauch versichert*

you/the goods are insured for £25,000 *Sie/die Waren sind für £25.000 versichert*

no-claims bonus	*Schadenfreiheitsrabatt m*
non-contributory pension	*beitragsfreie Rentenversicherung*
scheme	*f*
non-disclosure	*Nichtangabe f*
occupational pension scheme	*betriebliche Altersversorgung f*
other party	*Gegenpartei f*
particular average loss	*besondere Havarie f*
perishable goods	*verderbliche Waren fpl*
policy	*Police f*
policy-holder	*Versicherungsnehmer(in) m(f)*
premium	*Prämie f*
product liability insurance	*Produkthaftpflichtversicherung f*
proposal form	*Antragsformular nt*
reinsurance	*Rückversicherung f*
reinsurance pool	*Rückversicherungspool m*
reinsure	*rückversichern*
renew	*verlängern*
renewal	*Verlängerung f*
replacement cost	*Wiederbeschaffungskosten pl*
replacement value	*Wiederbeschaffungswert m*
risk	*Risiko nt*
salvage *n (act)*	*Bergung f*
salvage *n (payment)*	*Bergelohn m*
salvage *vb*	*bergen*
salvage costs	*Bergungskosten pl*
seaworthiness	*Seetüchtigkeit f*
settle *(claim)*	*regulieren*
small print	*Kleingedrucktes nt*
storm damage	*Sturmschaden m*
storm insurance	*Sturmversicherung f*
subrogation	*Subrogation f*
surrender	*rückkaufen*
surrender value	*Rückkaufswert m*
temporary cover	*vorübergehende Deckung f*
term insurance	*Risikolebensversicherung f*
theft	*Diebstahl m*
third-party insurance	*Haftpflichtversicherung f*
total loss	*Totalschaden m*
transport insurance	*Transportversicherung f*
travel insurance	*Reiseversicherung f*
underwrite	*versichern*
underwriter	*Versicherer m*

a high-risk/low-risk activity *eine risikoreiche/risikoarme Tätigkeit*
to take out insurance against ... *eine Versicherung gegen ... abschließen*

unlimited liability	*unbeschränkte Haftung f*
void *adj*	*nichtig*
whole-life insurance	*Lebensversicherung f auf den Todesfall m*
with particular average (WPA)	*mit besonderer Havarie*
with-profits endowment assurance	*Versicherung m auf den Erlebensfall f mit Gewinnbeteilung f*

to have unlimited cover *unbegrenzt versichert sein*
fair wear and tear *natürlicher Verschleiß*

See also **BANKING AND FINANCE**

above par	*über pari*
account	*Börsenhandelsperiode f*
allotment	*Zuteilung f*
A shares	*stimmrechtslose Aktien fpl*
asking price	*Verkaufskurs m*
bearer bond	*Inhaberobligation f*
bearish	*baisse-tendenziös*
bear market	*Baisse f*
below par	*unter pari*
benchmark	*Maßstab m*
Big Bang	*Big Bang m*
blue-chip investment	*sichere Wertpapieranlage f*
bonus issue	*Emission f von Gratisaktien fpl*
bonus share	*Gratisaktie f*
broker	*Makler(in) m(f)*
brokerage	*Maklergebühr f*
B shares	*nicht dividendenberechtigte Aktien fpl*
bucket shop	*unreelle Maklerfirma f*
bullish	*haussierend*
bull market	*Hausse f*
business news summary	*Zusammenfassung f der Wirtschaftsnachrichten fpl*
called-up capital	*eingefordertes Kapital nt*
call option	*Kaufoption f*
closing price	*Schlußkurs m*
commission	*Kommission f*
commodity exchange	*Warenbörse f*
common stock	*Stammaktien fpl*
consols	*Konsols mpl*
contango	*Report m*
contract note	*Effektenkaufabrechnung f*
convertible loan stock	*konvertierbarer Anleihestock m*
crash	*Börsenkrach m*
current yield	*Umlaufrendite f*
dealer	*Händler(in) m(f)*
dealing	*Effektenhandel m*

the market is buoyant *die Tendenz ist steigend*
to buy 1,000 shares in a company *1.000 Aktien einer Gesellschaft kaufen*
the share closed at 105 pence *die Aktie schloß mit 105 pence*
to corner the market in cotton/silver *die Baumwollvorräte/Silbervorräte aufkaufen*

dividend	*Dividende f*
dividend cover	*Dividendendeckung f*
Dow-Jones Average	*Dow-Jones-Index m*
earnings per share	*Gewinn m je Aktie*
equities	*Aktien fpl*
equity capital	*Eigenkapital nt*
Eurobond	*Eurobond m*
ex dividend	*ohne Dividende f*
ex rights	*ohne Bezugsrecht nt*
falling market	*Baissemarkt m*
flotation *(of a company)*	*Gesellschaftsgründung f*
flotation *(of shares)*	*Aktienemission f*
forward contract	*Terminabschluß m, Terminkontrakt m*
FT Index	*FT-Index m*
fully-paid share	*voll eingezahlte Aktie f*
futures	*Termingeschäfte ntpl*
gilt-edged securities	*Staatspapiere ntpl*
gold reserves	*Goldreserven fpl*
Government Broker	*Börsenmakler(in) m(f) im Auftrag der Bank of England*
government stock	*Staatsanleihe f*
Hang Seng Index	*Hang-Seng-Index m*
holding company	*Holdinggesellschaft f*
insider dealing	*Insiderhandel m*
investment	*Investition f*
investment company	*Investmentgesellschaft f*
investment income	*Erträge mpl aus Anlagen fpl*
investment portfolio	*Wertpapierportefeuille nt*
investment trust	*Investmenttrust m*
investor	*Investor(in) m(f)*
irredeemable	*nicht rückzahlbar*
issue *n*	*Emission f*
issue *vb (shares)*	*ausgeben*
issued capital	*ausgegebenes Kapital nt*
jobber	*Makler(in) m(f)*
joint-stock company	*Aktiengesellschaft f (AG f)*
listed company	*börsennotierte Firma f*

to float shares on the open market *Aktien auf den Markt bringen*
to sell one's holding in a company *seine Gesellschaftsanteile verkaufen*
we would like to invest £10,000 in shares/commodities *wir möchten £10.000 in Aktien/Waren investieren*
we have £10,000 available to invest *wir haben £10.000 für Investitionen zur Verfügung*
a sound/an unsound investment *eine sichere/unsichere Investition*

majority shareholder	Besitzer(in) m(f) der Aktienmehrheit f
majority shareholding	Mehrheitsbeteiligung f
minority interest	Anteile mpl in Fremdbesitz m
minority shareholder	Minderheitsaktionär(in) m(f)
minority shareholding	Minderheitsbeteiligung f
money market	Geldmarkt m
Nikkei Index	Nikkei Index m
non-voting shares	stimmrechtslose Aktien fpl
offer price	Angebotspreis m
opening price	Anfangskurs m
option	Option f
ordinary share	Stammaktie f
overcapitalize	überkapitalisieren
oversubscribed	überzeichnet
parent company	Muttergesellschaft f
partly-paid share	teileingezahlte Aktie f
par value	Nennwert m
Personal Equity Plan (PEP)	steuerfreier privater Aktienanlageplan m
portfolio	Portefeuille nt
preference shares	Vorzugsaktien fpl
preferred ordinary shares	bevorrechtigte Stammaktien fpl
privatization	Privatisierung f
privatize	privatisieren
put option	Verkaufsoption f
rally	sich erholen
rate of return	Rendite f
redeemable	rückzahlbar
return on investments (ROI)	Anlageverzinsung f
rights issue	Bezugsrechtsemission f
risk capital	Risikokapital nt
securities	Wertpapiere ntpl
share	Aktie f
share allocation	Aktienzuteilung f
share capital	Aktienkapital nt
share certificate	Aktienzertifikat nt

the bottom has fallen out of the market die Marktlage hat einen Tiefstand erreicht
to invest overseas im Ausland investieren
how are our shares in ... performing? wie stehen unsere ... Aktien?
a newly-privatized company eine erst kürzlich privatisierte Gesellschaft
to go public öffentliche Rechtsform annehmen
the shares are quoted on the stock exchange die Aktien sind an der Börse notiert

shareholder	*Aktionär(in) m(f)*
share index	*Aktienindex m*
share issue	*Aktienemission f*
share price	*Aktienkurs m*
shell company	*Mantelfirma f*
shorts *(securities)*	*Kurzläufer mpl*
short *(seller)*	*Baissespekulant m*
slump *n (in prices)*	*Sturz m*
slump *vb*	*(plötzlich) fallen*
speculate	*spekulieren*
speculation	*Spekulation f*
speculator	*Spekulant(in) m(f)*
spot price	*Kassapreis m, Lokopreis m*
stag	*Spekulant(in) m(f)*
statutory meeting	*Gründungsversammlung f*
statutory report	*Gründungsbericht m*
stock	*Wertpapier nt*
stockbroker	*Börsenmakler(in) m(f)*
stock exchange	*Börse f*
stockholder	*Aktionär(in) m(f)*
stock market	*Börse f*
stocks and shares	*(Aktien fpl und) Wertpapiere ntpl*
subscriber	*Zeichner(in) m(f)*
subscription	*Zeichnung f*
takeover bid	*Übernahmeangebot nt*
Tax Exempt Special Savings Account (TESSA)	*steuerfreies Sondersparprogramm nt*
tranche	*Tranche f*
transaction	*Transaktion f*
transfer of shares	*Aktienumschreibung f*
trend	*Tendenz f*
turn	*Provision f*
undated stock	*unkündbare Wertpapiere ntpl*

they have acquired a majority shareholding *sie haben die Aktienmehrheit erworben*

the share price has risen/fallen 25 pence since we bought the stock *seitdem wir die Aktien gekauft haben, sind sie um 25 pence gestiegen/ gefallen*

to attract small investors *kleinere Investoren anziehen*

the issue is oversubscribed/fully subscribed *die Emission ist überzeichnet/voll gezeichnet*

a good time to buy/sell *ein günstiger Zeitpunkt zu kaufen/verkaufen*

we will forward details of the transaction to you as soon as possible *wir werden Ihnen sobald wie möglich die Einzelheiten bezüglich der Transaktion zuschicken*

underwrite *(share issue)*	*garantieren*
underwriter *(bank)*	*Emissionsbank f*
underwriter *(person)*	*Garant m*
unissued capital	*noch nicht ausgegebenes Kapital nt*
unit trust	*Investmentfonds m*
unlisted company	*nicht börsennotierte Firma f*
Unlisted Securities Market (USM)	*Markt m für nicht notierte Wertpapiere ntpl*
venture capital	*Risikokapital nt*
white knight	*Investor m, der bei unerwünschter Übernahme mit einem einvernehmlichen Übernahmeangebot einschreitet*

these shares will yield a high/low return *diese Aktien bringen eine hohe/ niedrige Rendite*

EC citizens can work in any EC country without a work permit, and a residence permit (*Aufenthaltserlaubnis*) should be granted automatically if you have a job offer. It will usually be valid for five years. To work in Austria you will need a work permit (*Arbeitserlaubnis*), which will be valid initially for one year. You can apply for an extension, though for less specialist jobs there are quotas. Employers also need to apply for an employment permit. There are very strict restrictions on working in Switzerland for more than a holiday job and it is best to check with the Swiss Embassy about these.

Salaries are usually expressed per month in mainland Europe and are generally quoted gross. Companies may offer a thirteenth or even a fourteenth month's salary, i.e. one or two months' salary paid as a bonus at Christmas.

If you are sending your CV to a German-speaking company, it is helpful to translate your job title(s) and qualifications.

For more employment vocabulary, see **PERSONNEL**
For more information about letter-writing, see **MAKING CONTACT**
For job titles and names of departments, see **COMPANY STRUCTURES**
and the **GERMAN-ENGLISH GLOSSARY**

APPLYING FOR A JOB

OPENING THE LETTER

In reply to your advertisement for a regional sales director/ personal assistant in today's Daily News, I would be grateful if you could send me further details of this post, together with an application form *ich nehme Bezug auf Ihre Anzeige in der heutigen Ausgabe von "Daily News" und wäre Ihnen dankbar, wenn Sie mir nähere Angaben über die Stelle eines Regionalverkaufsleiters (einer Regionalverkaufsleiterin)/eines persönlichen Assistenten (einer persönlichen Assistentin) zusenden würden*

I saw your advertisement in today's Daily News and I would like to apply for the post of ... *ich habe Ihre Anzeige in der heutigen Ausgabe von "Daily News" gesehen und möchte mich um die Stelle eines/einer ... bewerben*

I am writing to you in the hope that you will be able to offer me employment in the field of ... *ich schreibe Ihnen in der Hoffnung, daß Sie mir eine Stelle im Bereich ... anbieten können*

I am writing to enquire about the possibility of joining your company for 3 months/6 months on work placement *ich möchte mich hiermit erkundigen, ob es möglich wäre, in Ihrer Firma ein dreimonatiges/sechsmonatiges Praktikum zu absolvieren*

GIVING YOUR BACKGROUND

I have three years' experience of this kind of work *ich habe drei Jahre Erfahrung in diesem Bereich*

I have the qualifications and experience for the job *ich habe die erforderlichen Qualifikationen und die nötige Erfahrung für diese Stelle*

I am currently working in the same field *ich arbeite zur Zeit in diesem Bereich*

I was trained as an engineer *ich bin ausgebildeter Ingenieur/ ausgebildete Ingenieurin*

I am very anxious to work in publishing/advertising *ich möchte unbedingt im Verlagswesen/bei einer Werbeagentur arbeiten*

I would like to work in Germany for approximately 6 months before starting university/beginning my training course *bevor ich mit meinem Universitätsstudium/meiner Ausbildung beginne, würde ich gerne 6 Monate in Deutschland arbeiten*

As you will see from my CV, I have worked in Germany/Austria/ Switzerland before *wie Sie meinem Lebenslauf entnehmen können, habe ich schon in Deutschland/Österreich/in der Schweiz gearbeitet*

I would like to work abroad (again) *ich würde gerne (wieder) im Ausland arbeiten*

As well as speaking fluent French, I have a working knowledge of German and can read Italian and Spanish *ich spreche fließend Französisch. Außerdem habe ich Grundkenntnisse in Deutsch und kann Italienisch und Spanisch lesen*

WHY YOU WOULD LIKE THE JOB

I would like to make better use of my languages *ich würde meine Sprache gerne etwas mehr einsetzen*

I would like to change jobs because ... *ich möchte meinen Arbeitsplatz wechseln, weil ...*

For personal/professional reasons *aus persönlichen/beruflichen Gründen*

CLOSING THE LETTER

I shall be available from the end of April *ich könnte die Stelle Ende April antreten*

My present salary is ... per annum/per month and I have four weeks holiday with pay *mein derzeitiges Gehalt ist ... pro Jahr/ pro Monat, und ich habe Anspruch auf vier Wochen Urlaub*

I am available for interview at any time *ich stehen jederzeit zu einem Vorstellungsgespräch zur Verfügung*

If possible, I would prefer to have my interview on a Friday/at the weekend *wenn möglich, würde ich lieber an einem Freitag/am*

Wochenende zu einem Vorstellungsgespräch kommen

Please do not contact my present employers *bitte setzen Sie sich nicht mit meinem derzeitigen Arbeitgeber in Verbindung*

Would you cover my relocation expenses? *würden Sie für meine Umzugskosten aufkommen?*

Would you help me to find accommodation? *würden Sie mir bei der Wohnungssuche behilflich sein?*

I enclose a stamped addressed envelope for your reply *ich füge einen frankierten Rückumschlag für Ihre Antwort bei*

I enclose an international reply coupon *ich füge einen internationalen Antwortschein bei*

I can supply references from my previous employers if you require them *wenn Sie wünschen, kann ich Ihnen Referenzen von früheren Arbeitgebern vorlegen*

Please find enclosed my CV and references *in der Anlage übersende ich Ihnen meinen Lebenslauf und Referenzen*

Please find herewith my completed application form *hiermit übersende ich Ihnen mein ausgefülltes Bewerbungsformular*

If you require any further information, please do not hesitate to contact me *für weitere Auskünfte stehe ich Ihnen jederzeit gern(e) zur Verfügung*

RECRUITING EMPLOYEES ABROAD

We are seeking to recruit ... *wir suchen ...*

We have vacancies for ... *wir haben Stellen für ...*

We are looking for experienced sales personnel *wir suchen erfahrenes Verkaufspersonal*

The successful candidate will be between 25–45 *der/die erfolgreiche Kandidat/Kandidatin sollte zwischen 25 und 45 Jahre alt sein*

Experience in the field is preferable but not essential *Erfahrung in diesem Bereich ist erwünscht, aber nicht unbedingt erforderlich*

Knowledge of English and at least one other European language is essential *Englischkenntnisse und mindestens eine weitere europäische Sprache sind erforderlich*

You will be travelling for two months of the year *Sie werden zwei Monate im Jahr auf Reisen sein*

You will have to be capable of working in a Team *Sie müssen im Team arbeiten können*

The closing date for application is 15 October *Bewerbungen müssen bis spätestens 15. Oktober eingehen*

Salary: ... p.a. plus commission/bonuses and a company car *Gehalt: ... pro Jahr zusätzlich Kommission/Prämien und Firmenwagen*

Salary on application *Auskunft über Gehalt auf Anfrage*
We will help you to find temporary accommodation *wir werden Ihnen gern(e) behilflich sein, vorübergehende Unterkunft zu finden*
We will arrange temporary accommodation for you free of charge *wir werden kostenlos vorübergehende Unterkunft für Sie arrangieren*
We will cover your relocation expenses up to ... *wir kommen für Umzugskosten bis zu einer Summe von ... auf*
For more details, contact:- *für weitere Einzelheiten wenden Sie sich an:-*

REPLYING TO AN APPLICANT

Thank you for your letter of application *vielen Dank für Ihr Bewerbungsschreiben*
I enclose an application form. Please fill it in and return it by 25 September *ich füge ein Bewerbungsformular bei. Bitte senden Sie es ausgefüllt bis zum 25. September an uns zurück*
We would like to invite you for an interview at the above address on 26 June at 2pm. Please contact us immediately if this is not convenient *wir möchten Sie hiermit zu einem Vorstellungsgespräch am 26. Juni um 14 Uhr unter obenstehender Adresse einladen. Falls Ihnen dieser Termin nicht paßt, setzen Sie sich bitte sofort mit uns in Verbindung*

ACCEPTING AND REFUSING

Thank you for your letter of 19 June. I shall be pleased to attend the interview at your offices in London on Thursday 4 July at 10am *vielen Dank für Ihr Schreiben vom 19. Juni. Ich komme gerne am Donnerstag, den 4. Juli um 10 Uhr zu einem Vorstellungsgespräch in Ihr Londoner Büro*
I am very pleased to say that I would like to accept your offer of the post of ..., commencing on 15 January *es freut mich sehr, Ihnen mitteilen zu können, daß ich Ihr Angebot für die Stelle als ... mit Arbeitsbeginn am 15. Januar gern(e) annehme*
Could you send me details about obtaining a work/residence permit? *können Sie mir bitte Informationen bezüglich Erhalt einer Arbeitserlaubnis/Aufenthaltsgenehmigung zusenden?*
I would very much like to accept the post which you have offered me. However, would it be possible to postpone my starting date until 1 March? *ich würde die Stelle, die Sie mir angeboten haben, sehr gerne annehmen. Wäre es jedoch möglich, das Anfangsdatum auf den 1. März zu verschieben?*

I would be very glad to accept your offer if you agreed to increase the salary to ... *ich würde Ihr Angebot sehr gerne annehmen, wenn Sie bereit wären, das Gehalt auf ... zu erhöhen*

Having given your offer all due consideration, I regret to say that I am forced to decline *ich möchte Ihnen mitteilen, daß ich mich nach reiflicher Überlegung leider gezwungen sehe, Ihr Angebot abzulehnen*

INFORMING THE SUCCESSFUL/UNSUCCESSFUL CANDIDATE

We are happy to offer you the post of ... *wir freuen uns, Ihnen hiermit die Stelle eines/einer ... anbieten zu können*

Please contact us in order to make the necessary arrangements *bitte setzen Sie sich mit uns in Verbindung, damit die nötigen Vorbereitungen getroffen werden können*

We regret to inform you that the post has already been filled *wir müssen Ihnen leider mitteilen, daß der Posten schon besetzt wurde*

We regret to inform you that your name has not been put on our short list *wir müssen Ihnen leider mitteilen, daß Sie nicht in die engere Auswahl gekommen sind*

We will keep your CV and application form on file *wir werden Ihren Lebenslauf und Ihre Bewerbung zu unseren Akten legen*

Please do not hesitate to reply to future advertisements for a similar post *bei künftigen Stellenangeboten können Sie sich gerne um einen ähnlichen Posten bewerben*

QUALIFICATIONS

Below is a list of the basic British academic qualifications and their approximate equivalent in Germany, Austria and Switzerland.

O levels, GCSEs, Standard Grades *Mittlere Reife f*

A levels, Higher Grades *Abitur nt (in Germany); Maturum nt (in Austria, Switzerland)*

A levels, Higher Grades in ... *Abitur nt/Maturum nt in den Fächern ...*

degree (in ...) *akademischer Abschluß m (in ...)*

OND (in ...) *zweijähriges Studium nt an einer technischen Fachschule (in ...)*

HND (in ...) *dreijähriges Studium nt an einer technischen Fachschule*

MA (in ...) *M.A. m (in ...)*

MBA *MBA m*

MSc (in ...) *Magister m der Naturwissenschaften (in ...)*

PhD (in ...) *Dr. (der/des ...)*

OTHER GERMAN QUALIFICATIONS

Diplom *nt* **(Dipl.)** *diploma after 5–6 years at university or technical college*
Dipl.-Ing *academically qualified engineer (with a Diplom)*
Dipl.-Kfm. *business school graduate (with a Diplom)*
Fachabitur *nt A levels in a specific subject, rather than the general Abitur*
FH *qualification from a Fachhochschule (technical college), e.g. Ing. FH (engineering qualification)*
Gesellenprüfung *f craftsman's certificate*
Lehre *f apprenticeship*
Meisterprüfung *f master craftsman's certificate*
Staatsexamen *nt first degree required before beginning teacher training*

ADDITIONAL VOCABULARY

applicant	*Bewerber(in) m/f*
application	*Bewerbung f*
application form	*Bewerbungsformular nt*
apply (for)	*sich bewerben (um +acc)*
aptitude test	*Eignungsprüfung f*
contract	*Arbeitsvertrag m*
CV (curriculum vitae)	*Lebenslauf m*
experience	*Erfahrung f*
handwritten letter	*handgeschriebener Brief m*
headhunter	*Kopfjäger m*
holiday job	*Ferienarbeit f*
international reply coupon	*internationaler Antwortschein m*
interview	*Vorstellungsgespräch nt*
job description	*Arbeitsplatzbeschreibung f*
job title	*Berufsbezeichnung f*
letter of application	*Bewerbungsschreiben nt*
medical certificate	*amtsärztliches Zeugnis nt*
qualifications	*Qualifikationen fpl*
recruit *vb*	*einstellen*
recruitment	*Einstellung f*
referee	*Referenz f*
reference	*Referenz f*
relocation expenses	*Umzugskosten pl*
sae (stamped addressed envelope)	*frankierter Rückumschlag m*

student	*Student (in) m(f)*
typewritten letter	*maschinengeschriebener Brief m*
unemployed	*arbeitslos*
vacancy	*freie Stelle f*
work *n*	*Arbeit f*
work *vb*	*arbeiten*
work placement	*Praktikum nt*

See also **COMPANY STRUCTURES** *and* **PERSONNEL**

John Dawes
89 Short Street
Glossop,
Derbys SK13 4AP
England

Glossop, den 15.9.1991

Maschinenbau Kaiser GmbH
Postfach 70
D-4000 Düsseldorf 1
Germany

Betr.: Bewerbung als Leiter der Exportabteilung
Bezug: Anzeige in der "Süddeutschen Zeitung" vom 12.9.1991

Sehr geehrte Damen und Herren,

hiermit möchte ich mich um die ausgeschriebene Stelle als Leiter
der Exportabteilung in Ihrem Verlag bewerben.

Neben Spezialkenntnissen im Bereich Maschinenbau verfüge ich
über Berufserfahrung in der Exportbranche. Außerdem habe ich
gute deutsche Sprachkenntnisse und bin mit der internationalen
Marktsituation vertraut. Ich bin kontaktfreudig und habe Freude
am selbständigen Arbeiten.

In der Anlage übersende ich Ihnen meine Bewerbungsunterlagen
sowie meinen Lebenslauf und Kopien meiner Zeugnisse.

Für weitere Auskünfte stehe ich Ihnen gerne jederzeit zur
Verfügung.

Ich würde mich freuen, bald von Ihnen zu hören.

Mit freundlichen Grüßen

John Dawes

John Dawes

Anlagen

Dear Sirs,

Re: Application for the post of Export Manager;
Ref: Advertisement in the "Süddeutsche Zeitung" of 12
September 1991

I wish to apply for the above-mentioned post of Export Manager
in your publishing house.

In addition to my specialized knowledge in the field of
machine manufacture, I have experience in exports. I also
have a good command of written and spoken German and am well
acquainted with the international market situation. I have an
outgoing personality and enjoy working independently.

Please find enclosed the documents in support of my
application, as well as my Curriculum Vitae and copies of my
references.

Please do not hesitate to contact me if you require any
further information.

I look forward to hearing from you.

Yours faithfully   Enc.

John Dawes

John Dawes

LEBENSLAUF

NAME **ANSCHRIFT**	John Alexander Dawes 89 Short Street Glossop Derbys SK13 4AP England Tel: 0457 864103
GEBURTSDATUM	15.10.58
GEBURTSORT	Sheffield, England
FAMILIENSTAND	Unverheiratet

SPRACHKENNTNISSE

English	(Muttersprache)
Deutsch	(fließend)
Französisch	(gute mündliche und schriftliche Kenntnisse)
Italienisch	(Grundkenntnisse)

BERUFLICHE TÄTIGKEITEN

Juni 1987 - heute	Export Manager (Leiter der Exportabteilung), Bawring Manufacturing plc, Derby
Okt 1984 - Mai 1987	Deputy Export Manager (Stellvertretender Leiter der Exportabteilung), Jones Machines, Welwyn Garden City
Okt 1981 - Mai 1983	Sales Representative (Vertreter), Smith and Sons, Sheffield
Juni 1980 - Sept 1980	Trainee Salesman (Firmenpraktikant), Fritz Wagner KG, Frankfurt

AUSBILDUNG

1983 - 1984	Diploma in Industrial Management (Diplom in Betriebsführung), London Polytechnic
1980 - 1981	Master of Business Administration (Magister in Betriebswirtschaftslehre), Hatfield Polytechnic
1977 - 1980	BSc in Mechanical Engineering (2i) (Diplom in Maschinenbau), Sheffield University
Mai 1977	4 A levels: German, French, Maths, Physics (Abitur in 4 Fächern: Deutsch, Französisch, Mathematik, Physik)

WEITERE INFORMATIONEN	EDV-Kenntnisse Führerschein Zahlreiche Auslandsaufenthalte in Europa und den Vereinigten Staaten

See also **PERSONNEL** *and* **PROPERTY**

absolute undertaking	*absolutes Versprechen nt*
acceptance of goods	*Warenabnahme f*
acceptance of offer	*Annahme f eines Angebots nt*
acceptor	*Akzeptant m*
accredited agent	*bevollmächtiger Vertreter(in) m(f)*
action	*Prozeß m*
actionable	*einklagbar*
adjudicate	*entscheiden*
adjudication	*gerichtliche Entscheidung f*
administration	*Verwaltung f*
administrative tribunal	*Verwaltungsgericht nt*
administrator	*Verwalter(in) m(f)*
advocate	*Anwalt m, Anwältin f*
affidavit	*Affidavit nt, eidesstattliche Erklärung f*
affirmation	*eidesstattliche Erklärung f*
agent	*Vertreter(in) m(f)*
(aggravated) damages	*(erhöhter) Schaden m*
agreement	*Vertrag m, Abkommen nt*
agreement to sell	*Verkaufsabkommen nt*
allow	*zugestehen*
anticipatory breach	*antizipierter Vertragsbruch m*
anti-trust legislation	*Kartellgesetzgebung f*
appeal *n*	*Berufung f*
appeal *vb*	*Berufung f einlegen*
appeal court	*Berufungsgericht nt*
appellant	*Berufungskläger(in) m(f)*
arbitration clause	*Schiedsklausel f*
arbitrator	*Schiedsrichter(in) m(f)*
article *(in contract)*	*Paragraph m*
articles of association	*Gesellschaftsvertrag m*
ascertained goods	*Speziessachen fpl*
assessment *(of damages)*	*Schadensfeststellung f*
assign	*übertragen*
assignee	*Zessionar m*
assignment	*Übertragung f*
assignor	*Zedent m*
attachment	*Pfändung f*
attorney	*Bevollmächtigte(r) f(m)*

I would like some advice regarding the law covering ... *ich möchte einen Rat, was das Gesetz über (+acc) ... betrifft*

Attorney-General *(UK)*	*Justizminister m*
Attorney-General *(US)*	*Generalstaatsanwalt m*
award *n*	*Zuerkennung f*
award *vb (contract)*	*vergeben*
award *vb (damages)*	*zuerkennen*
backdate	*rückdatieren*
bad faith	*Unredlichkeit f*
bail	*Kaution f*
bailee	*Gewahrsamsinhaber(in) m(f)*
bailment	*Verwahrung f*
bailor	*Hinterleger(in) m(f)*
bankrupt *adj*	*bankrott*
bankrupt *n*	*Konkursschuldner(in) m(f)*
go bankrupt	*Bankrott machen*
bankruptcy	*Bankrott m*
barrister	*Barrister m*
bearer	*Inhaber(in) m(f)*
bearer bill	*Inhaberwechsel m*
bilateral agreement	*bilaterales Abkommen nt*
bill of sale	*Übereignungsurkunde f*
bona fide	*bona fide, gutgläubig*
breach of contract	*Vertragsbruch m*
by(e-)law	*Satzung f*
case	*Fall m*
causation	*Verursachung f*
caveat emptor	*Mängelausschluß m*
charge	*Anklage f*
charter party	*Chartervertrag m*
civil law	*Zivilrecht nt*
clause	*Klausel f*
code of practice	*Standesordnung f*
codicil	*Testamentsnachtrag m, Kodizill nt*
commercial law	*Handelsrecht nt*
common law	*Gewohnheitsrecht nt*
common mistake	*gemeinsamer Irrtum m*
community law	*Gemeinschaftsrecht nt*
Companies Act	*Gesetz nt über die Kapitalgesellschaften fpl*
company law	*Gesellschaftsrecht nt*

they did not respect the relevant clause in the contract *sie haben die relevante Klausel im Vertrag nicht beachtet*
the law is quite clear on this matter *in dieser Sache ist das Gesetz ganz eindeutig*

compensation	*Entschädigung f*
complainant	*Kläger(in) m(f)*
completion	*Beendigung f*
compromise *n*	*Kompromiß m*
compromise *vb*	*einen Kompromiß m schließen*
conditional	*bedingt*
conditional sale agreement	*Kaufvertrag m unter Eigentumsvorbehalt m*
conditions of sale	*Verkaufsbedingungen fpl*
consignee	*Empfänger(in) m(f)*
consumer protection	*Verbraucherschutz m*
contract	*Vertrag m*
under contract	*unter Vertrag m*
contract law	*Schuldrecht nt*
contract of employment	*Arbeitsvertrag m*
contract of hire	*Mietvertrag m über bewegliche Sachen fpl*
contract of sale	*Kaufvertrag m*
contractual liability	*Vertragshaftung f*
contractual obligation	*vertragliche Verplichtung f*
conveyancing	*Eigentumsübertragung f*
cooling-off period	*Überdenkungsperiode f*
copyright	*Copyright nt*
costs	*Kosten pl*
counsel for the defence	*Verteidiger(in) m(f) der Anklager*
counter-claim *n*	*Gegenanspruch m*
counter-claim *vb*	*einen Gegenanspruch m geltend machen*
counter-offer *n*	*Gegenangebot nt*
counter-offer *vb*	*ein Gegenangebot einreichen*
Court of Appeal	*Berufungsgericht nt*
covenant	*vertragliches Versprechen nt*
creditor	*Gläubiger(in) m(f)*
criminal law	*Strafrecht nt*
damages	*Schaden(s)ersatz m*
debenture	*Obligation f*
debt	*Schuld f*

please sign one copy of the contract and return it to us *bitte senden Sie eine Kopie des Vertrags unterschrieben an uns zurück*
we will draw up a contract and submit it to you for inspection *wir werden einen Vertrag aufsetzen und Ihnen zur Begutachtung vorlegen*
this text is copyright *dieser Text ist urheberrechtlich geschützt*
does German/Swiss law cover this? *ist das nach deutschem/ schweizerischem Recht erlaubt?*

debt collection agency	*Inkassobüro nt*
debtor	*Schuldner(in) m(f)*
debtor-creditor-supplier agreement	*Abkommen nt zwischen Schuldner, Gläubiger und Lieferer*
deed	*Urkunde f*
deed of covenant	*Versprechensurkunde f*
default *(fail to appear)*	*nicht erscheinen*
default *(on a debt)*	*nicht bezahlen*
default notice	*Zahlungsaufforderung f*
defend	*verteidigen*
defendant	*Angeklagte(r) f(m)*
defraud	*betrügen*
deviation	*Abweichung f*
directive	*Direktive f*
disenfranchise	*Konzession f entziehen*
draft *n*	*Entwurf m*
draft *vb*	*entwerfen*
effective date	*Zeitpunkt m des Inkrafttretens nt*
embezzle	*unterschlagen*
embezzlement	*Unterschlagung f, Verantreuung f*
employment law	*Arbeitsrecht nt*
enforcement order	*Vollstreckungsauftrag m*
equitable	*gerecht*
equity	*Billigkeitsrecht nt, Equity-Recht nt*
escape clause	*Befreiungsklausel f*
estate	*Besitz m*
exclusion clause	*Freizeichnungsklausel f*
exclusive agency agreement	*Alleinvertretungsvertrag m*
exemption clause	*Freistellungsklausel f*
ex gratia payment	*Kulanzzahlung f*
expiry date	*Verfallstag m*
fees	*Honorar nt*
fiduciary	*Treuhänder(in) m(f)*
final demand *(bill)*	*letzte Zahlungsaufforderung f*
fixed-price contract	*Festpreisvertrag m*
formality	*Formalität f*
franchise *n*	*Konzession f, Franchise f*
franchise *vb*	*konzessionieren*
franchise agreement	*Franchisevereinbarung f*
franchisee	*Franchisenehmer(in) m(f)*
franchiser	*Franchisegeber(in) m(f)*
fraud	*Betrug m*
gentleman's agreement	*Gentleman's Agreement nt*

good faith	*Treu f und Glauben m*
goods and chattels	*Hab nt und Gut nt*
guarantee *n*	*Garantie f*
guarantee *vb*	*garantieren*
guarantor	*Bürge m, Bürgin f*
guilty party	*schuldige Partei f*
hire-purchase agreement	*Teilzahlungs(kauf)vertrag m*
illegal	*illegal*
illegality	*Illegalität f*
illegally	*illegal*
incidental damages	*Ersatz m des beiläufig entstandenen Schadens m*
indemnity clause	*Haftungsfreistellungsklausel f*
injunction	*einstweilige Verfügung f*
innocent party	*nichtschuldige Partei f*
insolvency	*Insolvenz f, Zahlungsunfähigkeit f*
intellectual property	*geistiges Eigentum nt*
international law	*internationales Recht nt*
judgement	*Gerichtsurteil nt*
jurisdiction	*Gerichtsbarkeit f*
justification	*Rechtfertigung f*
lapse of time	*Fristablauf m*
law	*Gesetz nt*
law court	*Gerichtshof m*
lawful	*gesetzlich*
Law Society	*Anwaltsverein m*
lawsuit	*Prozeß m*
lawyer	*Rechtsanwalt m, Rechtsanwältin f*
lease back	*rückvermieten*
leaseback arrangement	*Rückvermietungsabkommen nt*
legal	*gesetzlich*
legal department	*Rechtsabteilung f*

to operate within/outside the law *gesetzmäßig/gesetzwidrig handeln*
to bring a lawsuit against someone *jemanden verklagen*
you will be hearing from our lawyer in the very near future *Sie werden in Kürze von unserem Anwalt hören*
to take legal action to recover damages *Schadensersatz klagen*
we will be forced to take legal action if ... *wir sehen uns gezwungen, eine Klage zu erheben, wenn ...*
to seek *or* **take legal advice** *einen Anwalt m/eine Anwältin f zu Rate ziehen*
to give someone legal advice *jemanden juristisch beraten*
to have a legal right to something *einen Rechtsanspruch auf etwas (acc) haben*

legality	*Legalität f*
legally binding	*rechtsverbindlich*
legal requirement	*rechtliche Voraussetzung f*
legatee	*Vermächtnisnehmer(in) m(f)*
letter of intent	*Absichtserklärung f*
letters patent	*Patenturkunde f*
liability	*Haftung f*
liable	*haftbar*
licensing agreement	*Lizenzabkommen nt*
limited liability	*beschränkte Haftung f*
litigation	*Rechtsstreit m*
loophole	*Gesetzeslücke f*
magistrate	*Richter(in) m(f)*
mandate	*Mandat nt*
mandatory	*obligatorisch*
maritime law	*Seerecht nt*
maritime lawyer	*Seerechtsanwalt m,*
	Seerechtsanwältin f
misrepresentation	*falsche Darstellung f*
mitigation of loss	*Schadensminderung f*
moratorium	*Moratorium nt*
negligence	*Fahrlässigkeit f*
negligent	*fahrlässig*
negotiable	*verhandlungsfähig*
negotiation	*Verhandlung f*
non-payment	*Nichtzahlung f*
non-performance	*Nichterfüllung f*
notification	*Bescheid m*
nuisance	*Belästigung f*
null and void	*null und nichtig*
official receiver	*Konkursverwalter(in) m(f)*
out-of-court settlement	*außergerichtlicher Vergleich m*
partner	*Teilhaber(in) m(f),*
	Gesellschafter(in) m(f)
partnership *(company)*	*Personengesellschaft f*
partnership *(arrangement)*	*Partnerschaft f*
patent *n*	*Patent nt*
patent *vb*	*patentieren lassen*
patent office	*Patentamt nt*
patent rights	*Patentrechte ntpl*
penalty clause	*Strafklausel f*

to exploit a loophole in the law *eine Lücke im Gesetz ausnutzen*
the contract becomes null and void if ... *der Vertrag wird null und nichtig,*
  wenn ...

performance	*Erfüllung f*
plagiarism	*Plagiat nt*
plaintiff	*Kläger(in) m(f)*
power of attorney	*Vollmacht f*
precedent	*Präzedenzfall m*
prima facie	*prima facie*
principal	*Klient(in) m(f)*
promise *n*	*Versprechen nt*
promissory note	*Schuldschein m*
property *(ownership)*	*Eigentum nt*
proprietary goods	*Markenartikel mpl*
prosecute	*strafrechtlich verfolgen*
prosecuting counsel	*Staatsanwalt m, Staatsanwältin f*
quid pro quo	*Gegenleistung f*
ratification	*Ratifizierung f*
ratify	*ratifizieren*
receiver	*Konkursverwalter(in) m(f)*
receivership	*Konkursverwaltung f*
rectification	*Richtigstellung f*
registered trademark	*eingetragenes Warenzeichen nt*
regulation	*Vorschrift f*
repossess	*wieder in Besitz m nehmen*
repossession	*Wiederinbesitznahme f*
represent	*vertreten*
representation	*Vertretung f*
repudiation	*Nichtanerkennung f*
required notice	*vorgeschriebene Kündigungsfrist f*
restrictive trading agreement	*wettbewerbsbeschränkende Abmachung f*
return order	*Rückforderung f*
revocation	*Widerruf m*
revoke	*aufheben*
rider	*Anhang m, Zusatz m*
right	*Recht nt*
ruling	*Entscheidung f*
sale and lease back	*Verkauf m und Rückmiete f*
secured creditor	*gesicherter Gläubiger m*
security of tenure *(of tenant, worker)*	*Kündigungsschutz m*

I have a query regarding clause 4 of the contract *ich habe eine Rückfrage bezüglich Klausel 4 des Vertrags*
to go into receivership *den Konkurs eröffnen*

sequestration	*Sequestration f*
settle *(pay)*	*begleichen*
settlement *(payment)*	*Bezahlung f*
settlement *(of estate; agreement)*	*Regelung f*
signatory	*Unterzeichner m, Unterzeichnete(r) f(m)*
solicitor	*Rechtsanwalt m, Rechtsanwältin f*
specimen signature	*Unterschriftsprobe f*
statute	*Gesetz nt*
statutory	*gesetzlich*
subcontract *n*	*Subunternehmervertrag m*
subcontract *vb*	*einen Untervertrag m abschließen*
subject to confirmation	*vorbehaltlich einer Bestätigung f*
subject to contract	*vorbehaltlich eines Vertragsabschlusses m*
termination of contract	*Vertragskündigung f*
third party	*Dritter m*
tort	*Delikt nt*
Trade Descriptions Act	*Warenbeschreibungsgesetz nt*
trademark	*Warenzeichen nt*
trust	*Treuhandverhältnis nt*
trustee	*Treuhänder(in) m(f)*
unascertained goods	*Gattungssachen fpl*
unconditional	*bedingungslos*
undersigned	*Unterzeichnete(r) f(m)*
unilateral mistake	*einseitiger Fehler m*
void	*nichtig*
voidable contract	*anfechtbarer Vertrag m*
warrant	*Haftbefehl m*
warranty *(guarantee)*	*Garantie f*
warranty *(surety)*	*Gewährleistung f*
writ	*einstweilige Verfügung f*

to sue a company/somebody for damages *eine Firma/jemanden auf Schadensersatz verklagen*
the contract is valid for all countries *der Vertrag gilt für alle Länder*
to make void *ungültig machen*
to serve a writ on someone *jemanden vorladen*

MAKING CONTACT

BY PHONE

DIALLING CODES (UK ONLY)

To Austria	*010 43*	From Austria	*00 44*
To Germany	*010 49*	From Germany	*00 44*
To Luxembourg	*010 352*	From Luxembourg	*00 44*
To Switzerland	*010 41*	From Switzerland	*00 44*

When calling the UK from abroad, remember to knock the initial zero off the British dialling codes, e.g. when calling London from Germany you dial 00 44 71 or 00 44 81.

CALLING FROM A PAYPHONE
All Austrian payphones allow international direct dialling. Coin boxes have either three or four coin slots, the three-slot type having a red button (*Zahlknopf*), which you must press when you are connected so that the person you are calling can hear you. Phonecards can be bought in a *Tabak-Trafik*. For inland/international directory enquiries ring 16118/08.

German international payphones are marked *Europa* or *International*. You will need coins, as cashless calls are not possible in Germany. The cheap rate is Monday-Friday 18.00–08.00 and all day on Saturday and Sunday. For inland/international directory enquiries ring 01188/00118. If you dial the wrong number you will not hear a number unobtainable tone but a recorded message saying *kein Anschluß unter dieser Nummer*.

All call boxes in Luxembourg accept both Belgian and Luxembourg francs and can be used for international calls. Reverse-charge calls can only be made from the post office. For national/international enquiries ring 016/017.

You can phone abroad from all call boxes in Switzerland. All have dialling instructions in English. To make a reverse-charge call ring the operator on 114. For international enquiries ring 121. The cheap rate is Monday-Friday 21.00–08.00 and Saturday all day.

CALLING THE OPERATOR
Could you get me Bonn 42 57 86, please *ich hätte gern Bonn 42 57 86 (vier-zwo fünf-sieben acht-sechs or zweiundvierzig siebenundfünfzig sechsundachtzig)*
Would you give me Directory Enquiries, please *könnten Sie mich bitte mit der Auskunft verbinden?*
I'm looking for the phone number of ... *könnten Sie mir bitte die Nummer von ... geben?*
The address is ... *die Adresse ist ...*

What is the code for Frankfurt? *wie ist die Vorwahl von Frankfurt?*

I'd like to make a reverse-charge call to Glasgow/England *ich möchte ein R-Gespräch nach Glasgow/England anmelden*

I'd like a credit card call to Vienna *ich möchte ein Gespräch mit Kreditkarte nach Wien anmelden (NB: system does not exist in Germany)*

I want to make an international call *ich möchte im Ausland anrufen*

Can I dial direct to Colombia? *kann ich nach Kolombien durchwählen?*

I can't get through *ich komme nicht durch*

I'm getting "number unobtainable" *ich bekomme immer nur "Kein Anschluß unter dieser Nummer"*

My call was just cut off. Can you reconnect me? *das Gespräch ist unterbrochen worden. Können Sie mich noch mal verbinden?*

THE OPERATOR REPLIES

Welche Nummer haben Sie gewählt? *what number do you want?*

Ihre Nummer, bitte? *where are you calling from?*

Können Sie die Nummer bitte wiederholen? *would you repeat the number, please*

Sie können durchwählen *you can dial the number direct*

Legen Sie auf und wählen Sie dann noch einmal *replace the receiver and dial again*

Ich verbinde *go ahead, caller*

Der Teilnehmer 65 13 22 00 antwortet nicht *there's no reply from 65 13 22 00*

Ich versuche noch einmal, Sie zu verbinden *I'll try to reconnect you*

Bitte bleiben Sie am Apparat *hold the line, caller*

Ich versuche, Sie zu verbinden *I'm trying for you now*

Die Leitung ist besetzt *the line is engaged*

Wir haben ein Rufzeichen *ringing for you now*

Das Telefon ist gestört *their phone is out of order*

GETTING PAST THE SWITCHBOARD

Extension 3045 please *Apparat 3045 bitte*

Could I speak to Mr Müller, please? *könnte ich mit Herrn Müller sprechen?*

Could you put me through to Dr Meier, please? *könnten Sie mich zu Herrn Dr. Meier durchstellen, bitte?*

I'll hold *ich bleibe am Apparat*

I'll try again later *ich versuche es später noch einmal*

I'm phoning from England *ich rufe aus England an*

Does anyone speak English? *spricht irgend jemand Englisch?*

THE SWITCHBOARD OPERATOR REPLIES
Wer ist bitte am Apparat? *who is calling, please?*
Wen darf ich melden? *who shall I say is calling?*
Wissen Sie, welchen Apparat er hat? *do you know the extension number?*
Ich verbinde *I'm putting you through now*
Bitte bleiben sie am Apparat *sorry to keep you waiting*
Es meldet sich niemand *there's no reply*
Er spricht gerade auf der anderen Leitung *he is on the other line*
Hier spricht der automatische Anrufbeantworter *this is a recorded message*
Bitte sprechen Sie nach dem Piepston *please speak after the tone*

IF THE PERSON IS OUT
I'll call back later/tomorrow *ich rufe später/morgen noch mal an*
Is there anyone else I can speak to? *kann ich mit jemand anderem sprechen?*
Please transfer my call to ... *bitte stellen Sie mich zu ... durch*
Do you have a number where I can reach him/her? *wissen Sie unter welcher Nummer ich ihn/sie erreichen kann?*
When will he/she be in the office? *wann ist er/sie im Büro?*
Can you ask him/her to call me back? *können Sie ihn/sie bitten, mich zurückzurufen?*
Can I leave a message? *kann ich eine Nachricht hinterlassen?*
Who am I speaking to? *mit wem spreche ich?*

WHEN YOU GET THROUGH
My name is ... *mein Name ist ...*
I'm calling on behalf of ... *ich rufe im Auftrag von ... an*
You were recommended to me by Mr ... *Sie wurden mir von Herrn ... empfohlen*
I'm calling about ... *ich rufe wegen ... an*

RECEIVING A CALL FROM ABROAD
Speaking *am Apparat*
How can I help you? *was kann ich für Sie tun?*
Sorry, I don't speak German *ich spreche leider kein Deutsch*
Hold on a moment, please *einen Moment, bitte*
Who's calling? *wer ist bitte am Apparat?*
He's/she's out at the moment *er/sie ist im Augenblick nicht da*
Please call back tomorrow/this afternoon/in an hour *rufen Sie bitte morgen/heute nachmittag/in einer Stunde noch einmal an*
Can you speak a little louder/more slowly, please? *könnten Sie bitte etwas lauter/langsamer sprechen?*
This is a very bad line *die Verbindung ist sehr schlecht*

SAMPLE TELEPHONE CONVERSATION

VERMITTLUNG	: *Firma Walter & Co., guten Tag!*	
MS GRAY	: *Guten Tag, hier Gray von der Firma Best Books Ltd. in Glenrothes.* **Kann ich bitte mit Herrn Weber sprechen?**	*Can I speak to Mr Weber, please?*
VERMITTLUNG	: **Moment bitte, ich verbinde.**	*One moment, please. I'll put you through.*
SEKRETÄRIN	: *Schmidt, guten Tag!* **Was kann ich für Sie tun?**	*What can I do for you?*
MS GRAY	: *Gray von der Firma Best Books Ltd. in Glenrothes.* **Könnte ich** *bitte Herrn Weber sprechen?*	*Could I ...*
SEKRETÄRIN	: **Tut mir leid, aber** *Herr Weber ist heute nicht im Büro.* **Kann ich Ihnen helfen?**	*I'm sorry but ... Can I help you?*
MS GRAY	: *Ich hoffe ja.* **Es geht um folgendes.** *Ich werde vom 10. bis 15. September in Frankfurt sein und* **hatte mit Herrn Weber vereinbart, daß wir uns bei dieser Gelegenheit treffen.** *Wissen Sie, ob Herr Weber an einem der Tage noch frei ist?*	*It's about the following. had arranged with Mr Weber that we should meet on this occasion.*
SEKRETÄRIN	: *Einen Moment bitte,* **ich will mal nachsehen.** *Also, am 13. und 14. zwischen 9 und 11 Uhr morgens* **könnte ich noch Termine ausmachen. Würde Ihnen einer der beiden Tage passen?**	*I'll just check.* *I could give you an appointment. Would either of these days suit you?*
MS GRAY	: *Ja, der 14.* **September paßt ausgezeichnet. Sagen wir** *10 Uhr in der Cafeteria in Halle 3.*	*the 14th September is fine. Let's say ...*
SEKRETÄRIN	: *Gut, ich habe es notiert.*	*I've made a note of it.*
MS GRAY	: *Vielen Dank, Frau Schmidt und auf Wiederhören.*	
SEKRETÄRIN	: *Auf Wiederhören, Frau Gray.*	

LETTERS, FAXES AND TELEXES

STANDARD OPENING AND CLOSING FORMULAE

Used when you do not know the person's name	
Sehr geehrte Damen und Herren, Sehr geehrte Herren, Sehr geehrte gnädige Frau,	Mit freundlichen Grüßen Mit vorzüglicher Hochachtung
Used if you know the person's name	
Sehr geehrter Herr Wagner, Sehr geehrte Frau Professor Müller, Sehr geehrte Frau Kühn, sehr geehrter Herr Kühn,	As above, plus: Ich verbleibe, sehr geehrte Frau Professor, mit vorzüglicher Hochachtung Ihr/Ihre

TO ACQUAINTANCES AND FRIENDS

More formal	
Sehr geehrter Herr Dr. Braun, Liebe Freunde,	Mit freundlichen Grüßen Mit besten Grüßen
Fairly informal: 'Du' or 'Sie' forms may be used	
Lieber Peter, Liebe Ingrid, Lieber Ingrid, lieber Peter,	Es grüßt Sie Herzliche Grüße von Ihrem Viele Grüße an Euch beide

WRITING TO A FIRM OR AN INSTITUTION

Sehr geehrte Damen und Herren, Sehr geehrte Herren, Sehr geehrte Damen,	Mit freundlichen Grüßen Mit besten Empfehlungen (in business letters)
To someone in the same profession	
Sehr geehrter Herr Kollege, Lieber Kollege, Liebe Kollegin,	Mit freundlichen kollegiaten Grüßen

TO A PERSON IN AN IMPORTANT POSITION

Very formal	
Sehr geehrter Herr Bundesminister, Sehr geehrte Frau Präsidentin, Sehr verehrter, lieber Herr Professor,	Mit vorzüglicher Hochachtung

STARTING A LETTER

Thank you for your letter, which I have just received/which was passed to me by X *vielen Dank für Ihr Schreiben, das ich gerade erhalten habe/das von X an mich weitergeleitet wurde*

Please accept my apologies for the delay in replying to your letter *bitte entschuldigen Sie, daß ich erst jetzt auf Ihren Brief antworte*

With reference to your letter of 31 July *bezugnehmend auf Ihr Schreiben vom 21. Juli*

Further to our conversation of 4 December *ich nehme Bezug auf unser Gespräch vom 4. Dezember*

WITHIN THE LETTER

I was interested to hear that ... *ich habe mit Interesse erfahren, daß ...*

I regret to inform you that ... *es tut mir leid, Ihnen mitteilen zu müssen, daß*

I am happy to inform you that ... *ich freue mich, Ihnen mitteilen zu können, daß ...*

Please find enclosed ... *anbei (übersende ich Ihnen) ...*

I am sending separate cover ... *mit getrennter Post übersende ich Ihnen ...*

Could you please send us ... *könnten Sie uns bitte ... übersenden*

We would welcome your views on this matter *wir hätten gerne Ihre Ansicht in dieser Angelegenheit*

I hope you understand our point of view on this matter *ich hoffe, daß unsere Meinung in dieser Angelegenheit Ihr Verständnis findet*

I have received no reply to my letter of 3 August *auf mein Schreiben vom 3. August habe ich (noch) keine Antwort erhalten*

Please acknowledge receipt of this letter *bitte bestätigen Sie den Empfang dieses Schreibens*

ENDING A LETTER

I trust the foregoing is to your satisfaction *ich hoffe, Sie sind hiermit einverstanden*

I would be grateful if you could reply by return of post *ich wäre Ihnen dankbar, wenn Sie mir umgehend antworten würden*

If there is anything further I can do for you, please do not hesitate to contact me *wenn ich sonst noch etwas für Sie tun kann, setzen Sie sich bitte wieder mit mir in Verbindung*

Should you have any queries, I shall be pleased to discuss them with you *sollten Sie irgendwelche Fragen haben, werde ich sie Ihnen gerne beantworten*

I look forward to hearing from you *ich sehe Ihrer Antwort mit In-*

teresse entgegen

THANKS AND BEST WISHES
Thank you for taking the trouble to write to us *vielen Dank, daß Sie sich die Mühe gemacht haben, uns zu schreiben*
We greatly appreciate the time and trouble you took for us *wir danken Ihnen vielmals für Ihre Zeit und Mühe*
I have been asked to thank you on behalf of the Managing Director/Marketing Manager for the presentation you gave us *ich wurde gebeten, Ihnen im Namen des Geschäftsführers/ Marketing Managers für Ihre Präsentation zu danken*
We would ask you to accept our grateful thanks for all you have done for us *wir danken Ihnen vielmals für all Ihre Bemühungen*
Please give our most sincere thanks to your colleagues *bitte sprechen Sie Ihren Kollegen unseren herzlichsten Dank aus*

GETTING THE LETTER/FAX/TELEX SENT
to fax something to somebody *jemandem etwas faxen*
please type up this letter *könnten Sie bitte diesen Brief tippen?*
please send this today *bitte schicken Sie das heute noch ab*
this is urgent *das ist dringend*
send copies to ... *schicken Sie Kopien an ...*

AT THE POST OFFICE

In Austria, stamps and phonecards can be bought at the post office or at a *Tabak-Trafik*. In Vienna, there are 24-hour post offices at Westbahnhof, Südbahnhof, the central telegraph office of the Börseplatz, and the main post office, which is at Fleischmarkt 19, is also open 24 hours a day. The address of the poste restante service is Hauptpostlagernd, Fleischmarkt 19, 1010 Vienna.

International calls may be made from post offices in Germany, which also offer fax, telegram and banking services. The main post office in Bonn is the Hauptpostamt, Münsterplatz, 5300 BONN 1. There are around 15 large post offices in Berlin, one for each district.

Post office opening times in Luxembourg depend on the size of the office and on the services offered. The times given below are for the main post office only. Many post offices only open in the afternoon.

In Switzerland post offices also offer telephone and telegram facilities and the mail system itself is highly efficient. The main post office in Geneva is located in rue de Lausanne and is open from 06.30 to 23.00 every day.

SPIEL MIT KG

Spielwaren
Postfach 3178
D1000 BERLIN

The Magical Toybox
41 Apsley Street
Glasgow G11 7SN

Berlin, den 31.7 1991

Betr.: Produktvorführung Spieluhren
Bezug: Ihr Schreiben vom 26.7.91

Sehr geehrter Herr Aylwin,

vielen Dank für Ihr Schreiben vom 26.7.91, in dem Sie Ihr
Interesse an unserer neuen Serie von Spieluhren zum Ausdruck
bringen. Wir erlauben uns, Ihnen mit getrennter Post
unverbindlich einige Muster zur Ansicht zu senden.

Wir freuen uns über Ihre Interesse an unseren Produkten und
verbleiben

mit besten Empfehlungen

Inge Fuchs

SPIEL MIT KG
Inge Fuchs
Vertriebsleiterin

Anlage: Gesamtprospekt 1991

Dear Mr Aylwin,

Re: Product Demonstration of toy clocks
Ref: Yr letter of 26 July 1991

Thank you for your letter of 26 July enquiring about our new
range of toy clocks. We have pleasure in sending you some
samples, with no obligation to purchase on your part.

Thank you again for your interest in our products.

Yours sincerely,

Inge Fuchs

Inge Fuchs
Manager

Encl. 1991 catalogue

POST OFFICE OPENING HOURS

In Austria	*Mon-Fri*	*08.00–18.00*
In Germany	*Mon-Fri*	*08.00–17.00*
In Luxembourg	*Mon-Sun*	*06.00–20.00*
	Parcels	*08.00–12.00*
	and	*17.00–18.00*
In Switzerland	*Mon-Fri*	*07.30–12.00*
	and	*13.45–18.30*
	Sat	*09.30–11.00*

PHRASES USED BY THE CUSTOMER

Where's the nearest post office? *wo ist die nächste Post?*

Which window/counter sells stamps? *an welchem Schalter gibt es Briefmarken?*

Where is the poste restante? *wo ist der Schalter für postlagernde Sendungen?*

I'd like ten 1DM stamps please *ich hätte gerne zehn Briefmarken zu einer Mark*

I'd like some change for the phone/photocopier/stamp machine *ich hätte gerne Wechselgeld fürs Telefon/für den Kopierer/für den Briefmarkenautomat*

I'd like a money order for 100 DM *ich hätte gerne eine Zahlungsanweisung über hundert Mark*

Could I have a receipt? *kann ich eine Quittung haben?*

Can I send a fax from here? *kann ich von hier aus ein Fax schicken?*

Can I make photocopies here? *kann ich hier fotokopieren?*

How long will this letter/parcel take to arrive? *wie lange wird dieser Brief/dieses Päckchen brauchen?*

What's the quickest/cheapest way of sending this letter/parcel? *wie kann ich diesen Brief/dieses Päckchen auf die schnellste/billigste Art schicken?*

I'd like to send this letter/parcel ... *ich möchte diesen Brief/dieses Päckchen ... schicken*

by air *per Luftpost*

by registered post *per Einschreiben*

express delivery *per Expreß/per Eilboten*

special delivery *per Expreß/per Eilboten*

as printed matter *als Drucksache*

cheap rate *auf die billigste Art*

Which form should I fill out? *welches Formular muß ich ausfüllen?*

Could I have a registered post form/customs form/express delivery form? *kann ich bitte ein Einschreibeformular/Zollformular/Eilzustellungsformular haben?*

I don't know the post code. Where can I look it up? *ich weiß die Postleitzahl nicht. Wo könnte ich sie nachschlagen?*

PHRASES YOU ARE LIKELY TO HEAR
Da müssen Sie zum Schalter 4 gehen *I'm sorry, you'll have to go counter or window 4*
Wie wollen Sie das schicken? *how do you want to send this?*
Füllen Sie bitte dieses Formular aus *please fill out this form*
Können Sie sich ausweisen? *do you have any identification?*
Legen Sie das Päckchen bitte auf die Waage *put the parcel on the scales, please*
Dieses Päckchen ist nicht richtig verpackt *this parcel is not sealed/packed correctly*
Was ist im Päckchen? *what is in the parcel?*
Wie hoch ist der Wert? *what is the value of the contents?*

ADDITIONAL VOCABULARY

above-mentioned	*obengenannt*
acknowledge	*bestätigen*
address	*Adresse f*
airmail	*Luftpost f*
answer-back code	*Kennung f*
answering machine	*automatischer Anrufbeantworter m*
business address	*Geschäftsadresse f*
Business Reply Service	*Werbeantwort-Service m*
call *n*	*Anruf m*
call *vb*	*anrufen*
cardphone	*Kartentelefon nt*
car phone	*Autotelefon nt*
cellular telephone	*Funktelefon nt*
cheap rate	*Billigtarif m*
circular	*Wurfsendung f*
compliments slip	*Empfehlungszettel m*
conference call	*Konferenzschaltung f*
continuous tone	*Dauerton m*
cordless telephone	*schnurloses Telefon nt*
counter staff	*Schalterbeamter(-beamtin) m (f)*
courier service	*Kurierdienst m*
credit card call	*Anruf m mit Kreditkarte*
Datapost®	*Datapost®*
"date as postmark"	*Datum des Poststempels*
dialling tone	*Dauerton m*
dictate	*diktieren*

directory enquiries	*(Fernsprech)auskunft f*
draft *vb*	*aufsetzen*
draft *(letter) n*	*Entwurf m*
engaged tone	*Besetztzeichen nt*
envelope	*Umschlag m*
ex-directory number	*Geheimnummer f*
express delivery	*Eilzustellung f*
extension number	*Apparat m*
fax *n*	*Fax nt*
fax *vb*	*faxen*
fax machine	*Fax nt*
fax number	*Faxnummer f*
franking machine	*Frankiermaschine f*
Freefone®	*Freefone®*
Freepost®	*Freepost®, portofrei*
international reply coupon	*internationaler Rückantwortschein m*
letter	*Brief m*
local call	*Ortsgespräch nt*
long-distance call	*Ferngespräch nt*
memo	*Mitteilung f*
modem	*Modem nt*
operator	*Vermittlung f*
operator service	*Vermittlungsdienst m*
pager	*Funkrufempfänger m*
parcel	*Päckchen nt, Paket nt*
parcel post	*Paketpost f*
payphone	*Münzfernsprecher m*
peak rate	*Höchsttarif m*
personal call	*Privatgespräch nt*
phone box	*Telefonzelle f*
phone call	*Anruf m*
phonecard	*Telefonkarte f*
PO Box	*Postfach nt*
post *vb*	*aufgeben*
postage and packing	*Porto nt und Verpackung f*
postage rate	*Porto nt*
postal order	*Postanweisung f*
post box	*Postfach nt*
post code	*Postleitzahl f*
poste restante	*postlagernd*
postmark	*Poststempel m*
post office	*Postamt nt*
post paid	*portofrei*
prepaid envelope	*Freiumschlag m*

"private"	"vertraulich"
"private and confidential"	"streng vertraulich"
recorded delivery	eingeschriebene Sendung *f*
recorded message	Ansagetext *m*
re-dial *vb*	noch einmal wählen
registered post	Einschreiben *nt*
reply-paid postcard	Rückantwortkarte *f*
reverse-charge call	R-Gespräch *nt*
ringing tone	Rufzeichen *nt*
send	senden
special delivery	Eilzustellung *f*
stamp	(Brief)marke *f*
stamp machine	Briefmarkenautomat *m*
standard rate	Standardtarif *m*
surface mail	Post *f* auf dem Land-/Seeweg
switchboard	Vermittlung *f*
telephone *n*	Telefon *nt*
telephone box	Telefonzelle *f*
telephone directory	Telefonbuch *nt*
telex	Telex *nt*
telex directory	Telexverzeichnis *nt*
telex machine	Fernschreiber *m*
transfer charge call	R-Gespräch *nt*
trunk call	Ferngespräch *nt*
type *vb*	tippen
undermentioned	nachstehend
undersigned	unterzeichnet
videophone	Fernsehtelefon *nt*
window envelope	Fensterumschlag *m*
Yellow Pages®	Branchenverzeichnis *nt*, Gelbe Seiten *fpl*

acceptable quality level	*höchstzulässige Produktionsausschußquote f*
allow for	*einrechnen, einkalkulieren*
allowance *(discount)*	*Preisnachlaß m*
assembly line	*Fließband nt*
assembly plant	*Montagewerk nt*
automated	*automatisiert*
automation	*Automatisierung f*
backlog	*Rückstand m*
batch	*Charge f, Los nt*
batch production	*Serienproduktion f*
blueprint	*Entwurf m*
bottleneck	*Engpaß m*
bottling plant	*Abfüllanlage f*
breakdown *(of machine)*	*Ausfall m*
brewery	*Brauerei f*
built-in obsolescence	*geplantes Veralten nt*
by-product	*Nebenprodukt nt*
cannery	*Konservenfabrik f*
capital goods	*Kapitalgüter ntpl*
chemical plant	*Chemiefabrik f*
CIM (computer-integrated manufacture)	*CIM nt (rechnerintegrierte Fertigung f)*
component	*Bauteil nt*
computer-controlled	*computergesteuert*
control system	*Kontrollsystem nt*
custom-built	*kundenspezifisch*
cutting machine	*Schneidemaschine f*
defect	*Defekt m*
defective	*defekt*
depreciate *(machine)*	*sich abnutzen*
depreciation *(on machine)*	*Abnutzung f*
distillery	*Brennerei f*
division of labour	*Arbeitsteilung f*
downtime	*Ausfallzeit f*
drill *n*	*Bohrer m*
drill *vb*	*bohren*
economies of scale	*Größenvorteile mpl*

the plant is running 10% above/below capacity *das Werk arbeitet mit 10% über/unter Kapazität*
do you have sufficient capacity to handle an order of ...? *reicht Ihre Kapazität aus, um einen Auftrag von ... auszuführen?*
there is a manufacturing defect in this consignment *diese Warensendung weist einen Herstellungsfehler auf*

ergonomics	*Ergonomie f*
factory	*Fabrik f*
finished goods	*Fertigwaren fpl*
fitter	*Monteur(in) m(f)*
flaw	*Fehler m*
flawed	*fehlerhaft*
flow-line production	*Fließbandproduktion f*
foundry	*Gießerei f*
furnace	*Brennofen m*
hiccup	*Störung f*
idle capacity	*Leerlaufkapazität f*
idle time	*Leerlaufzeit f*
industrial goods	*Industrieprodukte ntpl*
job	*Stelle f*
job card	*Stechkarte f*
job number	*Auftragsnummer f*
joint venture	*Joint-venture nt*
just-in-time manufacturing	*Just-in-time Produktion f,*
	Produktion f auf Abruf
kite mark	*Standardnormstempel m*
latent defect	*verborgener Mangel m*
lathe	*Drehbank f*
lead time	*Lieferzeit f*
licensing agreement	*Lizenzabkommen nt*
off line	*off-line*
on line	*on-line*
machine	*Maschine f*
machine shop	*Maschinenhalle f*
machine tool	*Werkzeugmaschine f*
machinist	*Maschinist(in) m(f)*
maintenance shift	*Wartungsschicht f*
man-hour	*Arbeitsstunde f*
man-made	*künstlich*
manufacture *n*	*Herstellung f*
manufacture *vb*	*herstellen*
manufactured goods	*Fertigwaren fpl*
manufacturer	*Hersteller m*
manufacturing	*Herstellung f*
manufacturing cycle	*Herstellungszyklus m*

please advise me of the lead time for supply of ... *bitte teilen Sie mir die
Lieferzeit für ... mit*
to come on line *in Betrieb genommen werden*
to take something off line *etwas aus der Produktion nehmen*
they are clothes/car manufacturers *sie stellen Bekleidung/Autos her*

mass-produced items	*Massenartikel mpl*
mass production	*Massenproduktion f*
micrometer	*Mikrometer nt*
operating costs	*Betriebskosten pl*
operating profit	*Betriebsgewinn m*
order book	*Auftragsbuch nt*
output *n*	*Ausstoß m*
output *vb*	*produzieren*
overcapacity	*Überkapazität f*
overproduction	*Überproduktion f*
packaging *(wrapper)*	*Verpackung f*
packaging *(process)*	*Verpacken nt*
parameter	*Parameter m*
piece rate	*Leistungslohnsatz m*
plant *(factory)*	*Fabrik f*
plant *(machinery)*	*Maschinen fpl*
pottery *(factory)*	*Keramikfabrik f*
press *(machine)*	*Presse f*
primary products	*Grundstoffe mpl*
process *n*	*Prozeß m*
process *vb*	*verarbeiten*
processing plant	*Aufbereitungsanlage f*
product	*Produkt nt*
product design	*Produktdesign nt*
production	*Produktion f*
production control	*Produktionskontrolle f, Fertigungskontrolle f*
production line	*Fertigungsstraße f*
production planning	*Produktionsplanung f*
production problem	*Produktionsproblem nt*
productivity	*Produktivität f*
progress *(through factory)*	*fortschreiten*
pump	*Pumpe f*
quality assurance, quality control	*Qualitätssicherung f*
quality controller	*Qualitätsingenieur(in) m(f)*
raw materials	*Rohstoffe mpl*
recycled	*recycelt*

the factory is operational 24 hours a day *die Fabrik arbeitet 24 Stunden am Tag*

we would like to place an order for ... *wir möchten ... bestellen*

to increase/reduce output *die Produktion erhöhen/drosseln*

to output 30,000 units per day *30.000 Stück pro Tag produzieren*

the factory has an excellent record on delivery/quality/safety *die Fabrik hat einen sehr guten Ruf in Bezug auf Lieferzeit/Qualität/Sicherheit*

MANUFACTURING 166

refinery	*Raffinerie f*
robot	*Roboter m*
robotics	*Robotertechnik f*
running costs	*laufende Kosten pl*
safety standards	*Sicherheitsbestimmungen fpl*
semi-automated	*halbautomatisch*
service centre	*Service-Center nt*
shop floor	*Werkstatt f*
shrink-wrap	*einschweißen*
shrink-wrapped	*eingeschweißt*
shrink-wrapping *(material)*	*Schrumpfverpackung f*
shrink-wrapping *(process)*	*Einschweißen nt*
shut-down *n*	*vorübergehende Stillegung f*
shut down *vb*	*schließen*
specialization	*Spezialisierung f*
standardization	*Standardisierung f*
steelworks	*Stahlwerk nt*
stoppage	*Betriebsstörung f*
on stream	*in Betrieb*
subassembly	*Unterbaugruppe f*
substandard	*minderwertig*
throughput	*Durchsatz m*
time clock	*Stechuhr f*
tool	*Werkzeug nt*
turnaround time	*Umschlagzeit f*
undermanning	*Personalmangel m*
unit cost	*Kosten pl pro Einheit f*
unit price	*Preis m pro Einheit f*
vacuum-packed	*vakuumverpackt*
waste *n*	*Abfall m*
waste *vb*	*verschwenden, (übermäßig) verbrauchen*
wear and tear *(on machine)*	*Abnutzung f*
work in progress	*in Gang befindliche Arbeit f*
works	*Fabrik f*
workshop	*Werkstatt f*

the factory has high/low running costs *die Fabrik hat hohe/niedrige Betriebskosten*
a large-scale/small-scale manufacturer *ein Großbetrieb/Kleinbetrieb*
to come on stream *in Betrieb genommen werden*
is it possible to arrange a tour of the factory? *ist es möglich, eine Fabrikbesichtigung zu arrangieren?*
would you like to visit our factory? *möchten Sie unsere Fabrik besichtigen?*

See also **ADVERTISING AND MEDIA** *and* **BUYING AND SELLING**

advertise	*werben*
advertisement	*Anzeige f*
advertising campaign	*Werbekampagne f*
advertising manager	*Werbeleiter(in) m(f)*
advertising strategy	*Werbestrategie f*
after-sales service	*Kundendienst m*
appeal	*Aufforderung f*
artwork	*Design nt*
attitude survey	*Einstellungsuntersuchung f*
audience research	*Publikumsforschung f*
available market	*verfügbarer Markt m*
bad PR	*schlechte PR f*
bar chart	*Balkendiagramm nt*
blind test	*Blindtest m*
blurb	*Klappentext m*
brand	*Marke f*
brand acceptance	*Markenakzeptanz f*
brand awareness	*Markenbewußtsein nt*
brand image	*Markenimage nt*
brand loyalty	*Markentreue f*
brand manager	*Produktmanager(in) m(f)*
brief n	*Instruktionen fpl*
bring out	*auf den Markt m bringen*
brochure	*Werbeschrift f*
built-in obsolescence	*geplantes Veralten nt*
buyer's market	*Käufermarkt m*
buying behaviour	*Kaufverhalten nt*
canvass	*werben*
canvasser	*Kundenwerber(in) m(f)*
captive market	*regulierter Markt m*

who is the campaign aimed at? *auf wen ist die Kampagne abgezielt?*
is it possible to arrange a tour of the factory? *ist es möglich, eine Fabrikbesichtigung zu arrangieren?*
we would be happy to arrange a visit at your convenience *wir arrangieren gerne einen Besuch zu einem Ihnen angenehmen Zeitpunkt*
please arrange accommodation for our guests *bitte arrangieren Sie die Unterkunft für unsere Gäste*
to arrange for guests to be met/taken care of *das Abholen/die Betreuung von Gästen arrangieren*
to increase/reinforce brand awareness *Markenbewußtsein vergrößern/verstärken*
what is your brief? *was sind Ihre Anweisungen?*
our brief is to ... *unsere Anweisungen sind, zu ...*

catalogue	*Katalog m*
circular	*Wurfsendung f*
client	*Kunde m, Kundin f*
competition	*Wettbewerb m, Konkurrenz f*
competitive advantage/edge	*Wettbewerbsvorteil m*
concessionaire	*Konzessionär(in) m(f)*
consumer	*Verbraucher m*
consumer behaviour	*Verbraucherverhalten nt*
consumer credit	*Verbraucherkredit m*
consumer durables	*Gebrauchsgüter ntpl*
consumer goods	*Konsumgüter ntpl*
consumerism	*Konsumdenken nt*
consumer market	*Verbrauchermarkt m*
control group	*Kontrollgruppe f*
convenience goods	*Güter ntpl des täglichen Bedarfs m*
corporate entertaining	*Entertainment nt*
corporate identity	*Corporate Identity f*
corporate image	*Firmenimage nt*
corporate logo	*Firmenlogo nt*
corporate planning	*Unternehmensplanung f*
corporate strategy	*Unternehmensstrategie f*
customer	*Kunde m, Kundin f*
customer profile	*Kundenprofil nt*
cut-throat competition	*existenzgefährdende Konkurrenz f*
demand	*Nachfrage f*
demand forecasting	*Nachfragevorausschau f*
derived demand	*abgeleiteter Bedarf m*
desk research	*sekundärstatistische Auswertung f*
direct-mail advertising	*Postwurfwerbung f*
direct marketing	*Direktabsatz m*
direct selling	*Direktverkauf m*
distributor	*Verteiler m*
distributor policy	*Verteilerpolitik f*
diversification	*Diversifikation f*
diversify	*diversifizieren*

to capture 40% of the market *40% des Markts erobern*
to corner the market in ... *den Markt für ... beherrschen*
to project a strong corporate image *ein starkes Firmenimage projizieren*
to create a demand for a product *Nachfrage für ein Produkt schaffen*
the demand for ... has increased (dramatically) *die Nachfrage nach ... ist (enorm) gestiegen*

down-market	*für den Massenmarkt m*
end product	*Endprodukt nt*
end user	*Endverbraucher(in) m(f)*
exhibition centre	*Ausstellungszentrum nt*
falling market	*rückläufiger Markt m*
feasibility study	*Rentabilitätsstudie f*
feature	*Merkmal nt*
feedback	*Feedback nt*
field research	*Primärerhebung f*
follow-up	*Nachfassen nt*
freebie	*Werbegeschenk nt*
fringe market	*Marginalmarkt m*
gimmick	*Gag m*
good PR	*gute PR f*
growth market	*Nachfragemarkt m*
guesstimate	*grobe Schätzung f*
halo effect	*Ausstrahlungseffekt m*
house style	*Hausstil m*
hype *n*	*Ausloben nt*
hype *vb*	*ausloben*
image	*Image nt*
impact	*Stoßwirkung f*
impulse buying	*Impulskaufen nt*
impulse purchase	*Impulskauf m*
indirect demand	*indirekte Nachfrage f*
junk mail	*Postwurfsendungen fpl*
launch *n*	*Lancierung f*
launch *vb*	*lancieren*
liaise	*als Verbindungsperson f fungieren*
lifestyle	*Lebensstil m*
logo	*Logo nt*
loss leader	*Lockangebot nt*
mailing list	*Adressenliste f*
mail shot	*Briefwerbung f*
market *n*	*Markt m*
market *vb*	*vermarkten*
marketable	*marktgängig*

to go down-market *an weniger anspruchsvolle Kunden verkaufen*
to flood the market (with ...) *den Markt (mit ...) überschwemmen*
the market for ... is growing very fast *der Markt für ... wächst rapide*
who is coming to the launch? *wer kommt zur Lancierung?*
are you on our mailing list? *sind Sie auf unserer Adressenliste?*
please add our name to your mailing list *bitte setzen Sie uns auf Ihre Adressenliste*

market analysis	*Marktanalyse f*
market demand	*Marktbedarf m*
market development manager	*Manager(in) m(f) für Marktentwicklung f*
marketer	*Vermarkter m*
market forces	*Marktkräfte fpl*
marketing	*Marketing nt*
marketing campaign	*Marketing-Kampagne f*
marketing concept	*Marketing-Konzept nt*
marketing intelligence	*Marketing-Informationen fpl*
marketing manager	*Marketing-Manager(in) m(f)*
marketing mix	*Marketing-Mix nt*
marketing plan	*Marketing-Plan m*
marketing strategy	*Marketing-Strategie f*
market leader	*Marktführer m*
market penetration	*Marktdurchdringung f*
market potential	*Marktpotential nt*
market price	*Marktpreis m*
market profile	*Marktprofil nt*
market research	*Marktforschung f*
market rigging	*Marktmanipulation f*
market share	*Marktanteil m*
market test	*Markttest m*
market trends	*Marktentwicklung f*
market value	*Marktwert m*
mass-market	*für den Massenmarkt m*
media research	*Medienforschung f*
merchandising	*Merchandising nt*
mid-market	*mittelmäßig*
mock-up	*Modell nt*
new business manager	*Manager(in) m(f) für neue Kunden*
niche	*Marktlücke f*

is there a market for ...? *besteht eine Nachfrage nach ...?*
there is no market for this product *dieses Produkt findet keinen Absatz*
to be on the market *auf dem Markt sein*
the bottom has fallen out of the market *die Marktlage hat einen Tiefstand erreicht*
they have priced themselves out of the market *sie haben sich durch zu hohe Preise konkurrenzunfähig gemacht*
our products have found a ready market *unsere Produkte haben guten Absatz gefunden*
what is the marketing strategy for these products? *wie sieht die Marketing-Strategie für diese Produkte aus?*
to have a 30% market share *einen Marktanteil von 30% haben*

niche marketing	*Niche-Marketing nt*
open day, open house	*Tag m der offenen Tür*
own brand	*Hausmarke f*
packaging	*Verpackung f*
photo call	*Fototermin m*
photo opportunity	*Fotogelegenheit f*
pie chart	*Kreisdiagramm nt*
pilot scheme	*Pilotprojekt nt*
point of sale (POS)	*Verkaufsort m, Point of Sale m (P.O.S. m)*
point-of-sale advertising	*Werbung f am Verkaufsort*
point-of-sale material	*Werbematerial nt am Verkaufsort*
postal survey	*Umfrage f per Post*
PR	*PR f*
premium offer	*Zugabeangebot nt*
press call	*Pressetermin m*
press conference	*Pressekonferenz f*
press officer	*Pressesprecher(in) m(f)*
press release	*Presseverlautbarung f*
PR exercise	*PR Arbeit f*
price-cutting	*Preissenkung f*
price maintenance agreement	*Preisbindungsabkommen nt*
pricing policy	*Preisgestaltungspolitik f*
PR man/woman	*PR Mann m, PR Frau f*
product	*Produkt nt*
product manager	*Produktmanager(in) m(f)*
product range	*Produktpalette f*
promote	*werben für*
promotion	*Werbung f*
proprietary brand	*Hausmarke f*
prospectus	*Prospekt m, Werbeschrift f*
PR people	*PR Leute pl*
public n	*Öffentlichkeit f*
publicity	*Publicity f*
publicity event	*Publicity-Veranstaltung f*
publicize	*bekanntmachen*
public relations	*Public Relations fpl*

to perform well (against the competition) *(gegenüber der Konkurrenz) gut abschneiden*
to present the company's viewpoint *den Standpunkt der Firma vertreten*
you can contact our press officer on 3501306. He/she will be pleased to deal with your enquiry *Sie können unseren Pressesprecher/unsere Pressesprecherin unter der Nummer 3501306 erreichen. Er/sie wird Ihnen gerne Ihre Fragen beantworten*
it's good for public relations to … *es ist gut für die PR, wenn …*

public relations consultant	*Public Relations Berater(in) m(f)*
public relations event	*Public Relations Veranstaltung f*
public relations firm	*Public Relations Firma f*
public relations officer (PRO)	*Pressesprecher(in) m(f)*
reply-paid postcard	*Rückantwortkarte f*
retail outlet	*Einzelhandelsverkaufsstelle f*
retail price	*Einzelhandelspreis m*
sales campaign	*Verkaufskampagne f*
sales conference	*Versammlung f des Verkaufsstabs m*
sales drive	*Verkaufskampagne f, Verkaufsvorstoß m*
sales figures	*Absatzziffern fpl, Verkaufsziffern fpl*
seller's market	*Verkäufermarkt m*
shift in demand	*Nachfrageverlagerung f*
showcard	*Schaufensterplakat nt*
showroom	*Ausstellungsraum m*
spin-off	*Nebenprodukt nt*
spokesman/woman	*Sprecher(in) m(f)*
stand	*Stand m*
standard of living	*Lebensstandard m*
static market	*statischer Markt m*
target market	*Zielmarkt m*
target marketing	*Target-Marketing nt*
teaser	*Neugier weckende Werbung f*
telemarketing	*Telemarketing nt*
testimonial	*Empfehlung f*
trade fair	*Messe f*
unique selling point (USP)	*einmaliges Verkaufsargument nt (USP m)*
unofficial market	*inoffizieller Markt m*
unsolicited goods	*unverlangte Waren fpl*
up-market	*anspruchsvoll*
user-friendly	*benutzerfreundlich*
visitor	*Besucher(in) m(f)*
wrapper	*Verpackung f*

please send details of the results of the marketing campaign *bitte senden Sie Einzelheiten über die Ergebnisse der Marketing-Kampagne*
we are targeting young people *wir zielen auf junge Leute ab*
the market is unsettled *der Markt ist schwankend*
to go up-market *an anspruchsvollere Kunden verkaufen*
X and Y will be visiting the plant/our offices on 2 August *X und Y werden am 2. August die Fabrik/unsere Firma besuchen*

See also **CONFERENCES AND PUBLIC SPEAKING**

MEETINGS

When addressing someone, you should always use his or her full title and surname, e.g. *Herr Doktor Köberle, Frau Seeberger, Frau Professor Müller-Wirth*, unless it has been made very clear that you are on first name terms.

SETTING UP THE MEETING

Please suggest a convenient time and date for our meeting *bitte schlagen Sie einen günstigen Termin für unsere Besprechung vor*

I shall be free to meet you some time during the week commencing 20 March *ich habe in der Woche vom 20. März Zeit für eine Besprechung mit Ihnen*

I'm afraid I can't manage the date/time you suggest *tut mir leid, aber an diesem Tag/zu dieser Zeit geht es nicht*

I will be happy to meet you at your office at the time you suggest *ich komme gerne zu dem von Ihnen angegebenen Zeitpunkt zu Ihrem Büro*

I will be in Düsseldorf on 2 February, and would be free to meet you from 2pm to 5pm *ich bin am 2. Februar in Düsseldorf und könnte Sie zwischen 14 und 17 Uhr treffen*

Should you need to change the time/date of our meeting, please contact me/my secretary as soon as possible *sollten Sie den Termin für unsere Besprechung ändern müssen, dann setzen Sie sich bitte so bald wie möglich mit mir/meiner Sekretärin in Verbindung*

The date/time of the meeting has been brought forward/put back to ... *das Datum/die Zeit für die Besprechung wurde auf ... vorverlegt/wurde verschoben auf ...*

I'd like to bring forward/postpone/cancel the meeting if possible *wenn möglich, würde ich die Besprechung gern vorverlegen/verschieben/absagen*

INTRODUCTORY REMARKS

Pleased to meet you, Mr/Ms Foster *angenehm (the person's name is not used in German)*

It's good to see you again *schön, Sie wiederzusehen*

I'm very glad of this opportunity to speak to you in person *ich freue mich über die Gelegenheit, mit Ihnen persönlich sprechen zu können*

I'm afraid Mr Murdoch can't be with us today *Herr Murdoch kann heute leider nicht anwesend sein*

Allow me to introduce ... *darf ich Ihnen ... vorstellen*

CONDUCTING THE MEETING

First and foremost *zu allererst*

I'd just like to say *ich möchte nur bemerken*

May I point out that ...? *darf ich darauf aufmerksam machen, daß ...?*

The way I see it *so wie ich das sehe*

That's an interesting question/comment *das ist eine interessante Frage/ein interessanter Kommentar*

I think it might be better to discuss this issue later *ich glaube, es ist besser, wenn wir diesen Punkt später besprechen*

The next item on the agenda is ... *der nächste Punkt auf der Tagesordnung ist ...*

Please stress that in the minutes *bitte heben Sie das im Protokoll hervor*

Could you/may I expand on that? *könnten Sie/darf ich das weiter ausführen?*

The problem is that ... *das Problem ist, daß ...*

Does anyone have any suggestions? *hat irgend jemand einen Vorschlag?*

What do you think of ...? *was halten Sie von ...?*

Would anyone object to .../if ... *hätte irgend jemand etwas einzuwenden, wenn ...?*

When shall we reconvene? *wann sollen wir uns wieder versammeln?*

AGREEING

I totally agree *da bin ich voll und ganz einverstanden*

I'm glad we agree *ich bin froh, daß wir uns da einig sind*

We are all very enthusiastic about this *wir sind alle ganz begeistert davon*

We will give your idea our total backing *wir werden Ihre Idee voll unterstützen*

We will make sure this gets top priority *wir werden dafür sorgen, daß dieser Punkt vorrangig behandelt wird*

I agree to a certain extent, but I think ... *im großen und ganzen stimme ich mit Ihnen überein, aber ich glaube ...*

I think we are in broad agreement on the fundamental issues *in den wichtigsten Fragen stimmen wir im großen und ganzen überein*

I take your point *ich akzeptiere, was Sie sagen*

DISAGREEING

We must agree to differ on this one, I'm afraid *ich fürchte, hier*

werden wir uns nicht einig werden
There is only one point I can't agree with *es gibt nur einen Punkt, dem ich nicht zustimmen kann*
It's not really feasible to do that at this stage *zum gegenwärtigen Zeitpunkt ist das eigentlich nicht durchführbar*
Are you sure that is correct? *sind Sie sicher, daß das richtig ist?*
In that case, I'm afraid we have to decline your offer *in diesem Fall müssen wir Ihr Angebot leider ablehnen*

NEGOTIATIONS

NEGOTIATING CONDITIONS
The following is a list of typical conditions you may wish to discuss during negotiations, along with related phrases.

cancellation clause (*Rücktrittsklausel f*)
There will be a 50% charge on orders cancelled less than 6 weeks before due delivery *für Bestellungen, die bis zu 6 Wochen vor der fälligen Lieferung storniert werden, erheben wir eine Stornierungsgebühr von 50%*

commission (*Provision f*)
3% commission on sales up to 2,000 DM and 5% on sales thereafter *3% Provision bei einem Umsatz bis zu 2.000 DM and 5% bei höheren Umsätzen*
2% commission on sales up to 1,500 DM and 5% on total sales when sales exceed this figure *2% Provision bei einem Umsatz bis zu 1.500 DM und 5% vom Gesamtumsatz, wenn der Umsatz diesen Betrag überschreitet*

credit period (*Laufzeit f eines Kredits*)
90 days after receipt of invoice *90 Tage nach Erhalt der Rechnung*
60 days after invoice for standard orders, 6 months after invoice for goods on consignment *bei Standardbestellungen 60 Tage nach Rechnungsausstellung, bei Waren auf Kommission 6 Monate nach Rechnungsausstellung*

delivery (*Lieferung f*)
We require delivery by 2 February *die Lieferung muß spätestens bis zum 2. Februar bei uns eingehen*
Delivery will be 2 weeks from receipt of order *Lieferzeit ist 2 Wochen nach Erhalt der Bestellung*

discount (*Rabatt m*)
early settlement discount *Rabatt bei prompter Zahlung*
2% discount for payment within 14 days *2% Skonto bei Zahlung innerhalb von 14 Tagen*

exclusivity (*Alleinverkaufsrecht nt*)
We must have exclusivity over the Hamburg region *wir benötigen das Alleinverkaufsrecht für die Hamburger Gegend*
You would have absolute exclusivity over the West Coast *Sie hätten den Alleinvertrieb für die Westküste*
The exclusive agency agreement will be reviewed annually *der Alleinvertretungsvertrag wird jährlich neu überprüft*

minimum order (*Mindestbestellung f*)
A minimum order of 5,000 units *eine Mindestbestellung von 5.000 Stück*

payment method (*Zahlungsweise f*)
confirmed irrevocable letter of credit *bestätigtes unwiderrufliches Akkreditiv nt*
bill of exchange *Wechsel m*

penalty clause (*Strafklausel f*)
The penalty clause is 4% for each month of delay *die Strafklausel besagt 4% je Monat Verzug*

quantity discount (*Mengenrabatt m*)
We can offer 3% on orders over 10,000 DM/on orders of more than 600 units *bei Bestellungen über 10.000 DM/von mehr als 600 Stück geben wir 3% Skonto*

royalty on sales (*Ertragsanteil m*)
3% of turnover on sales under licence *3% des Umsatzes bei Lizenzverkäufen*

sales targets (*Verkaufsziele ntpl*)
Sales targets will be reviewed on a monthly basis *die Verkaufsziele werden jeden Monat neu überprüft*

staff training (*Personalausbildung f*)
We would insist on/require an intensive staff training course for sales personnel/engineers *wir bestehen auf einem/verlangen einen intensiven Ausbildungskurs für Verkaufspersonal/Techniker*
Staff training would be ongoing for the first year of the contract

Personalausbildung findet im ganzen ersten Jahr der Anstellung statt

unit price (*Stückpreis m*)
We propose a unit price of 500 DM *wir schlagen einen Stückpreis von 500 DM vor*
On orders up to 1,000 the unit price is 100 DM *bei Bestellungen bis zu 1.000 Stück ist der Stückpreis 100 DM*

warranty (*Garantie f*)
Our products will carry an 18 month warranty from date of sale/ installation *auf unsere Produkte ist 18 Monate Garantie ab Verkaufsdatum/Installation*
Warranty will be 12 months parts and labour followed by 6 months parts only *12 Monate Garantie auf Ersatzteile und Installation und danach 6 Monate nur auf Ersatzteile*

PRESENTING YOUR POSITION

INTRODUCTORY
We have a lot to discuss *wir haben viel zu besprechen*
I'm sure our discussions will be mutually beneficial *ich bin sicher, daß beide Seiten von unserer Besprechung profitieren werden*
I think there's some room for negotiation *ich glaube, wir haben eine Verhandlungsbasis*
I'm confident we'll reach agreement *ich bin zuversichtlich, daß wir zu einer Übereinkunft kommen*
I look forward to hearing your proposals *ich sehe Ihren Vorschlägen mit Interesse entgegen*
I think you'll be interested/pleasantly surprised by our proposals *ich glaube, unsere Vorschläge werden Sie interessieren/ angenehm überraschen*

OPENING THE DISCUSSION
Shall we begin? *wollen wir anfangen?*
Perhaps I could start by ... *vielleicht fange ich am besten damit an, ... zu ...*
This is how we see it *das ist unsere Ansicht*
Our position on warranty/exclusivity is as follows *unsere Auffassung bezüglich Garantiezeit/Alleinvertretung ist wie folgt*
We believe it's reasonable/appropriate to ... *wir erachten es als vernünftig/angemessen, ... zu ...*
If I could just outline our proposals *wenn ich kurz unsere Vorschläge skizzieren darf*
What we propose is ... *wir schlagen vor, daß ...*

CLOSING THE DISCUSSION

Does anyone have any further questions? *gibt es noch Fragen?*

Let's take a break for some refreshments/lunch *lassen Sie uns eine Pause für Erfrischungen/eine Mittagspause machen.*

If no one wishes to add anything further, perhaps we can bring the meeting to a close *wenn niemand mehr etwas hinzufügen möchte, können wir jetzt vielleicht Schluß machen*

It has been a very fruitful discussion *die Diskussion war sehr lohnend*

I hope we have clarified our position *ich hoffe, wir haben unsere Position klar gemacht*

May I suggest we continue discussions at a later date? *darf ich vorschlagen, daß wir die Besprechung zu einem späteren Zeitpunkt fortsetzen?*

Thank you (all) for coming *vielen Dank, daß Sie (alle) gekommen sind*

When will we hear from you? *wann werden wir von Ihnen hören?*

We will be in touch very soon *wir werden uns bald mit Ihren in Verbindung setzen*

ADDITIONAL VOCABULARY

adjourn	*vertagen*
adjournment	*Vertagung f*
agenda	*Tagesordnung f*
AGM (annual general meeting)	*JHV f (Jahreshauptversammlung f)*
AOCB (any other competent business)	*Sonstiges*
attend	*besuchen, teilnehmen*
audio conferencing	*Audio-Konferenzschaltung f*
board meeting	*Vorstandssitzung f*
board (of directors)	*Vorstand m*
brainstorming (session)	*Brainstorming nt*
breakfast meeting	*Arbeitsfrühstück nt*
briefing	*Einsatzbesprechung f*
business dinner	*Arbeitsessen nt*
business lunch	*Arbeitsessen nt*
cancel	*absagen*
casting vote	*ausschlaggebende Stimme f*
chairman	*Vorsitzende(r) m*
chairwoman	*Vorsitzende f*
composite motion	*Sammelantrag m*
concession	*Konzession f*
consensus	*Übereinstimmung f*

decide	*(sich) entscheiden*
decision	*Beschluß m*
deal	*Geschäft nt*
delegate *n*	*Delegierte(r) f(m)*
delegate *vb*	*delegieren*
delegation	*Delegation f*
dialogue	*Dialog m*
discussion	*Besprechung f*
EGM (extraordinary general meeting)	*a.o. HV f (außerordentliche Hauptversammlung f)*
feedback	*Feedback nt*
flip-chart	*Flip-Chart f*
interpreter	*Dolmetscher(in) m(f)*
lunch meeting	*Arbeitsessen nt*
meeting	*Besprechung f*
minute book	*Protokollbuch nt*
minutes	*Protokoll nt*
mover	*Antragsteller(in) m/f*
negotiate	*verhandeln über (+acc)*
negotiation	*Verhandlung f*
overhead projector	*Overheadprojektor m*
point of order	*Geschäftsordnungspunkt m*
report *n*	*Bericht m*
statutory meeting	*Gründungsversammlung f*
subject to confirmation	*vorläufig*
video conferencing	*Video-Konferenzschaltung f*
working breakfast	*Arbeitsfrühstück nt*
working dinner	*Arbeitsessen nt*
working lunch	*Arbeitsessen nt*

acknowledge	*bestätigen*
acknowledgement (slip)	*Empfangsbestätigung f*
addressing machine	*Adressiermaschine f*
agenda	*Tagesordnung f*
answering machine	*(automatischer) Anrufbeantworter m*
archive *n*	*Archiv nt*
archive *vb*	*archivieren*
audio-typing	*Schreiben nt nach Diktiergerät nt*
audio-typist	*Phonotypistin f*
automatic document feeder	*automatischer Papiervorschub m*
azerty keyboard	*Azerty-Tastatur f*
box file	*Flachordner m*
business card	*Visitenkarte f, Karte f*
calculator	*Rechner m*
carbon copy	*Durchschlag m*
card index	*Kartei f*
circular	*Rundschreiben nt*
clerical staff	*Schreibkräfte fpl*
collate	*kollationieren*
compliments slip	*Empfehlungszettel m*
computer	*Computer m*
console	*Konsole f*
continuous stationery	*Endlospapier nt*
copy holder	*Dokumentenständer m*
copy paper	*Kopierpapier nt*
copy typist	*Schreibkraft f*
correcting fluid	*Korrekturflüssigkeit f*
correction ribbon/tape	*Korrekturband nt*
daisy wheel printer	*Typenraddrucker m*
data processing (DP)	*Datenverarbeitung f (DV f)*
dead file	*abgelegte Akte f*
desk	*Schreibtisch m*
desk diary	*Tischkalender m*
desk light	*Schreibtischlampe f*
desk pad	*Schreibunterlage f*
desktop computer	*Desktop-Computer m*
desktop copier	*Desktop-Kopierer m*
dictaphone ®	*Diktaphon ® nt*
dictate	*diktieren*
dictation	*Diktat nt*

I need access to a fax machine/computer *ich brauche Zugang zu einem Fax/Computer*
to take dictation *ein Diktat aufnehmen*

dictionary	*Wörterbuch nt*
disk box	*Diskettenkasten m*
diskette	*Diskette f*
duplicate *n*	*Duplikat nt*
duplicate *vb*	*ein Duplikat machen*
electric typewriter	*elektrische Schreibmaschine f*
electronic mail	*elektronische Post f*
enlarge	*vergrößern*
enlargement	*Vergrößerung f*
eraser	*Radiergummi m*
ergonomics	*Ergonomie f*
extension	*Nebenanschluß m*
extension number	*Apparat m*
fax *n*	*Fax nt*
fax *vb*	*faxen*
fax machine	*Fax nt*
file *n*	*Aktenhefter m*
file *vb*	*ablegen*
file copy	*Ablage f*
filing	*Aktenablage f*
filing cabinet	*Aktenschrank m*
filing system	*Ablagesystem nt*
floppy disk	*Floppy-Disk f*
folder	*Aktendeckel m*
franking machine	*Frankiermaschine f*
guillotine	*Papierschneidemaschine f*
intercom	*(Gegen)sprechanlage f*
internal memo	*hausinterne Mitteilung f*
in-tray	*Ablage f für Eingänge mpl*
keyboard	*Tastatur f*
laser printer	*Laserdrucker m*
letterhead *(writing paper)*	*Geschäfts(brief)papier nt*
lever arch file	*Leitz-Ordner ® m*
memorandum	*Mitteilung f*
memory typewriter	*Speicherschreibmaschine f*
microfiche	*Mikrofiche m or nt*
microfiche reader	*Microfiche-Leser m*
microfilm	*Mikrofilm m*
microfilm reader	*Mikrofilm-Leser m*
mouse	*Maus f*
office	*Büro nt*
office building	*Bürogebäude nt*
office equipment	*Bürogeräte ntpl*
office hours	*Dienstzeit f*
office manager	*Büroleiter(in) m(f)*

office staff	*Büroangestellten m/fpl*
office supplies	*Büroartikel mpl*
office worker	*Büroangestellte(r) f(m)*
open-plan office	*Großraumbüro nt*
out-tray	*Ablage f für Ausgänge mpl*
overhead projector	*Overheadprojektor m*
paper	*Papier nt*
paper clip	*Büroklammer f*
paper punch	*Locher m*
paperwork	*Schreibarbeit f*
pending tray	*Ablage f für unerledigte Arbeit*
petty cash	*Portokasse f*
photocopier	*Fotokopiergerät nt*
photocopy *n*	*Fotokopie f*
photocopy *vb*	*fotokopieren*
portable (computer)	*Portable nt*
printer	*Drucker m*
print-out	*Ausdruck m*
qwerty keyboard	*Qwerty-Tastatur f*
reception area	*Empfangsbereich m*
ribbon	*Farbband nt*
ring binder	*Ringbuch nt*
screen	*Bildschirm m*
secretary	*Sekretär(in) m(f)*
shredder	*Reißwolf m*
single-line display	*einzeilige Darstellung f*
single-sheet feed	*Einzelblattzuführung f*
stapler	*Hefter m*
stationery *(general)*	*Schreibwaren fpl*
stationery *(letter paper)*	*Briefpapier nt*

is ... in the office today? *ist ... heute im Büro?*

I will be in the office all day/from 9am/until 2pm *ich werde den ganzen Tag/ab 9 Uhr morgens/bis 2 Uhr nachmittags im Büro sein*

is there a photocopier/fax machine in the office? *ist hier im Büro ein Kopierer/ein Fax?*

could you provide me with an office from 1 to 22 April? *können Sie mir vom 1. bis 22. April ein Büro zur Verfügung stellen?*

what are your office hours? *wie sind Ihre Geschäftszeiten?*

our normal office hours are from 9 to 5 *unser Büro ist normalerweise von 9 bis 5 geöffnet*

I'd like three photocopies of this, please *kann ich hiervon bitte drei Kopien haben?*

I will need secretarial help *ich brauche eine Schreibkraft*

you will be sharing an office with ... *Sie werden Ihr Büro mit ... teilen*

who speaks English in the office? *wer spricht Englisch im Büro?*

stationery cupboard	*Regal nt mit Schreib- und Korrespondenzunterlagen fpl*
street map	*Stadtplan m*
suspension file	*Hängemappe f*
telephone *n*	*Telefon nt*
telephone *vb*	*anrufen*
telephone directory	*Telefonbuch nt*
telex *n*	*Telex nt*
telex *vb*	*telexen*
telex *vb (somebody)*	*ein Telex schicken (+dat)*
telex (machine)	*Fernschreiber m, Telex nt*
time clock	*Stechuhr f*
toner	*Toner m*
type	*tippen*
typewriter	*Schreibmaschine f*
VDU (visual display unit)	*Bildschirmgerät nt*
visitor's book	*Gästebuch nt*
window envelope	*Fensterumschlag m*
word processor	*Textverarbeitungsanlage f*
words per minute (wpm)	*Wörter ntpl pro Minute f (WpM)*
work station	*Arbeitsplatz m*

to type up notes *Notizen mit der Maschine ins Reine schreiben*

See also **JOB APPLICATIONS** *and* **COMPANY STRUCTURES**

absenteeism	*Nichterscheinen nt am Arbeitsplatz m*
across-the-board wage increase	*allgemeine Lohnerhöhung f*
agreed procedure	*vereinbarte Verfahrensordnung f*
agreement	*Vereinbarung f*
appeal (against) *n*	*Einspruch m (gegen +acc)*
appeal (against) *vb*	*Einspruch m erheben (gegen +acc)*
appraisal interview	*Beurteilungsgespräch nt*
appraisal method	*Beurteilungsmethode f*
apprentice	*Auszubildende(r) f(m) (Azubi m/f)*
apprenticeship	*Lehre f*
aptitude test	*Eignungsprüfung f*
arbitration	*Schiedsverfahren nt*
arbitrator	*Schiedsrichter(in) m(f)*
assess	*einschätzen*
assessment	*Einschätzung f*
back pay	*Nachzahlung f*
back shift	*Spätschicht f*
basic wage	*Grundlohn m*
benefit-in-kind	*Sachleistung f*
block release	*bezahlte Freistellung f für längere Zeit*
blue-collar worker	*Arbeiter(in) m(f)*
bonus	*Bonus m, Zulage f*
career development	*Laufbahnentwicklung f*
casual worker	*Gelegenheitsarbeiter(in) m(f)*
clock in/on	*stempeln, stechen*
clock out/off	*stempeln, stechen*
closed shop	*Closed Shop m*
code of practice	*Verfahrensregeln fpl*
collective agreement	*Betriebsvereinbarung f*
collective bargaining	*Tarifverhandlungen fpl*
complainant	*Beschwerdeführer(in) m(f)*
conciliation	*Schlichtung f*
conditions of employment	*Anstellungsbedingungen fpl*
constructive dismissal	*fingierte Entlassung f*
consultation	*Konsultation f, Beratung f*
contract of employment	*Arbeitsvertrag m*
contributory pension scheme	*beitragspflichtige Rentenversicherung f*

an across-the-board wage increase *eine allgemeine Gehaltserhöhung*
to pay/receive a bonus payment *eine Prämie zahlen/erhalten*

day release	*bezahlte Freistellung f für einen Tag*
day shift	*Tagschicht f*
delegate	*delegieren*
delegation	*Delegation f*
demarcation	*Abgrenzung f*
demote	*zurückstufen*
demotion	*Zurückstufung f*
derecognition	*Aberkennung f*
direct labour	*Arbeiter(in) m(f) in der Produktion*
discrimination	*Diskriminierung f*
dismiss	*entlassen*
dismissal	*Entlassung f*
dispute	*Kontroverse f*
double time	*doppelter Tarif m (für Nacht- oder Feiertagarbeit)*
downgrade *(post)*	*zurückstufen*
early retirement	*vorzeitige Pensionierung f*
education	*Ausbildung f*
employ	*anstellen*
employee	*Angestellte(r) f(m)*
employee benefits	*Sachbezüge pl für Angestellten m/fpl*
employer	*Arbeitgeber(in) m(f)*
employers' association	*Arbeitgeberverband m*
employer's contribution	*Arbeitgeberanteil m*
employer's liability	*Arbeitgeberhaftpflicht f*
employment agency	*Arbeitsvermittlung f*
employment law	*Arbeitsrecht nt*
equality	*Gleichheit f*
equal opportunities employer	*Arbeitgeber(in) m(f), der Chancengleichheit praktiziert*
equal pay	*gleicher Lohn m*
evaluation	*Leistungsbewertung f*
expense account	*Spesenkonto nt*
expenses	*Spesen pl*
fixed term contract	*Vertrag m mit bestimmter Dauer*
flat rate	*Pauschalsatz m*
flexitime	*Gleitzeit f*
foreman/woman	*Vorarbeiter(in) m(f)*

does German/Swiss employment law cover this? *ist das nach deutschem/schweizerischem Arbeitsrecht erlaubt?*
we are expanding our staff *wir stellen mehr Personal ein*

freelance *adj*	*freiberuflich*
freelance *vb*	*freiberuflich arbeiten*
fringe benefit	*Lohnnebenleistungen fpl*
general strike	*Generalstreik m*
golden handcuffs	*Bindung f einer Führungskraft an eine Gesellschaft durch Vergünstigungen*
golden handshake	*hohe Abfindung f bei Entlassung f*
golden hello	*Einstellungsprämie f*
golden parachute	*großzügiges Abfindungsversprechen nt für den Fall einer Übernahme*
graduate	*Akademiker(in) m(f)*
grievance	*Beschwerde f*
grievance procedure	*Beschwerdeverfahren nt*
guaranteed wage	*garantierter Mindestlohn m*
headhunter	*Kopfjäger(in) m(f)*
health and safety	*Gesundheit f und Sicherheit f*
health insurance	*Krankenversicherung f*
homeworker	*Heimarbeiter(in) m(f)*
house style	*Hausstil m*
human relations	*Human Relations pl, innerbetriebliche Mitarbeiterbeziehungen fpl*
human resources	*Arbeitskräfte fpl*
human resources development (HRD)	*Ausbildung f der Arbeitskräfte*
incentive	*Anreiz m*
incentive scheme	*Anreizsystem nt*
increment	*Zulage f*
individual bargaining	*Einzeltarifverhandlungen fpl*
induction	*Induktion f*
induction course	*Einführungskurs m*
industrial accident	*Arbeitsunfall m*
industrial action	*Arbeitskampfmaßnahmen fpl*
industrial dispute	*Arbeitsstreitigkeit f*
industrial relations	*Arbeitgeber-/ Arbeitnehmerbeziehungen fpl*
industrial tribunal	*Arbeitsgericht nt*
industry-wide agreement	*industrieweite Abmachung f*
in-house training	*betriebsinterne Ausbildung f*
job description	*Arbeitsplatzbeschreibung f*
job losses	*Arbeitsplatzverluste mpl*
job satisfaction	*berufliche Zufriedenheit f*

job security	Sicherheit f des Arbeitsplatzes m
job specification	Arbeitsplatzbeschreibung f
/job title	Berufsbezeichnung f
labour market	Arbeitsmarkt m
last in, first out (LIFO)	zuletzt geheuert, zuerst gefeuert
lay-off n	Entlassung f wegen Arbeitsmangel m
lay off vb	entlassen
length of service	Dienstjahre ntpl
lock-out	Aussperrung f
luncheon voucher	Essensmarke f
management consultant	Unternehmensberater(in) m(f)
man management	Personalführung f
manpower forecast	Arbeitskräfteprognose f
maternity benefit	Mutterschaftsgeld nt
maternity leave	Mutterschaftsurlaub m
merit pay	Leistungszulage f
minimum wage	Mindestlohn m
mobility of labour	Mobilität f der Arbeitskräfte fpl
moonlighting	Schwarzarbeit f
national insurance	Sozialversicherung f
natural wastage	natürliche Personalreduzierung f
negotiate	verhandeln
negotiation	Verhandlung f
net pay	Nettolohn m
night shift	Nachtschicht f
non-contributory pension scheme	beitragsfreie Rentenversicherung f
occupational accident	Arbeitsunfall m
occupational hazard	Berufsrisiko nt
official strike	gewerkschaftlich organisierter Streik m
off-the-job training	außerbetriebliche Ausbildung f
on-the-job training	innerbetriebliche Ausbildung f
organizational culture	Unternehmensstil m
overstaffed	überbesetzt
overtime	Überstunden fpl
overtime ban	Überstundenverbot nt
paid holidays	bezahlter Urlaub m
part-timer	Teilzeitbeschäftigte(r) f(m)
paternity leave	Vaterschaftsurlaub m

to lay staff off (temporarily) *Personal (vorübergehend) entlassen*
to achieve cuts by natural wastage *Kosteneinsparungen durch natürliche Personalreduzierung erreichen*

payment-by-results system	*Leistungslohnsystem nt*
payroll	*Lohnliste f*
pay slip	*Lohnstreifen m*
pension scheme	*Rentenversicherung f*
performance-related pay	*leistungsbezogener Lohn m*
performance review	*Leistungsbesprechung f*
personnel department	*Personalabteilung f*
personnel management	*Personalführung f*
personnel manager	*Personalchef(in) m(f)*
picket	*Streikposten m*
placement *(as trainee)*	*Praktikum nt*
placement *(finding job)*	*Vermittlung f*
plant bargaining	*Betriebsvereinbarungen fpl*
probationary period	*Probezeit f*
proficiency test	*Leistungstest m*
profit-sharing	*Gewinnbeteiligung f*
profit-sharing scheme	*Gewinnbeteiligungsplan m*
promote	*befördern*
promotion	*Beförderung f*
pro rata *adj, adv*	*anteilmäßig*
rationalize	*rationalisieren*
recruit	*einstellen*
recruitment	*Einstellung f*
recruitment drive	*Anwerbungskampagne f*
redeployment	*Umsetzung f (der Arbeitskräfte fpl)*
redundancy	*Entlassung f*
redundancy agreement	*Entlassungsvereinbarung f*
redundancy payment	*Entlassungsabfindung f*
redundant	*arbeitslos*
reinstate	*wiedereinstellen*
reinstatement	*Wiedereinstellung f*
relocation	*Umzug m*
retire	*in den Ruhestand m treten*
retirement	*Ruhestand m*
salary	*Gehalt nt*
salary increase	*Gehaltserhöhung f*

we have 2,000 employees on our payroll *wir haben 2.000 Beschäftigte*
to picket a factory *Streikposten vor eine Fabrik aufstellen*
to recruit from abroad *Personal aus dem Ausland anwerben*
we are recruiting 50 new employees this month *diesen Monat stellen wir 50 neue Arbeitskräfte ein*
the company has had to make 30 staff redundant *die Firma mußte 30 Angestellte entlassen*
to get the sack *entlassen werden*

salary review	*Gehaltsüberprüfung f*
salary scale	*Besoldungsordnung f*
security of tenure	*Kündigungsschutz m*
self-employed	*selbständig*
semi-skilled worker	*angelernte Arbeitskraft f*
shiftwork	*Schichtarbeit f*
shiftworker	*Schichtarbeiter(in) m(f)*
shop steward	*gewerkschaftliche Vertrauensperson f*
short-staffed	*unterbesetzt*
short time	*Kurzarbeit f*
shut-down	*vorübergehende Stillegung f*
sick pay	*Krankengeld nt*
single status	*gleichberechtigt*
sit-in	*Sit-in nt*
skilled worker	*Facharbeiter(in) m(f)*
staff *n*	*Personal nt*
staff *vb*	*mit Personal besetzen*
statutory deductions	*gesetzliche Abzüge mpl*
strike *n*	*Streik m*
strike *vb*	*streiken*
striker	*Streikende(r) f(m)*
take-home pay	*Nettolohn m*
teamworking	*Arbeiten nt im Team nt*
termination date	*Inkrafttreten nt der Kündigung f*
termination of employment	*Kündigung f eines Arbeitsvertrages m*
threshold agreement	*Lohnschwellenvereinbarung f*
time-and-a-half	*Arbeitszeit f zu anderthalbfachem Tarif*
time card	*Stechkarte f*
time clock	*Stechuhr f*
time-sheet	*Stechkarte f*
trade dispute	*Arbeitsstreitigkeit f*
trade union	*Gewerkschaft f*
trade union agreement	*Gewerkschaftsabkommen nt*
trade union recognition	*Anerkennung f der Gewerkschaft*
training	*Ausbildung f*
training course	*Ausbildungskurs m*
training officer	*Ausbildungsleiter(in) m(f)*
understaffed	*unterbesetzt*
unfair dismissal	*unfaire Entlassung f*

to go on strike *in (den) Streik treten*
to be on strike *streiken*

union dues	*Gewerkschaftsbeitrag m*
unskilled worker	*ungelernter Arbeiter m,*
	ungelernte Arbeiterin f
vacancy	*freie Stelle f*
vocational guidance	*Berufsberatung f*
vocational training	*Berufsausbildung f*
voluntary deductions	*freiwillige Abgaben fpl*
voluntary redundancy	*freiwillige Aufgabe f des*
	Arbeitsplatzes m
wage differential	*Lohngefälle nt*
wage freeze	*Lohnstopp m*
wage negotiations	*Tarifverhandlungen fpl*
wages	*Lohn m*
wages policy	*Lohnpolitik f*
white-collar worker	*Angestellte(r) f(m)*
wildcat strike	*wilder Streik m*
workforce	*Arbeitskräfte fpl*
work-in	*Fabrikbesetzung f*
working conditions	*Arbeitsbedingungen fpl*
working week	*Arbeitswoche f*
workload	*Arbeitspensum nt*
work measurement	*Arbeitszeitstudie f*
work permit	*Arbeitserlaubnis f*
work placement	*Praktikum nt*
work-to-rule *n*	*Bummelstreik m*
work to rule *vb*	*nach Vorschrift f arbeiten*
wrongful dismissal	*ungerechtfertigte Entlassung f*

action	*Aktion f*
activity chart	*Arbeitsgliederungsplan m*
agenda	*Tagesordnung f*
allow for	*einrechnen, einkalkulieren*
brief *n*	*Instruktionen fpl*
brief *vb*	*instruieren*
budget *n*	*Budget nt*
budget *vb (prepare a budget)*	*den Haushaltsplan m aufstellen*
contingency	*Eventualität f*
contingency plan	*Ausweichplan m*
contingency planning	*Planung f für Eventualfälle*
corporate planning	*Unternehmensplanung f*
cost *n*	*Kosten pl*
cost *vb (have a price)*	*kosten*
cost *vb (calculate cost of)*	*Kosten pl berechnen*
costing	*Kalkulation f*
crisis management	*Krisenmanagement nt*
critical path analysis	*kritische Pfadanalyse f*
deadline	*Frist f, Fristablauf m*
decision	*Entscheidung f*
decision-making	*Entscheidungfindung f*
delegate	*delegieren*
department manager	*Abteilungsleiter(in) m(f)*
diversification	*Diversifikation f*
early warning system	*Frühwarnsystem nt*
efficiency	*Leistungsfähigkeit f*
ergonomics	*Ergonomie f*
extrapolation	*Extrapolation f*
financial management	*Finanzmanagement nt*
flowchart	*Flußdiagramm nt*
forecast *n*	*Voraussage f*
forecast *vb*	*voraussagen*
histogram	*Säulendiagramm nt*
inefficiency	*Inkompetenz f*
inventory control	*Bestandskontrolle f*
junior management	*unteres Management nt*

to allot time for something *Zeit für etwas vorsehen*
to keep to budget *das Budget einhalten*
to go over budget *das Budget überschreiten*
we are budgeting for sales/losses of ... *wir veranschlagen einen Umsatz/ Verluste von ...*
to chase someone up on something *jemandem wegen etwas (gen) hinterher sein*
to meet/miss a deadline *eine Frist einhalten/überschreiten*
to set an unrealistic deadline *eine unrealistische Frist ansetzen*

long-term	*langfristig*
manage	*leiten*
management *(process)*	*Management nt*
(the) management	*(das) Management nt*
management appraisal	*Leistungsbeurteilung f des Managements*
management audit	*Prüfung f und Bewertung f der Manager-Leistung f*
management by crisis	*Management nt durch Krisen fpl*
management by objectives	*Unternehmensführung f mit Zielvorgabe f*
management committee	*geschäftsführender Ausschuß m*
management consultant	*Unternehmensberater(in) m(f)*
management course	*Managementkurs m*
management development	*Förderung f der Führungskräfte fpl*
management information system (MIS)	*Management-Informations-System nt (MIS nt)*
management style	*Führungsstil m*
management team	*Management Team nt*
management training	*Ausbildung f der Führungskräfte fpl*
manager(ess)	*Manager(in) m(f)*
managerial level	*Führungsebene f*
managerial staff	*leitendes Personal nt*
man-hour	*Arbeitsstunde f*
man management	*Personalführung f*
manpower planning	*Personalplanung f*
middle management	*mittleres Management nt*
motivate	*motivieren*
motivation	*Motivation f*
office manager	*Büroleiter(in) m(f)*
organization chart	*Organisationsplan m*
overspend	*zuviel ausgeben*
phase	*Phase f*
plan n	*Plan m*

a well-/badly-managed project *ein gutorganisiertes/schlechtorganisiertes Projekt*
efficient/inefficient management *fähiges/unfähiges Management*
the decision must be taken at managerial level *die Entscheidung muß auf Managementebene getroffen werden*
the next phase is scheduled to begin this month *die nächste Phase soll diesen Monat beginnen*
the project is entering its final phase *das Projekt tritt in seine Endphase ein*

plan *vb*	*planen*
procedure	*Verfahren nt*
programme	*Programm nt*
progress *n*	*Fortschritt m*
progress *vb*	*vorankommen*
progress chaser	*Terminjäger m*
progress report	*Tätigkeitsbericht m*
project *n*	*Projekt nt*
project *vb*	*planen*
projected	*geplant*
projection	*Projektion f*
project manager	*Projektleiter(in) m(f)*
rationalization	*Rationalisierung f*
redeployment	*Umsetzung f (der Arbeitskräfte pl)*
reminder	*Mahnung f*
reschedule	*verlegen (auf +acc)*
schedule *n*	*Zeitplan m*
schedule *vb*	*planen*
scheduling	*Planung f*
short-term	*kurzfristig*
status report	*Lagebericht m*
strategy	*Strategie f*
think tank	*Planungsstab m*
timescale	*Zeitvorgabe f*
work measurement	*Arbeitszeitstudie f*
work study	*Arbeitsstudie f*

to plan for all contingencies *alle Eventualitäten einplanen*
to follow progress *die Entwicklung im Auge behalten*
everything is progressing smoothly *es geht alles gut voran*
on schedule *plangemäß, planmäßig*
ahead of/behind schedule *dem Zeitplan voraus/hinterher*
to draw up a schedule *einen Zeitplan aufstellen*
to stick to a schedule *einen Zeitplan einhalten*
to schedule something for next week/month/year *etwas für nächste Woche/nächsten Monat/nächstes Jahr vorsehen*
please provide a status report on the project *bitte legen Sie einen Lagebericht über das Projekt vor*

See also **THE LAW AND CONTRACTS** *and* **BUYING AND SELLING**

access	*Zugang m*
acre	*Morgen m*
advertise	*werben*
advertisement	*Anzeige f*
advertising rates	*Anzeigentarif m*
agricultural land	*landwirtschaftlich genutztes Grundstück nt*
air conditioning	*Klimaanlage f*
apartment	*Wohnung f*
apartment building	*Wohnblock m*
architect	*Architekt(in) m (f)*
attic	*Dachboden m*
attic room	*Mansarde f*
balcony	*Balkon m*
basement	*Untergeschoß nt, Souterrain nt*
bathroom	*Badezimmer nt*
bay window	*Erkerfenster nt*
bedroom	*Schlafzimmer nt*
bridging loan	*Überbrückungskredit m*
brochure	*Prospekt m*
builder	*Bauunternehmer(in) m (f)*
building *(house, offices etc)*	*Gebäude nt*
building *(process)*	*Bau m*
building land	*Bauland nt*
building site	*Baustelle f*
building society	*Bausparkasse f*

the property offers accommodation for four offices *in der Immobilie können vier Büros untergebracht werden*
to advertise a property for sale *eine Immobilie durch Anzeige zum Verkauf anbieten*
I would like to place an advertisement in your "properties for sale"/"to let" section *ich möchte eine Anzeige in Ihrem Immobilienteil "zu verkaufen"/"zu vermieten" aufgeben*
I saw your advertisement in Property Magazine of 1 July and am interested in ... *ich habe Ihre Anzeige in der Ausgabe "Property Magazine" vom 1. Juli gesehen und bin interessiert an (+dat) ...*
the airport is an hour away by car/train/bus *der Flughafen ist eine Autostunde/Zugstunde/Busstunde entfernt*
how far away is the airport/station/city centre? *wie weit ist der Flughafen/der Bahnhof/das Stadtzentrum entfernt?*
three/four-bedroomed house *ein Haus mit vier/fünf Zimmern, Küche und Bad (NB the Germans measure in terms of rooms, not bedrooms)*
to the rear/front/side of the building *hinter/vor/neben dem Gebäude*
the house was built in 1981 *das Haus wurde 1981 gebaut*

buy	*kaufen*
buyer	*Käufer(in) m(f)*
buyer's market	*Käufermarkt m*
cable television	*Kabelfernsehen nt*
car park	*Parkplatz m*
carpet	*Teppich m*
ceiling	*Decke f*
cellar	*Keller m*
central heating	*Zentralheizung f*
city centre	*Stadtmitte f*
commission	*Provision f, Kommission f*
completion *(of sale)*	*Verkaufsabschluß m*
completion *(of work)*	*Fertigstellung f*
construction *(work)*	*Bauarbeiten fpl*
contract	*Vertrag m*
conversion	*Umbau m*
convert	*umbauen*
conveyancing	*Eigentumsübertragung f*
cottage	*Cottage nt*
demolition	*Abbruch m*
detached house	*Einzelhaus nt*
details	*Details ntpl*
dining room	*Eßzimmer nt*
double glazing	*Doppelfenster ntpl*
downstairs *adj*	*unten*
downstairs *adv*	*(nach) unten*
electricity	*Elektrizität f*
endowment mortgage	*Hypothek f mit Lebensversicherung f*
entrance	*Eingang m*
entrance hall	*Eingangshalle f*
entryphone	*Türsprechanlage f*
estate *(residential)*	*Siedlung f*
estate *(around large house)*	*Gut nt*
estate agency	*Maklerbüro nt*
estate agent	*Immobilienmakler(in) m(f)*
estate manager	*Gutsverwalter(in) m(f)*
facade	*Fassade f*
fair rent	*angemessene Miete f*

the property comprises ... over a surface area of 200m² *die Immobilie hat ... auf einer Grundfläche von 200m²*
to develop a site *ein Grundstück erschließen*
to be equipped/fitted with ... *eingerichtet/ausgestattet sein mit ...*
to exchange contracts *einen Kaufvertrag abschließen*

fees	*Honorar* nt
fire escape *(stairs, ladder)*	*Feuertreppe f, Feuerleiter f*
fire exit	*Notausgang m*
fireplace	*Kamin m*
fixtures and fittings	*Einbauten mpl und Zubehör nt*
flat	*Wohnung f*
floor *(of room)*	*Fußboden m*
floor *(storey)*	*Stock m*
floor-to-ceiling	*vom Fußboden m bis zur Decke f*
forecourt	*Vorhof m*
foundations	*Fundament nt*
freehold	*Eigentumsrecht nt*
freehold property	*(freier) Grundbesitz m*
front *(of a building)*	*Vorderfront f*
fully-equipped	*gut ausgestattet*
furnished	*möbliert*
garden	*Garten m*
gas	*Gas nt*
good-sized	*ziemlich groß*
ground floor	*Erdgeschoß nt*
ground rent	*Erbbauzins m*
grounds	*Anlagen fpl*
hotel	*Hotel nt*
house	*Haus nt*
industrial building	*gewerblich genutztes Gebäude nt*
industrial estate	*Industriegebiet nt*
insurance	*Versicherung f*
interior *n*	*Innere nt*
interior decoration	*Innenausstattung f*
interior decorator	*Innenausstatter(in) m(f)*
kitchen	*Küche f*
land	*Land nt*

all fixtures and fittings are included in the sale/rental price *alle Einbauten und Zubehör sind im Verkaufspreis/Mietpreis inbegriffen*
what floor is it on? *auf welchem Stock(werk) ist es?*
the property is situated on the first/second floor *die Immobilie liegt im ersten/zweiten Stock*
a first/second-floor flat *eine Wohnung im ersten/zweiten Stock*
how many rooms are there? *wieviele Zimmer hat es/sie?*
how many square metres does the property cover? *was ist die gesamte Grundfläche?*
what does the price include? *was ist im Preis inbegriffen?*
you will get the keys to the property on Monday *die Schlüsselübergabe ist am Montag*

landing	*Treppenabsatz m*
landlady	*Vermieterin f*
landlord	*Vermieter m*
lawyer	*Rechtsanwalt m, Rechtsanwältin f*
lease *n*	*Pachtvertrag m*
lease *vb (from)*	*pachten (von +dat)*
lease *vb (to)*	*verpachten (an +acc)*
leasehold	*Pachtbesitz m*
leasehold property	*Pachtbesitz m*
legal fees	*Anwaltshonorar nt*
let *n*	*see phrases below*
let *vb (to)*	*vermieten (an +acc)*
to let	*zu vermieten*
lift	*Fahrstuhl m*
loft	*Dachboden m, Loft m*
lounge	*Wohnzimmer nt*
mains sewage	*Kanalisation f*
mains water	*Wasseranschluß m*
mortgage	*Hypothek f*
neighbour	*Nachbar(in) m(f)*
obtain	*erhalten*
occupied	*bewohnt*
offer *n*	*Angebot nt*
offer *vb*	*anbieten*
office accommodation	*Büroraum m*
office block	*Bürogebäude nt*
office space	*Büroraum m*
overpriced	*zu teuer*
owner	*Besitzer(in) m(f)*
parking facilities	*Parkmöglichkeiten fpl*
partition wall	*Trennwand f*
penthouse	*Penthouse nt*
picture window	*Panoramafenster nt*

to take out a long/short lease on a property *einen langfristigen/ kurzfristigen Pachtvertrag abschließen*
to have a house/flat on a long/short let *ein Haus/eine Wohnung langfristig/kurzfristig mieten*
to put a property on the market *eine Immobilie zum Verkauf anbieten*
the building has been on the market for two months *das Gebäude steht seit 2 Monaten zum Verkauf*
to take out a mortgage on ... *eine Hypothek für ... aufnehmen*
in poor/fair/good/excellent order *in schlechtem/akzeptablem/gutem/ ausgezeichnetem Zustand*
parking for four cars *Stellplätze für vier Wagen*

planning permission	*Baugenehmigung f*
plumbing	*sanitäre Installation f*
power point	*Steckdose f*
price	*Preis m*
private	*privat*
property	*Immobilie f*
property developer *(business)*	*Grundstückserschließungsunternehmen nt*
property development	*Grundstückserschließung f*
property management	*Grundstücksverwaltung f*
property manager	*Grundstücksverwalter(in) m(f)*
property market	*Immobilienmarkt m*
radiator	*Heizkörper m*
real estate	*Immobilien fpl*
rebuild	*wieder aufbauen*
redecorated	*neu tapeziert*
refurbished	*renoviert*
refurbishment	*Renovierung f*
rent *n*	*Miete f*
rent *vb (from)*	*mieten (von +dat)*
rent *vb (to)*	*vermieten (an +acc)*
for rent	*zu vermieten*
replumbed	*mit neuen sanitären Installationen fpl*
request	*bitten um (+acc)*
residential area	*Wohngegend f*
residential building	*Wohngebäude nt*
for residential use	*für Wohnzwecke mpl*
restored	*wiederhergestellt*
rewired	*mit neu verlegten Leitungen fpl*
roof	*Dach nt*
room	*Zimmer nt*
sale	*Verkauf m*
for sale	*zu verkaufen*
satellite dish	*Satellitenantenne f*
security guard	*Wache f*
sell	*verkaufen*
seller	*Verkäufer(in) m(f)*
seller's market	*Verkäufermarkt m*
semidetached house	*Doppelhaushälfte f*
services	*öffentliche Dienstleistungen fpl*

when was the building refurbished? *wann wurde das Gebäude renoviert?*
who is responsible for the cleaning/upkeep of ...? *wer ist für die Reinigung/Wartung (+gen) ... verantwortlich?*

shower (room)	Dusche *f*
sitting tenant	*(derzeitiger) Mieter m*
skylight	*Dachfenster nt*
solicitor	*Rechtsanwalt m, Rechtsanwältin f*
spacious	*geräumig*
speculation	*Spekulation f*
stairs	*Treppe f*
storey	*Stock m, Stockwerk nt*
structural engineer	*Bauingenieur(in) m(f)*
structurally sound	*baulich einwandfrei*
structural repairs	*bauliche Reparaturen fpl*
structural report	*Baubericht m*
sublet	*untervermieten*
subsidence	*Bodensenkung f*
suburb	*Vorort m*
survey *n (report)*	*Gutachten nt*
survey *vb*	*begutachten*
survey fee	*Honorar nt für Gutachten nt*
surveyor	*Gutachter(in) m(f)*
tenancy	*Mietverhältnis nt*
tenant	*Mieter(in) m(f)*
terraced house	*Reihenhaus nt*
tinted window	*getönte Scheibe(n) f(pl)*
toilet	*Toilette f*
town centre	*Stadtmitte f*
underground car park	*Tiefgarage f*
underpriced	*zu billig*
unfurnished	*unmöbliert*
unoccupied	*unbewohnt*
unsold	*unverkauft*
upstairs *adj*	*im oberen Stock m*
upstairs *adv*	*(nach) oben*
utility room	*Allzweckraum m*
vacant	*unbewohnt*
vacant possession	*verlassener Grundbesitz m*
valuation	*Wertbestimmung f*
video entry system	*Sichtsprechanlage f*

**the property is situated in the centre of .../just outside .../within easy
reach of ...** *die Immobilie liegt im Zentrum von .../etwas außerhalb von
.../ist von ... leicht zu erreichen*
to get a property surveyed *eine Immobilie begutachten lassen*
the property was valued at over/under £500,000 *die Immobilie wurde auf
über/unter £500.000 geschätzt*

villa	*Villa f*
wall *(inside)*	*Wand f*
wall *(outside)*	*Mauer f*
wallpaper	*Tapete f*
wall-to-wall carpeting	*Teppichboden m*
warehouse	*Lager(haus) nt*
waste disposal	*Müllbeseitigung f*
window	*Fenster nt*
wiring	*elektrische Leitungen fpl*

AI (artificial intelligence)	*KI f (künstliche Intelligenz f)*
application	*Anwendung f*
application development	*Anwendungsentwicklung f*
applied research	*angewandte Forschung f*
automation	*Automatisierung f*
breakthrough	*Durchbruch m*
CAD/CAM (computer-assisted design/manufacture)	*CAD/CAM nt (rechnergestütztes Konstruieren nt/ rechnergestützte Fertigungssteuerung f)*
computer model	*Computermodell nt*
concept	*Konzept nt*
customer trial	*Ausprobieren nt durch den Kunden*
cybernetics	*Kybernetik f*
demonstration	*Vorführung f*
design *n*	*Design nt*
design *vb*	*entwerfen*
designer	*Designer(in) m(f)*
design team	*Designteam nt*
develop	*entwickeln*
development	*Entwicklung f*
development costs	*Entwicklungskosten pl*
devise	*konstruieren, erfinden*
ergonomics	*Ergonomie f*
industrial design	*Industriedesign nt*
industrial espionage	*Industriespionage f*
innovation	*Innovation f*
innovative	*innovativ*
innovator	*Neuerer m*
invent	*erfinden*
invention	*Erfindung f*
inventor	*Erfinder(in) m(f)*
laboratory	*Labor nt*
laboratory manager	*Laborleiter(in) m(f)*
laboratory technician	*Labortechniker(in) m(f)*
man-year costs	*Kosten pl pro Arbeitskraft pro Jahr*
market trial	*Markttest m*

we hope to recover all development costs within 5 years *wir hoffen, daß wir die Entwicklungskosten innerhalb von 5 Jahren zurückbekommen*
a forward-looking R & D policy *eine zukunftsorientierte Forschungs- und Entwicklungspolitik*
to invest money in research *Geld in Forschung investieren*

mock-up	*Modell* nt
modernize	*modernisieren*
new technology	*neue Technologie* f
out of date	*überholt*
patent n	*Patent* nt
patent vb	*patentieren lassen*
payback time	*Amortisationszeit* f
pilot plant	*Pilotanlage* f
pilot project	*Pilotprojekt* nt
preproduction	*Vorfertigung* f
product	*Produkt* nt
product design	*Produktdesign* nt
product development	*Produktentwicklung* f
prototype	*Prototyp* m
pure research	*reine Forschung* f
R & D (research and development)	*FuE* f *(Forschung* f *und Entwicklung* f*)*
research n	*Forschung* f
research (into) vb	*Forschungen* fpl *anstellen (über +acc)*
research and development (R & D)	*Forschung* f *und Entwicklung* f *(FuE* f*)*
research budget	*Forschungsbudget* nt
research department	*Forschungsabteilung* f
researcher	*Forscher(in)* m(f)
research laboratory	*Forschungslabor* nt
research manager	*Leiter(in)* m(f) *der Forschungsabteilung* f
research programme	*Forschungsprogramm* nt
research worker	*wissenschaftlicher Mitarbeiter* m, *wissenschaftliche Mitarbeiterin* f
robotics	*Robotertechnik* f
technological	*technologisch*
technology	*Technologie* f
test n	*Test* m

to find a marketable application for an invention *eine gut verkäufliche Anwendung für eine Erfindung finden*
to take out a patent on something *ein Patent für etwas anmelden*
the prototype will be ready in September *der Prototyp wird im September fertig sein*
to undertake research in the field of ... *Forschung im Bereich (+gen) ... betreiben*
this research will pay for itself within 5 years *diese Forschungsarbeit wird sich innerhalb von 5 Jahren selbst tragen*

test *vb*	*testen*
trial	*Versuch m*
up-to-date	*modern*
user-friendly	*benutzerfreundlich*

to carry out trials of a new product *ein neues Produkt einer Versuchsreihe unterziehen*

the new product will be unveiled at the trade fair in Paris/Berlin *das neue Produkt wird auf der Fachmesse in Paris/Berlin vorgestellt*

See also **IMPORT-EXPORT AND SHIPPING**

bin card/tag	*Lagerfachkarte f*
buffer stocks	*Ausgleichslager nt*
computerized stocktaking	*computerisierte Warenbestandsaufnahme f*
depository *(place)*	*Hinterlegungsstelle f*
inventory	*Inventar nt*
inventory control	*Bestandsüberwachung f*
last in, first out (LIFO)	*zuletzt eingekauft - zuerst verbraucht*
overstocking	*Überbevorratung f*
procurement	*Beschaffung f*
stock *n*	*Bestand m*
stock *vb*	*führen*
in stock	*auf Lager nt*
out of stock	*nicht vorrätig*
stock code	*Lagercode m*
stock control	*Lagerkontrolle f*
stock controller	*Lagerhalter(in) m(f)*
stock-in-trade	*Warenbestand m*
stock level	*Höhe f des Lagerbestands m*
stocklist	*Lagerliste f*
stock management	*Lagerhaltung f*
stocktaking	*Inventur f*
stock turnover	*Lagerumschlag m*
stock up	*auffüllen*
take stock	*Bestandsaufnahme f machen*
warehouse	*Lager(haus) nt*
warehouse capacity	*Lagerkapazität f*
warehousing costs	*Lagerkosten pl*

to buy in 500 units of ... *500 Stück von ... kaufen*
to make an inventory *eine Bestandsliste aufstellen*
what is the position regarding stocks of ...? *wie sieht es mit Vorrat von ... aus?*
we have 30,000 units in stock *wir haben 30.000 Stück auf Lager*
this item is out of stock *dieser Artikel ist nicht auf Lager*
the stock level is getting low *der Lagerbestand nimmt ab*
to maintain stock levels of ... *einen Lagerbestand von ... aufrechterhalten*
to stock up on something *einen Vorrat von etwas anlegen*
we regret that the following items are unavailable at the moment *leider sind folgende Artikel momentan nicht erhältlich*

ad valorem tax	*Vermögenssteuer f*
after tax	*nach Steuern*
allowance	*Steuerfreibetrag m*
anti-dumping duty	*Antidumpingzoll m*
back duty	*Steuerrückstand m*
basic rate	*Anfangssteuersatz m*
before tax	*vor Steuern*
Budget *(of government)*	*Haushalt m*
capital gains tax (CGT)	*Kapitalertragssteuer f*
capital transfer tax	*Kapitalverkehrssteuer f*
corporation tax	*Körperschaftssteuer f*
council tax	*Gemeindesteuer f*
customs duty	*Zoll m*
customs regulation	*Zollbestimmung f*
customs union	*Zollunion f*
death duty	*Erbschaftssteuer f*
direct taxation	*direkte Besteuerung f*
double taxation agreement	*Doppelbesteuerungsabkommen nt*
double taxation relief	*Befreiung f von Doppelbesteuerung f*
earned income	*Arbeitseinkommen nt*
excise duty	*Verbrauchssteuer f*
fiscal policy	*Fiskalpolitik f*
fiscal year	*Steuerjahr nt*
free of tax	*steuerfrei*
income	*Einkommen nt*
income tax *(general)*	*Einkommenssteuer f*
income tax *(on salary)*	*Lohnsteuer f*
indirect taxation	*indirekte Besteuerung f*
Inland Revenue (IR)	*britisches Finanzamt nt*
Internal Revenue Service (IRS)	*amerikanisches Steueramt nt*
investment income	*Erträge mpl aus Anlagen fpl*
luxury tax	*Luxussteuer f*
mortgage relief	*Steuervorteil m durch Hypothek f*
non-taxable	*steuerfrei*

profits before/after tax *Gewinn vor/nach Steuern*
a favourable/an unfavourable Budget *ein günstiger/ungünstiger Haushalt*
to sell at pre-Budget prices *zu Preisen vor Verkündigung des Haushalts verkaufen*
the increase/reduction will come into force as of 1 January *die Erhöhung/ Reduzierung tritt am 1. Januar in Kraft*
to pay duty *Zoll zahlen*
to buy something duty-free *etwas duty-free kaufen*

non-taxable income	nicht zu versteuerndes Einkommen nt
PAYE (pay as you earn)	Quellenabzugsverfahren nt
personal allowance	persönlicher Steuerfreibetrag m
pre-tax	vor Steuern
profits tax	Ertragssteuer f
progressive taxation	Progressivbesteuerung f
property tax	Vermögenssteuer f
stamp duty	Stempelgebühr f
standard rate	Einheitssteuersatz m
tax n	Steuer f
tax vb	besteuern
taxable	steuerpflichtig
tax accountant	Steuerberater(in) m(f)
tax allowance	Steuerfreibetrag m
tax avoidance	Steuerumgehung f
tax bill	Steuerbescheid m
tax bracket	Steuerklasse f
tax code	Steuerkennziffer f
tax collection	Steuererhebung f
tax collector	Finanzbeamter m, Finanzbeamtin f
tax concession	Steuervergünstigung f
tax consultant	Steuerberater(in) m(f)
tax credit	Steuergutschrift f
tax cut	Steuersenkung f
tax-deductible	abzugsfähig
tax evasion	Steuerhinterziehung f
tax exemption	Steuerbefreiung f
tax-free	steuerfrei
tax haven	Steuerparadies nt
tax holiday	steuerfreie Periode f
tax increase	Steuererhöhung f
tax loophole	Steuerlücke f
tax loss	Steuerverlust m
tax rebate	Steuerrückvergütung f

to recover VAT paid on something Mehrwertsteur für etwas zurückerstattet bekommen
these goods are taxed at 15% diese Waren sind mit 15% besteuert
to have a tax bill of over ... Steuern von über ... bezahlen müssen
to benefit from tax concessions von Steuererleichterungen profitieren
please advise us of the tax implications regarding this deal bitte teilen Sie uns mit, welche steuerlichen Auswirkungen dieses Geschäft für uns hat
to exploit a tax loophole eine Steuerlücke ausnutzen
to do something for tax purposes etwas aus steuerlichen Gründen tun

tax relief	*Steuervergünstigung f*
tax reserve certificate	*Wertpapier nt für angelegte*
	Steuerrücklagen
tax return	*Steuererklärung f*
tax schedules	*Steuertabelle f*
tax shelter	*Verhinderung f steuerlicher*
	Belastung f
tax tables	*Steuertabelle f*
tax year	*Steuerjahr nt*
unearned income	*Einkünfte fpl aus*
	Kapitalvermögen nt
VAT (value-added tax)	*MwSt f (Mehrwertsteuer f)*
VAT-exempt	*befreit von Mehrwertsteuer f*
wealth tax	*Vermögenssteuer f*
zero-rated	*befreit von Mehrwertsteuer f*
zero-rating	*Mehrwertsteuerbefreiung f*

GETTING INTO THE COUNTRY

EC citizens have free access to all EC countries for up to three months at a time. Austria's application for membership of the EC is to be reviewed once the single market has been implemented, but there are no restrictions on EC nationals entering the country.

If you intend to spend more than eight days on business in Switzerland in any three month period, you must register with the local authorities (*Einwohnerkontrolle*).

Commercial samples imported into any European country must be declared and accompanied by the appropiate import documents.

TRAVELLING

For German fast long-distance trains (*Intercity, Interregio*) you will have to pay a supplement (*ein Zuschlag*) and it is advisable to get a seat reservation (*Platzkarte*).

Cities are well-provided with public transport. Larger cities will have not only buses but a *U-bahn* (underground), and an *S-bahn* (tram system). In South Germany and Austria, the *S-Bahn* is called the *Trambahn*.

If you are driving your own car, you will need a Green Card for insurance cover overseas and, if you are driving a vehicle hired or leased in the UK, you will need a VE103 certificate. It is compulsory to display a country of origin sticker and to carry a warning triangle for use in case of a breakdown. It is strongly recommended that you carry spare bulbs for headlights and indicators. If you have a British vehicle, you must also convert your headlights for driving on the right. The motoring organizations will be able to give you advice on any other requirements.

The EC driving licence is recognized in all EC countries and in Switzerland but non-EC licence-holders require an international driving licence.

Motorways in Germany and Austria are toll-free, though some Austrian mountain roads charge a toll. For Swiss motorways you will need to buy an annual disc (*vignette*), costing about £12.50, and display it on your windscreen. It can be bought at border crossings or tourist offices in Switzerland, or from the motoring organizations in the UK. Although there is no legal speed limit on most German motorways, it is recommended that you keep below 130kph (about 80mph) and there are certain stretches of motorway where, for a trial period, a compulsory speed limit is being imposed. You should look out for the warnings to this effect.

The German *Verkehrsfunk* (motorists' radio) gives details of traffic jams (*Stau*), queues at border crossings (*Wartezeiten an den Grenzen*), diversions (*Umleitungen*) and blocked mountain passes (*nicht befahrbare Pässe*). Wavelengths are shown on blue road signs along the motorways.

See also **AT THE HOTEL**

ARRANGING THE BUSINESS TRIP

Please meet me at the airport/at my hotel *bitte holen Sie mich vom Flughafen/vom Hotel ab*
I will be on flight BA007, arriving at 8.45pm *ich komme um 20.45 Uhr mit dem Flug BA007 an*
I will make my own way to my hotel/the meeting *ich finde schon selbst zum Hotel/zur Besprechung*
I have never been to Brussels before *ich war noch nie in Brüssel*
I know Luxembourg quite well already *ich kenne Luxemburg schon recht gut*

BOOKING A PLANE/TRAIN TICKET

How much is a return/single to London? *(plane) was kostet ein Hinund Rückflug/ein einfacher Flug nach London?; (train) was kostet eine Rückfahrkarte/eine einfache Fahrt nach London?*
When is the next/last plane to Berlin? *wann geht die nächste/ letzte Maschine nach Berlin?*
When is the next/last train to Berlin? *wann fährt der nächste/ letzte Zug nach Berlin?*
What time does the plane take off/land? *wann fliegt das Flugzeug ab/wann landet das Flugzeug?*
What time does the train leave/arrive? *wann fährt der Zug ab/ kommt der Zug an?*
What is the latest check-in time? *wann muß ich spätestens beim Check-in sein?*
I'd like a non-smoking window seat *ich hätte gerne einen Fenster-sitz, Nichtraucher*
Not over the wing *nicht über dem Flügel*
I'd like a seat facing the engine/with my back to the engine *ich hätte gerne einen Platz in Fahrtrichtung/in Gegenfahrtrichtung*
I'd like to book two seats *ich möchte zwei Plätze buchen*
I'd like to confirm my booking *ich möchte meine Buchung bestäti-gen*
Is there a direct flight? *gibt es einen Direktflug?*
How long is the stopover? *wie lange dauert die Zwischenlan-dung?*

Can I go via Brussels? *kann ich über Brüssel reisen?*

I'd like to change my reservation *ich möchte meine Buchung ändern*

I'd like to upgrade my ticket to first class *ich möchte mein Ticket auf "Erste Klasse" umschreiben lassen*

Is there any room left in first class? *ist in der ersten Klasse noch Platz frei?*

Is there any room left in non-smoking/smoking? *(plane) ist im Nichtraucher/Raucher noch Platz frei?; (train) ist im Nichtraucherabteil/Raucherabteil noch Platz frei?*

Is there an earlier/later flight/train? *gibt est noch einen früheren/späteren Flug/Zug?*

If I go on stand-by, what chance is there that I'll get a seat? *wenn ich Standby fliege, welche Chance habe ich, noch mitzukommen?*

I'd like a vegetarian/salt-free meal *ich hätte gerne ein vegetarisches/salzloses Gericht*

I an diabetic, can I get a special meal? *ich bin Diabetiker(in), kann ich ein spezielles Gericht haben?*

Are meals served on that train/plane? *hat dieser Zug einen Speisewagen?/wird auf diesem Flug Essen serviert?*

AT THE AIRPORT/RAILWAY STATION

Where can I hire a car? *wo kann ich ein Auto mieten?*

Where can I change money? *wo kann ich Geld wechseln?*

Where can I buy magazines/a newspaper? *wo kann ich Zeitschriften/eine Zeitung kaufen?*

Is the 18.30 to Geneva due to leave on time? *wird der Zug/die Maschine nach Genf um 18.30 Uhr pünktlich abfahren/abfliegen?*

I am due to meet a Mr Pyke here. Could you page him please? *ich soll hier einen Herrn Pyke treffen. Können Sie ihn bitte ausrufen lassen?*

Do you have facilities for the disabled? *haben Sie Einrichtungen für Behinderte?*

AIRPORT

Where is the British Airways desk, please? *wo ist der British Airways Schalter, bitte?*

I have only one piece of hand luggage *ich habe nur ein Stück Handgepäck*

Can I book my luggage straight through to ...? *kann ich das Gepäck gleich nach ... durchchecken?*

My luggage hasn't arrived *mein Gepäck ist nicht angekommen*
Can I check in for the 14.30 to London yet? *kann ich schon für den Flug um 14.30 Uhr nach London einchecken?*
Is the Lufthansa flight to Manchester boarding yet? *sollen sich die Passagiere des Lufthansa Flugs nach Manchester schon zum Flugsteig begeben?*
Has the 12.20 to Glasgow been called yet? *ist der Flug um 12.20 Uhr nach Glasgow schon aufgerufen worden?*
I am in transit *ich bin Transitreisende(r)*
How often do shuttles leave for the city centre? *wie oft fahren die Busse ins Stadtzentrum?*
Does this shuttle go to terminal 2? *fährt dieser Pendelbus zum Terminal 2?*
I would prefer not to put these diskettes through the X-ray machine *ich möchte diese Disketten lieber nicht durch die Röntgenkontrolle gehen lassen*

RAILWAY STATION

Where is platform 14, please? *wo ist Bahnsteig 14, bitte?*
Is this the right platform for Brussels? *ist das der richtige Bahnsteig für Brüssel?*
Which platform does the London train leave from? *von welchem Gleis fährt der Zug nach London ab?*
Which window sells international tickets? *welcher ist der Auslandsschalter?*
Can I buy a ticket on the train? *kann ich eine Fahrkarte im Zug lösen?*

PHRASES YOU ARE LIKELY TO HEAR AT THE AIRPORT OR RAILWAY STATION
Raucher oder Nichtraucher? *smoking or non-smoking?*
Haben Sie Gepäck? *do you have any luggage?*
Dieser Flug ist völlig ausgebucht *that flight is fully-booked*
Möchten Sie Standby fliegen? *would you like to go on standby?*
Sie müssen zu Flugsteig 35 *you will be boarding at Gate 35*
Bitte, gehen Sie sofort zu Flugsteig 35 *please go straight to Gate 35*
Ihr Flug wird um 9 Uhr aufgerufen *your flight will be called at 9am*
Ihr Flug/Zug hat Verspätung *your flight/train has been delayed*
Abflug/Abfahrt ist voraussichtlich um 21 Uhr *take-off/departure is now scheduled for 9pm*
Wie wollen Sie zahlen? *how will you be paying?*

ON THE PLANE OR TRAIN

Could I change seats? *kann ich mich auf einen anderen Platz setzen?*
I'd prefer to be by the window/in the aisle seat *ich hätte lieber einen Fensterplatz/einen Platz am Gang*
What time will breakfast/lunch/dinner be served? *wann wird das Frühstück/Mittagessen/Abendessen serviert?*
What time is it, local time? *wie spät ist es nach Ortszeit bitte?*
What time will we arrive in Paris? *wann kommen wir in Paris an?*
I'm sorry, but you're sitting in my seat *tut mir leid, aber das ist mein Platz*
Excuse me, this is a non-smoking compartment/section *Entschuldigung, hier ist Nichtraucher*

PLANE

Please do not wake me up *bitte wecken Sie mich nicht*
I ordered a special meal *ich habe ein spezielles Gericht bestellt*
All the lockers are full. Where can I put my bag? *die Gepäckablagen sind alle voll. Wo kann ich meine Tasche hintun?*
Could I have a washing kit, please? *könnte ich bitte Waschzeug haben?*
I suffer from airsickness *mir wird beim Fliegen immer schlecht*

TRAIN

Is it all right if I open/close the window? *macht es Ihnen etwas aus, wenn ich das Fenster öffne/zumache?*
Where should I change for Amsterdam? *wo muß ich nach Amsterdam umsteigen?*
I was told that I could buy a ticket on the train *man hat mir gesagt, daß ich eine Fahrkarte im Zug lösen könnte*
Is there a telephone on the train? *gibt es ein Telefon im Zug?*

AT CUSTOMS

I am here on business *ich bin geschäftlich hier*
I represent Clarke & Co *ich vertrete die Firma Clarke & Co*
I will be spending three days here *ich bleibe drei Tage hier*
I have nothing to declare *ich habe nichts zu verzollen*
I have the usual allowance of cigarettes and alcohol *ich habe (nur) die erlaubte Menge an Zigaretten und Alkohol*
I will be re-exporting these samples *ich werde diese Muster wieder ausführen*

Could I have a receipt? *könnte ich eine Quittung haben?*

PHRASES YOU ARE LIKELY TO HEAR AT CUSTOMS
Was ist der Zweck Ihrer Reise? *what is the purpose of your visit?*
Wie lange bleiben Sie hier im Land? *how long will you be staying in the country?*
Machen Sie Ihre Tasche bitte auf *open your bag, please*
Haben Sie etwas zu verzollen? *have you anything to declare?*
Auf diese Sachen müssen Sie Zoll zahlen *you will have to pay duty on these items*

TAKING A TAXI

Could you order me a taxi, please? *könnten Sie mir bitte ein Taxi bestellen?*
Where can I get a taxi? *wo kann ich einen Taxistand finden?*
Take me to this address, please *fahren Sie mich bitte zu dieser Adresse*
How much to the airport/railway station? *wieviel kostet es zum Flughafen/Bahnhof?*
I'm in a hurry *ich habe es eilig*
Please wait here *bitte warten Sie hier*
Stop here, please *bitte halten Sie hier*
How much is that? *wieviel macht das?*
Can I pay you in sterling? *kann ich in Pfund zahlen?*
Keep the change *stimmt so*
Can I have a receipt? *kann ich eine Quittung haben?*
Please pick me up here at 4 o'clock *bitte holen Sie mich um 16 Uhr hier ab*
But the meter says only ... *aber auf dem Zähler stehen nur ...*
This is the third time we've been down this street *jetzt sind wir schon das dritte Mal durch diese Straße gefahren*

HIRING AND DRIVING A CAR

Where can I hire a car? *wo kann ich ein Auto mieten?*
I reserved a car. My name is Dawes *ich habe ein Auto auf den Namen Dawes reservieren lassen*
I'd like a two-door/four-door model *ich hätte gern(e) ein Auto mit zwei/vier Türen*
I'd like an Opel Ascona for 3 days *ich hätte gern(e) einen Opel Ascona für 3 Tage*
Have you got a larger/smaller car? *haben Sie ein größeres/kleineres Auto?*
What does the hire price include? *was ist im Mietpreis inbegrif-*

fen?

Is mileage/insurance included? *ist Kilometerpauschale/Versicherung inbegriffen?*

Can I return the car outside office hours? *kann ich den Wagen außerhalb der Öffnungszeiten zurückbringen?*

Can you show me the controls? *können Sie mir die Schalter zeigen?*

Can you tell me the way to ...? *können Sie mir sagen, wie ich nach ... komme?*

How far is the next service station? *wie weit ist die nächste Tankstelle entfernt?*

Can I park here? *darf man hier parken?*

I'd like to check the tyres *ich hätte gern(e) den Reifendruck geprüft*

Fifty litres, please *fünfzig Liter, bitte*

Fill her up, please *volltanken, bitte*

Could you check the tyre pressure/oil/water? *würden Sie bitte den Reifendruck/Ölstand/Kühlwasserstand prüfen?*

Could you clean the windscreen? *können Sie bitte die Windschutzscheibe waschen?*

Can you take me to the nearest garage? *können Sie mich zur nächsten Autowerkstatt bringen?*

Can you give me a tow? *können Sie mich abschleppen?*

How long will it take to repair? *wie lange dauert die Reparatur?*

PHRASES YOU ARE LIKELY TO HEAR WHEN DRIVING

Ihren Führerschein, bitte *could I see your driving licence?*

Sind Sie schon mal in Deutschland Auto gefahren? *have you driven in Germany before?*

Versicherung kostet extra *insurance costs extra*

Nur siebenhundert Kilometer sind dabei *the mileage limit is 700km*

Können Sie sich anderweitig ausweisen? *have you any other form of identification?*

ILLNESS AND EMERGENCIES

In EC countries, EC citizens can have medical treatment and medication partially refunded by filling in an E111 form (available in the UK from the Department of Social Security or Post Offices), which will generally ensure that you receive a 70–75% refund on medical expenses paid to chemists and doctors or hospitals working within the state health service. You must get the form filled in at the time of treatment.

In Austria, treatment in a public hospital is free but other medical services must be paid for.

Non-EC citizens should have private medical insurance, as should EC citizens travelling to Switzerland or other non-EC countries.

I feel ill *mir ist nicht gut*
I feel sick *mir ist schlecht*
I feel faint *mir wird schwindelig*
My ... hurts *mein(e) ... tut weh*
I have a pain in the ... *ich habe Schmerzen im/in der ...*
I am allergic to penicillin/milk products *ich habe eine Allergie gegen Penizillin/Milchprodukte*
I have a headache *ich habe Kopfschmerzen*
I have a high temperature *ich habe Fieber*
I think I have broken ... *ich glaube, ich habe meinen/meine/mein ... gebrochen*
I have been stung by a bee/wasp *ich bin von einer Biene/Wespe gestochen worden*
I have been bitten by a dog *ich bin von einem Hund gebissen worden*
My companion is ill *mein(e) Begleiter(in) ist krank*
He/she is unconscious *er/sie ist bewußtlos*
I'd like to see a doctor/dentist immediately *ich brauche sofort einen Arzt/Zahnarzt*
Can you give me a prescription for ...? *können Sie mir ... verschreiben?*
This is an emergency *es handelt sich um einen Notfall*
Please call an ambulance/the fire brigade/the police *bitte rufen Sie einen Krankenwagen/die Feuerwehr/die Polizei*
There is a fire *es brennt*
There has been an accident *da ist ein Unfall passiert*
I have been attacked/robbed *ich bin überfallen/ausgeraubt worden*
I have lost my ... *ich habe meinen/meine/mein ... verloren*
Help! *Hilfe!*

ADDITIONAL VOCABULARY

accident *(general)*	*Unglück nt*
accident *(car)*	*Unfall m*
aeroplane	*Flugzeug nt*
airport	*Flughafen m*
airport police	*Flughafenpolizei f*
airport tax	*Flughafengebühr f*
airsickness	*Luftkrankheit f*

aisle seat	*Sitz m am Gang*
ambulance	*Krankenwagen m*
APEX ticket	*APEX ticket nt*
arrivals *(area at airport/station)*	*Ankunft f*
arrivals board *(at airport)*	*Ankunftsanzeige f*
arrivals board *(at railway station)*	*Ankunftstafel f*
aspirin	*Aspirin ® nt*
baggage allowance	*zugelassenes Gepäck nt*
baggage reclaim	*Gepäckausgabe f*
bank	*Bank f*
bar	*Bar f*
blood group	*Blutgruppe f*
boarding pass	*Bordkarte f*
boat train	*Zug m mit Fährenanschluß*
breakdown	*Panne f*
breakdown van	*Abschleppwagen m*
buffet car	*Speisewagen m*
business class	*Business-Klasse f*
business trip	*Geschäftsreise f*
cafeteria	*Cafeteria f*
cancellation	*Stornierung f*
cancelled	*storniert, abgesagt*
car	*Auto nt*
car hire	*Autovermietung f*
car hire firm	*Autoverleih m*
car park *(long-term)*	*Parkplatz m für Dauerparker*
car park *(short-term)*	*Parkplatz m für Kurzparker*
car phone	*Autotelefon nt*
cash dispenser	*Geldautomat m*
charter flight	*Charterflug m*
check in *vb*	*sich einchecken*
check-in desk	*Abflugschalter m*
club class	*Club-Klasse f*
coach	*Reisebus m, Bus m*
compartment	*Abteil nt*
confirm	*bestätigen*
confirmation	*Bestätigung f*
couchette	*Liegewagenplatz m*
customs	*Zoll m*
customs declaration	*Zollerklärung f*
customs officer	*Zollbeamte m, Zollbeamtin f*
delayed	*verspätet*
dentist	*Zahnarzt m, Zahnärztin f*
departure lounge	*Abflughalle f*
departures *(area at airport)*	*Abflug m*

departures *(area at railway station)*	*Abfahrt f*
departures board *(at airport)*	*Abfluganzeige f*
departures board *(at railway station)*	*Abfahrtstafel f*
diabetic	*Diabetiker(in) m(f)*
diarrhoea	*Durchfall m*
diesel (fuel)	*Diesel nt*
dining car	*Speisewagen m*
doctor	*Arzt m, Ärztin f*
domestic arrivals	*Ankunft f Inland*
domestic departures	*Abflug m Inland*
domestic flight	*Inlandsflug m*
driver	*Fahrer(in) m(f)*
driving licence	*Führerschein m*
duty	*Zoll m*
duty-free goods	*zollfreie Waren fpl*
duty-free shop	*Duty-free-Shop m*
economy class	*Touristenklasse f*
emergency exit	*Notausgang m*
emergency telephone	*Notruftelefon nt*
excess baggage	*Übergepäck nt*
executive class	*Executive Class f*
exit *(general)*	*Ausgang m*
exit *(on motorway)*	*Ausfahrt f*
express train	*Schnellzug m*
ferry	*Fähre f*
filling *(in tooth)*	*Füllung f, Plombe f*
fire brigade	*Feuerwehr f*
firm booking	*feste Buchung f*
first aid post	*Sanitätswache f*
first class	*erste Klasse f*
first class lounge	*Aufenthaltsraum m für erste Klasse*
flat tyre	*Reifenpanne f*
flight	*Flug m*
flying time	*Flugzeit f*
food poisoning	*Lebensmittelvergiftung f*
fully booked	*ausgebucht*
gate	*Flugsteig m*
guard *(on train)*	*Schaffner(in) m(f)*
guidebook	*Reiseführer m*
hand luggage	*Handgepäck nt*
headphones	*Kopfhörer mpl*
hire *vb*	*mieten*

hire price	*Mietpreis m*
hospital	*Krankenhaus nt*
hovercraft	*Luftkissenboot nt, Hovercraft nt*
hydrofoil	*Tragflügelboot nt*
immigration	*Einwanderungsstelle f*
information desk	*Information f*
injection	*Spritze f*
insulin	*Insulin nt*
insurance	*Versicherung f*
international arrivals	*Ankunft f Ausland*
international departures	*Abflug m Ausland*
international flight	*Auslandsflug m*
itinerary	*Reiseroute f*
land *vb*	*landen*
landing	*Landung f*
left-luggage locker	*Schließfach nt*
left-luggage office/counter	*Gepäckaufbewahrung f*
lost property office	*Fundbüro nt*
luggage locker *(on plane)*	*Gepäckfach nt*
map *(of country)*	*Landkarte f*
map *(of town)*	*Stadtplan m*
medical insurance	*Krankenversicherung f*
meter *(in taxi)*	*Zähler m*
mileage	*Kilometergeld nt, Kilometerpauschale f*
motorway	*Autobahn f*
non-smoking (compartment/ section) *(plane)*	*Nichtraucher m*
non-smoking (compartment/ section) *(train)*	*Nichtraucherabteil nt*
no-show	*fehlender Passagier m*
oil	*Öl nt*
one-way ticket	*einfache Fahrkarte f*
open return *(plane)*	*offener Rückflug m*
overbook	*überbuchen*
overbooked	*übergebucht*
passport	*Reisepaß m*
passport control	*Paßkontrolle f*
petrol	*Benzin nt*
platform	*Bahnsteig m*
police	*Polizei f*
policeman/woman	*Polizist(in) m(f)*
police station	*Polizeiwache f*
porter	*Gepäckträger m*
post office	*Postamt nt*

pregnant	*schwanger*
prescription	*Rezept nt*
puncture	*Reifenpanne f*
railway police	*Bahnhofspolizei f*
reservation	*Reservierung f, Buchung f*
reserve *vb*	*reservieren, buchen*
restaurant car	*Speisewagen m*
return ticket *(plane)*	*Rückflugticket nt*
return ticket *(train)*	*Rückfahrkarte f*
safety belt	*Sicherheitsgurt m*
sample	*Muster nt*
scheduled flight	*Linienflug m*
seasickness	*Seekrankheit f*
seatbelt	*Sicherheitsgurt m*
second class	*zweite Klasse f*
service station	*Tankstelle f*
shuttle *(to/from airport)*	*Airport Bus m/Flughafenbus m*
shuttle *(flight)*	*Pendelflug m*
single ticket *(train)*	*Einzelfahrkarte f*
single ticket *(plane)*	*Einzelticket nt*
sleeping car	*Schlafwagen m*
smoking (compartment/ section) *(plane)*	*Raucher m*
smoking (compartment/ section) *(train)*	*Raucherabteil nt*
speed limit	*Geschwindigkeitsbegrenzung f*
stand-by ticket	*Standby-Ticket nt*
station	*Bahnhof m*
stationmaster	*Bahnhofsvorsteher m*
steward	*Steward m*
stewardess	*Stewardeß f*
stopover	*Zwischenlandung f*
supplement	*Extragebühr f*
take off *vb*	*abfliegen, starten*
take-off *n*	*Abflug m, Start m*
taxi	*Taxi nt*
taxi driver	*Taxifahrer(in) m(f)*
taxi rank	*Taxistand m*
terminal *(airport)*	*Terminal nt*
terminal *(rail)*	*Endbahnhof m*
terminal *(bus)*	*Endstation f*
through train	*durchgehender Zug m*
ticket *(plane)*	*Ticket nt, Flugschein m*
ticket *(train, bus)*	*Fahrkarte f*
ticket office	*Fahrkartenschalter m*

toilet	*Toilette f*
toothache	*Zahnschmerzen mpl*
train	*Zug m*
transit lounge	*Transitraum m*
transit stop	*Transitstop m*
travel agency	*Reisebüro nt*
traveller's cheque	*Reisescheck m*
travel sickness	*Reisekrankheit f*
underground	*Untergrundbahn f, U-bahn f*
unleaded petrol	*bleifreies Benzin nt*
unlimited mileage	*unbegrenzte Kilometer mpl*
vaccination	*Impfung f*
vaccination certificate	*Impfschein m*
visa	*Visum nt*
waiting room	*Warteraum m*
wheelchair	*Rollstuhl m*
window	*Fenster nt*
window seat	*Fensterplatz m*

To help you translate business material from German, this glossary contains all the German words given as translations in the first section of the book and their translations in a business context. In addition, for the most common words translations of basic meanings are also provided.

Abbau *m quarrying; mining; reduction; breakdown*

Abbildung *f figure; diagram; reproduction*

abbrechen *to demolish; to abort; to escape; to stop*

Abbruch *m demolition; stopping*

Abendsitzung *f evening session*

Aberkennung *f derecognition*

abfahren *to leave; to (set) sail*

Abfahrt *f departure; exit*

Abfahrtstafel *f departures board*

Abfall *m waste; rubbish; garbage*

Abfallentsorgung *f waste management*

Abfallminimierung *f waste minimization*

Abfallprodukt *nt waste product*

Abfindung *f compensation*

abfliegen *to take off*

Abflug *m take-off; departure*

Abfluganzeige *f departures board*

Abflughalle *f departure lounge*

Abflugschalter *m check-in desk*

Abfluß *m outflow; outlet; drain*

Abfüllanlage *f bottling plant*

abgelegte Akte *f dead file*

abgeleiteter Bedarf *m derived demand*

abgesagt *cancelled; refused*

Abgrenzung *f demarcation*

abheben *to withdraw; to pick up; to take off*

Abhebung *f withdrawal*

abholen *to collect*

Abholgebühr *f collection rate; collection charge*

Abholung *f collection*

Abkommen *nt agreement*

Ablage *f file copy; filing*

Ablage *f* **für Ausgänge** *mpl out-tray*

Ablage *f* **für Eingänge** *mpl in-tray*

Ablage *f* **für unerledigte Arbeit** *pending tray*

ablagern *to deposit; to store; to dump*

Ablagesystem *nt filing system*

ablegen *to file; to store*

abmelden *log off/out*

sich abnutzen *to wear out; to depreciate*

Abnutzung *f wear and tear; depreciation*

Abraum *m spoil; slag*

Abrechnung(en) *f(pl) accounting; balancing; bill; deduction*

Abrechnungszeitraum *m accounting period*

abreisen *to leave; to check out*

Abreisezeit *f departure time; check-out time*

Abruf *m retrieval; request; call*

abrufen *to retrieve; to request delivery of*

absagen *to cancel; to refuse*

Absatz *m sales; paragraph*

Absatzanalyse *f sales analysis*

Absatzbericht *m sales report*

Absatzkosten *pl distribution costs*

Absatzmöglichkeit *f outlet; market*

Absatzplanung *f sales planning*

Absatzprognose *f sales forecast*

Absatzweg *m channel of distribution*

Absatzziffern *fpl sales figures*

Abschleppwagen *m breakdown van*

abschreiben *to write off; to copy; to deduct*

Abschreibung *f write-off; deduction; allowance*

Absichtserklärung *f letter of intent*

absolutes Versprechen *nt absolute undertaking*

Absorption *f absorption*

abstürzen *to fall; to crash*

Abteil *nt compartment*

Abteilung *f department; section*
Abteilung *f* **für Reklamationen** *complaints department*
Abteilungs- *departmental*
Abteilungsleiter(in) *m(f) department manager(ess); head of department*
Abweichung *f difference; variance; deviation*
abwerten *to devalue*
Abwertung *f devaluation*
abzielen auf *to target*
abzugsfähig *tax-deductible*
Adresse *f address*
Adressenliste *f mailing list*
Adressiermaschine *f addressing machine*
Aerosolspray *nt aerosol spray*
Affidavit *nt affidavit*
Agent *m agent*
Agentur *f agency*
aggressiv *aggressive; hard-hitting*
aggressive Verkaufsstrategie *f commando selling; hard sell*
aggressive Verkaufstaktik *f commando selling; hard sell*
Akademiker(in) *m(f) graduate*
Akkreditiv *nt letter of credit*
Aktenablage *f filing*
Aktendeckel *m folder*
Aktenhefter *m file*
Aktenschrank *m filing cabinet*
Aktie *f share*
voll eingezahlte Aktie *f fully-paid share*
Aktien *fpl shares; stock; equities*
Aktienbank *f joint-stock bank*
Aktienemission *f share issue; flotation*
Aktiengesellschaft *f* **(AG** *f)* *public limited company (plc); public company; joint-stock company*
Aktienindex *m share index*
Aktienkapital *nt share capital*
Aktienkurs *m share price*
Aktienmehrheit *f majority shareholding*
Aktienumschreibung *f transfer of shares*
Aktienzertifikat *nt share certificate*

Aktienzuteilung *f share allocation*
Aktion *f action*
Aktionär(in) *m(f) shareholder; stockholder*
Aktiva *pl assets*
Aktualisieren *nt update*
aktualisieren *to update*
Aktualisierung *f update*
Aktuar(in) *m(f) actuary*
Akzept *nt acceptance*
Akzeptant *m acceptor*
alleinstehende Anzeige *f solus*
Alleinverkaufsrecht *nt exclusivity*
Alleinvertreter(in) *m(f) sole agent*
Alleinvertretungsvertrag *m exclusive agency agreement*
Allgefahrenpolice *f all-risks policy*
allgemeine Abnutzung *f fair wear and tear*
allgemeine Lohnerhöhung *f across-the-board wage increase*
Allgemeines Zoll- und Handelsabkommen *nt* **(GATT)** *General Agreement on Tariffs and Trade (GATT)*
Allzweckraum *m utility room*
alphanumerisch *alphanumeric*
Amortisation *f amortization*
Amortisationszeit *f payback time*
amtsärztliches Zeugnis *nt medical certificate*
analog *analog*
Analog-Digital-Umsetzer *m* **(ADU** *m)* *A/D converter*
anbieten *to offer*
Anerkennung *f recognition*
Anfall *m accrual; yield; amount*
Anfangskurs *m opening price*
Anfangssteuersatz *m basic rate of tax*
anfechtbarer Vertrag *m voidable contract*
Angebot *nt bid; tender; offer*
Angebotspreis *m asking price; offer price*
Angebot *nt* **und Nachfrage** *f supply and demand*
Angeklagte(r) *f(m) defendant*
Angeld *nt earnest money*
angelernte Arbeitskraft *f semi-*

skilled worker

angemessene fair; appropriate

Angestellte(r) f(m) employee; white-collar worker

angewandte Forschung f applied research

angrenzende Zimmer ntpl connecting rooms

Anhang m codicil; appendix; rider

Ankunft f arrival

Ankunftsanzeige f arrivals board

Ankunftstafel f arrivals board

Anlage f plant; park; equipment; installation(s); conception; investment; capital

Anlagen fpl grounds; installations

Anlagenabschreibung f capital allowance

Anlageverzinsung f return on investments (ROI)

anlegen to invest; to draw up; to create; to dock

Anleihekapital nt debenture capital

anmelden to apply; to register; to log in/on

sich anmelden to check in; to register; to enrol

Annahme f acceptance

annullieren to cancel

Anreiz m incentive

Anreizsystem nt incentive scheme

Anruf m (phone) call

Anrufbeantworter m answering machine

anrufen to ring; to call; to telephone

Ansagetext m recorded message

Anschlag m keystroke; poster; placard; estimate

Anschluß m connection; extension; contact; power point; port

Ansprechzeit f response time

Anspruch m claim; right

Ansprüche mpl **geltend machen** to claim

anspruchsvoll up-market; (high-) quality

anstellen to employ; to turn on; to do

Anstellungsbedingungen fpl conditions of employment

Anteile mpl **in Fremdbesitz** m minority interest; minority shareholder

anteilmäßig pro rata; proportional; proportionate

Antidumpingzoll m anti-dumping duty

Antiqua f roman (type)

antizipierter Vertragsbruch m anticipatory breach

Antragsformular nt proposal form

Antragsteller(in) m(f) mover

Anwalt m, **Anwältin** f advocate; lawyer

Anwaltshonorar nt legal fees

Anwartschaftsrente f deferred annuity

Anwenderpaket nt application package; application software

Anwendung f application; use

Anwendungsentwicklung f application development

Anwerbungskampagne f recruitment drive

Anzahlung f depoit; down payment

(als) Anzahlung f (on) account

Anzeige f advertisement

Anzeigenblatt nt freesheet

Anzeigenetat m advertising budget

Anzeigenrabatt m advertising allowance

Anzeigenraum m advertising space

Anzeigentarif m advertising rates

Apparat m apparatus; appliance; telephone; extension (number)

Arbeit f work; labour

arbeiten to work

arbeitendes Kapital nt capital employed; working capital

Arbeiter(in) m(f) worker; blue-collar worker

Arbeitgeber(in) m(f) employer

Arbeitgeberanteil m employer's contribution

Arbeitgeberhaftpflicht f employer's liability

Arbeitgeberverband m employers' association

Arbeitnehmer(in) m(f) employee

Arbeitsbedingungen *fpl* *working conditions*
Arbeitsdiskette *f working disk*
arbeitseinkommen *nt earned income*
Arbeitserlaubnis *f work permit*
Arbeitsessen *nt business lunch; business dinner; lunch meeting; working lunch; working dinner*
Arbeitsfrühstück *nt breakfast meeting; working breakfast*
Arbeitsgericht *nt industrial tribunal*
Arbeitsgliederungsplan *m activity chart*
Arbeitsgruppe *f working group*
arbeitsintensiv *labour-intensive*
Arbeitskampfmaßnahmen *fpl industrial action*
Arbeitskräfte *fpl workforce; human resources*
Arbeitskräfteprognose *f manpower forecast*
arbeitslos *unemployed; redundant*
Arbeitslosigkeit *f unemployment*
Arbeitsmangel *m lack of work*
Arbeitsmarkt *m labour market*
Arbeitspensum *nt workload*
Arbeitsplatz *m workplace; work station*
Arbeitsplatzbeschreibung *f job description; job specification*
Arbeitsplatzbewertung *f job evaluation*
Arbeitsplatzverluste *mpl job losses*
Arbeitsrecht *nt employment law*
Arbeitsstreitigkeit *f industrial dispute; trade dispute*
Arbeitsstudie *f work study*
Arbeitsstunde *f man-hour*
Arbeitsteilung *f division of labour*
Arbeitsunfall *m industrial accident; occupational accident*
Arbeitsvermittlung *f employment agency; employment exchange; placement*
Arbeitsvertrag *m employment contract*
Arbeitswoche *f working week*
Arbeitszeit *f working hours*
Arbeitszeitstudie *f work measure-ment*

Architekt(in) *m(f) architect*
Archiv *nt archive; records department*
archivieren *to archive*
Artikel *m article; item*
Arzt *m*, **Ärztin** *f doctor*
ASCII(-Datei *f) ASCII (file)*
Assistent(in) *m(f) assistant*
assoziierte Mitgliedstaaten *mpl associated states*
Atmosphäre *f atmosphere*
Atomindustrie *f nuclear industry*
Atommüll *m nuclear waste*
Audio-Konferenzschaltung *f audio conferencing*
aufbauen *to construct; to build*
Aufbereitungsanlage *f processing plant*
Aufforderung *f appeal; request; demand*
auffüllen *to stock up; to fill up*
Aufgabe *f job; task; giving up*
aufgeben *to post; to place; to register; to give up*
aufgelaufene Kosten *pl accrued charges*
aufgelaufene Zinsen *mpl accrued interest*
aufgeschoben *deferred*
aufheben *to revoke; to abolish; to offset*
Aufheller *m optical brightener*
Aufkauf *m acquisition; buying up*
aufkaufen *to buy up; to buy out*
Auflage(nhöhe) *f circulation*
Auflegung *f flotation; issue*
hohe Auflösung *f high resolution*
Aufnahmestudio *nt recording studio*
aufnehmen *to record; to photograph; to admit; to absorb*
aufschieben *to put off; to defer*
aufsetzen *to draft; to land*
Aufsicht *f supervision; supervisor*
Aufsichtsbehörde *f regulator*
Aufsichtsratsmitglied *nt non-executive director*
Auftragsbearbeitung *f order processing*

Auftragsbuch *nt order book*
Auftragsnummer *f job number*
Aufwand *m expenditure*
Aufwertung *f revaluation; increase in value*
Aufzeichnung *f note; sketch; record*
augenfällig *conspicuous*
ausbauen *to upgrade; to convert; to elaborate*
ausbaufähig *upgradeable*
Ausbeutung *f exploitation; utilization*
Ausbildung *f education; training*
Ausbildungskurs *m training course*
Ausbildungsleiter(in) *m(f) training officer*
Ausdruck *m print-out; expression*
Ausfahrt *f exit; departure*
Ausfall *m breakdown; loss; stoppage*
Ausfallzeit *f downtime*
Ausfuhrgenehmigung *f export licence*
Ausgabe *f edition; issue; version; print-out*
Ausgabedaten *fpl output (data)*
Ausgaben *fpl expenses; expenditure; outgoings*
ausgeben *to spend; to pay out; to issue; to print out; to output; to dump*
ausgebucht *fully-booked*
ausgegebenes Kapital *nt issued capital*
ausgleichen *to balance; to settle; to compensate for*
Ausgleichslager *nt buffer stocks*
Aushilfspersonal *nt temporary staff*
Auskunft *f information; directory enquiries*
Auslage *f display; expense*
Ausland *nt abroad; foreign countries; foreigners*
Auslandsabsatz *m foreign sales*
Auslandsflug *m international flight*
Auslandsinvestition *f foreign investment*
Ausloben *nt hype*
ausloben *to hype; to offer as a prize*

ausprobieren *to try out; to test-drive*
ausschlaggebende Stimme *f casting vote*
ausschneiden und einfügen *cut and paste*
Außendienstleiter(in) *m(f) field sales manager*
Außenhandel *m overseas trade*
Außenministerium *nt Foreign Office*
außerbetriebliche Ausbildung *f off-the-job training*
außerbetrieblicher Wirtschaftsprüfer *m external auditor*
außergerichtlicher Vergleich *m out-of-court settlement*
außerordentliche Hauptversammlung *f* **(a.o.HV** *f) EGM (extraordinary general meeting)*
Aussperrung *f lock-out*
ausstehend *outstanding; owing; receivable*
ausstehende Gelder *ntpl monies due*
ausstellen *to display; to exhibit*
Aussteller(in) *m(f) exhibitor; issuer; drawer*
Ausstellungshalle *f exhibition hall*
Ausstellungsraum *m showroom*
Ausstellungszentrum *nt exhibition centre*
Ausstoß *m output*
Ausstrahlungseffekt *m halo effect*
Auswahl *f range; choice*
Ausweichplan *m contingency plan*
Auswertung *f evaluation; analysis; utilization*
Auswirkung *f impact; effect*
Auswirkung *f* **haben (auf** +*acc) to impact (on); to have an effect (on)*
Auszubildende(r) *f(m) apprentice; trainee*
Auto *nt car*
Autobahn *f motorway*
Automat *m machine; vending machine; dispenser*
automatischer Papiervorschub *m automatic document feeder*
automatisiert *automated*

Automatisierung *f automation*
Automobilindustrie *f car industry*
Autor(in) *m(f) author*
autorisiertes Aktienkapital *nt authorized capital*
Autotelefon *nt car phone*
Autoverleih *m car hire; car hire firm*
Azerty-Tastatur *f azerty keyboard*
Azubi *m/f apprentice; trainee*
Bad *nt bath; bathroom*
Badezimmer *nt bathroom*
Bahnhof *m railway station*
Bahnhofspolizei *f railway police*
Bahnhofsvorsteher(in) *m(f) station-master*
Bahnsteig *m platform*
Baisse *f fall; slump; bear market*
Baissemarkt *m falling market; bear market*
Baissespekulant *m short (seller); bear*
baisse-tendenziös *bearish*
Balkendiagramm *nt bar chart*
Balkon *m balcony*
Bandbreite *f bandwidth*
Bank *f bank*
Bankangestellte(r) *f(m) bank employee*
Bankauskunft *f banker's reference*
Bankdienstleistungen *fpl banking facilities/services*
Bankdirektor(in) *m(f) bank manager*
Bankeinlage *f bank deposit*
Bank *f* **für Internationalen Zahlungsausgleich (BIZ** *f) Bank for International Settlements (BIS)*
Bankgebühren *fpl bank charges*
Bankier *m banker*
Bankkonto *nt bank account*
Bankkredit *m bank loan*
Bankleitzahl *f sort code*
Banknote *f banknote*
Bankrott *m bankruptcy*
bankrott *bankrupt*
Bankrott machen *to go bankrupt*
Banktratte *f bank(er's) draft*
Bankwesen *nt banking*
Bar *f bar*

Baratterie *f barratry*
Barbestand *m cash-in-hand*
Bar-Code *m bar code*
Bar-Code-Leser *m bar code reader*
Bardividende *f cash bonus*
Bargeld *nt cash*
Bargeldkassenbuch *nt petty cash book*
bargeldlose Überweisung *f credit transfer*
Bargeldreserven *fpl cash reserves*
Barrister *m barrister*
Barscheck *m open cheque; uncrossed cheque*
Barwertrechnung *f discounted cash flow*
Barzahlung *f* **bei Lieferung** *cash on delivery (COD)*
Bau *m building*
Bauarbeiten *fpl construction*
Baubericht *m structural report*
Baudrate *f baud rate*
Baugenehmigung *f planning permission*
Bauindustrie *f construction industry*
Bauingenieur(in) *m(f) structural engineer*
Bauland *nt building land*
baulich einwandfrei *structurally sound*
bauliche Reparaturen *fpl structural repairs*
Bausparkasse *f building society*
Baustelle *f building site*
Bauteil *nt component*
Bauunternehmer(in) *m(f) builder*
Bearbeitungsgebühr *f handling charge*
Bedienung *f service charge*
bedingt *conditional*
bedingungslos *unconditional*
Beendigung *f completion*
Befehl *m order; command*
befördern *promote*
Beförderung *f promotion*
befreit von Mehrwertsteuer *f VAT-exempt; zero-rated*
Befreiungsklausel *f escape clause*
Befreiung *f* **von Doppelbesteuerung** *f double taxation relief*

begleichen to pay; to settle
Begünstigte(r) f(m) beneficiary
begutachten survey
behandeln to deal with; to treat
Behörde f authority; office
Beilage f insert; supplement; enclosure
beitragsfreie Rentenversicherung f non-contributory pension scheme
beitragspflichtige Rentenversicherung f contributory pension scheme
bekanntmachen to publicize; to announce; to publish
(be)laden load
Belästigung f nuisance
Beleg m voucher
Belletristik f poetry and fiction
Benachrichtigung f notification
Benutzer(in) m(f) user
benutzerfreundlich user-friendly
Benutzername m username
Benzin nt petrol
Berater(in) m(f) consultant
Beratung f consultancy; consultation
Beratungsunternehmen nt consultancy
berechnen to calculate; to estimate
Berechnung f calculation; estimation
Bereitstellung f appropriation
Bergbau m mining
Bergelohn m salvage
bergen salvage (money)
Bergung f salvage
Bergungskosten pl salvage costs
Bericht m report
Berichterstattung f coverage; reporting
berufliche Zufriedenheit f job satisfaction
Berufsausbildung f vocational training
Berufsberatung f vocational guidance
Berufsbezeichnung f job title
Berufsrisiko nt occupational hazard
Berufung f appeal
Berufung f einlegen to appeal

Berufungsgericht nt appeal court
Berufungskläger(in) m(f) appellant
berührungsempfindlich touch-sensitive
beschädigen to damage
beschädigt damaged
Beschaffung f procurement
Bescheid m notification; information
beschlagnahmen to impound
Beschluß m decision; resolution
beschränkte Haftung f limited liability
Beschwerde f grievance; complaint; appeal
Beschwerdeführer(in) m(f) complainant
Beschwerdeverfahren nt grievance procedure
Besetztzeichen nt engaged tone
Besitz m estate; property; possession
Besitzer(in) m(f) owner
Besoldungsordnung f salary scale
besondere Havarie f particular average loss
frei von besonderer Havarie free of particular average (FPA)
mit besonderer Havarie f with particular average (WPA)
besprechen to discuss; to review
Besprechung f meeting; discussion
Besprechungsraum m meeting room
Bestand m stock; lease
Bestandsaufnahme f **machen** to take stock
Bestandskontrolle f stock control; inventory control
Bestandsüberwachung f stock control; inventory control
bestätigen to confirm; to acknowledge
Bestätigung f confirmation; acknowledgement
bestellen to order
Bestellformular nt order form
Bestellnummer f order number
Bestellung f (purchase) order
besteuern to tax

frei Bestimmungsbahnhof *free to receiving station*
Bestimmungsort *m destination*
Bestseller *m bestseller*
besuchen *to visit; to attend*
Besucher(in) *m(f) visitor*
Besuchshäufigkeit *f call frequency*
Besuchsrhythmus *m calling cycle*
Beteiligungsgesellschaft *f associated company*
Betrieb *m operation; running; business; factory*
außer Betrieb *out of order; off stream; not in use*
in Betrieb *on stream; in operation; in use*
betriebliche Altersversorgung *f occupational pension scheme*
Betriebsausgabe(n) *f(pl) revenue expenditure*
Betriebsergebnisrechnung *f operating statement*
Betriebsführung *f management*
Betriebsgewinn *m operating profit*
Betriebsingenieur(in) *m(f) plant engineer*
betriebsinterne Ausbildung *f in-house training*
betriebsinterne Buchprüfung *f internal audit*
betriebsinterner Wirtschaftsprüfer *m internal auditor*
Betriebskapital *nt working capital*
Betriebskonto *nt trading account*
Betriebskosten *pl operating costs*
Betriebsrat *m works council*
Betriebsstörung *f stoppage*
Betriebssystem *nt operating system*
Betriebsunkosten *pl plant cost*
Betriebsvereinbarung *f collective agreement*
Betriebsvereinbarungen *fpl plant bargaining*
Betrug *m fraud; deceipt*
betrügen *to defraud; to deceive*
Bett *nt bed*
Beurteilungsgespräch *nt appraisal interview*
Beurteilungsmethode *f appraisal method*

bevollmächtiger Vertreter(in) *m(f) accredited agent*
Bevollmächtigte(r) *f(m) attorney*
nicht bevorrechtigter Gläubiger *m deferred creditor*
bevorrechtigte Stammaktien *fpl preferred ordinary shares*
sich bewerben (um) *to apply (for)*
Bewerber(in) *m(f) applicant*
Bewerbungsformular *nt application form*
Bewerbung(sschreiben *nt) f (letter of) application*
Bewertung *f assessment; evaluation*
bewohnt *occupied*
bezahlen *to pay (for)*
Bezahlung *f payment; settlement*
Bezahlung *f bei Auftragserteilung cash with order (cwo)*
Bezirksleiter(in) *m(f) area manager*
Bezogene(r) *f(m) drawee*
ohne Bezugsrecht *nt ex rights*
Bezugsrechtsemission *f rights issue*
bieten *to bid; to offer*
Big Bang *m Big Bang*
Bilanz *f balance (sheet); financial statement*
Bilanzaufstellung *f balance sheet*
Bilanzbuchhalter(in) *m(f) accountant*
Bilanzeinheit *f profit centre*
Bilanzierungsrichtlinien *fpl accounting standards*
bilateraler Handel *m bilateral trade*
bilaterales Abkommen *nt bilateral agreement*
Bildplatte *f videodisc*
Bildschirm *m screen*
Bildschirmgerät *nt VDU (visual display unit)*
Bildschirmtext *m Viewdata ®*
Bildunterschrift *f caption*
billig *cheap*
billiges Geld *nt cheap money; easy money*
Billigkeitsrecht *nt equity*
Billigladen *m discount store*
Billigtarif *m cheap rate*
Binärcode *m binary code*

binär-kompatibel *binary compatible*
Bindung *f commitment; relationship*
(Europäischer) Binnenmarkt *m single (European) market*
biologisch abbaubar *biodegradable*
Biosphäre *f biosphere*
Bit *nt bit*
bitten um *(+acc) to request; to ask for*
Blankokredit *m unsecured loan*
Blasenspeicher *m bubble memory*
bleifreies Benzin *nt unleaded petrol*
Blindtest *m blind test*
blockierte Währung *f blocked currency*
Bodensenkung *f subsidence*
bohren *to drill*
Bohrer *m drill*
Bonus *m bonus*
Bonuspackung *f bonus pack*
Bordkarte *f boarding pass*
Börse *f stock exchange; stock market*
Börsenhandelsperiode *f account*
Börsenkrach *m (stock market) crash*
Börsenmakler(in) *m(f) stockbroker*
börsennotierte Firma *f listed company*
Boulevardblatt *nt tabloid*
bpi (Bits *ntpl* **pro Inch** *m*) *bpi (bits per inch)*
bps (Bits *ntpl* **pro Sekunde** *f*) *bps (bits per second)*
brachliegendes Kapital *nt idle money*
Brainstorming *nt brainstorming (session)*
Branchenverzeichnis *nt Yellow Pages* ®
brandbeschädigt *fire-damaged*
Brauerei *f brewery*
Break-Even-Analyse *f break-even analysis*
Break-Even-Punkt *m break-even point*
Brennerei *f distillery*
Brennofen *m furnace*
Brief *m letter*
Briefmarke *f stamp*

Briefmarkenautomat *m stamp machine*
Briefpapier *nt note paper; stationery*
Briefumschlag *m envelope*
Briefwerbung *f mail shot*
Bruchschaden *m breakage*
Bruttogewinn *m gross profit*
Bruttoinlandsprodukt *nt* **(BIP** *nt*) *gross domestic product (GDP)*
Bruttosozialprodukt *nt* **(BSP** *nt*) *gross national product (GNP)*
Bruttoumsatz *m gross sales*
buchen *to reserve*
Bücher *ntpl books; accounts*
Buchführung *f book-keeping; accounting*
Buchführungssystem *nt accounting system*
Buchführungsverfahren *nt accounting procedures*
Buchhaltung *f accounts (department)*
Buchprüfung *f audit*
Buchrechte *ntpl book rights*
Buchung *f reservation*
Buchwert *m book value*
Budget *nt budget*
Bulletin Board *nt bulletin board*
Bummelstreik *m work-to-rule*
Bürge *m,* **Bürgin** *f guarantor*
Büro *nt office*
Büroangestellte(r) *f(m) office worker; clerk*
Büroartikel *mpl office supplies*
Bürogebäude *nt office block; office building*
Bürogeräte *ntpl office equipment*
Bürohilfe *f office junior*
Büroklammer *f paper clip*
Büroleiter(in) *m(f) office manager*
Büroraum *m office accommodation; office space*
Business-Klasse *f business class*
Byte *nt byte*
CAD *nt* **(rechnergestütztes Konstruieren** *nt*) *CAD (computer-assisted design)*
CAD/CAM *nt* **(rechnergestütztes Konstruieren** *nt/***rechnergestützte**

Fertigungssteuerung *f*) *CAD/CAM (computer-assisted design/ manufacture)*

CAL *nt* (**rechnergestütztes Lernen** *nt*) *CAL (computer-assisted learning)*

CAM *nt* (**rechnergestützte Fertigungssteuerung** *f*) *CAM (computer-assisted manufacture)*

Cash-flow *m* *cash flow*

Cash-flow Aufstellung *f* *cash-flow statement*

Caterer *m* *caterer*

CD *f* (**Compact-disc** *f*) *CD (compact disc)*

CERN *CERN (Conseil Européen pour la Recherche Nucléaire)*

Charge *f* *batch*

Charterflug *m* *charter flight*

Chartervertrag *m* *charter party*

Chef(in) *m(f)* *boss*

Chemiefabrik *f* *chemical plant*

chemische Industrie *f* *chemical industry*

Chip *m* *chip*

cif (**Kosten, Versicherung und Fracht inkl.**) *CIF (cost, insurance and freight)*

cif & c (**Kosten, Versicherung, Fracht und Provision inkl.**) *CIF & C (cost, insurance, freight and commission)*

cif & i (**Kosten, Versicherung, Fracht und Bankzinsen inkl.**) *CIF & I (cost, insurance, freight and interest)*

CIM *nt* (**rechnerintegrierte Fertigung** *f*) *CIM (computer input from microfilm)*

CIM (**computer input from microfilm**) *CIM (computer input from microfilm)*

Clearingbank *f* *clearing bank*

Clearingstelle *f* *clearing house*

Closed Shop *m* *closed shop*

Club-Klasse *f* *club class*

Code *m* *code*

Company Secretary *m* *company secretary*

Computer *m* *computer*

Computerabteilung *f* *computing department*

Computerfirma *f* *computer agency*

computergesteuert *computer-controlled*

computerisiert *computerized*

Computermodell *nt* *computer model*

Computerspiel *nt* *computer game*

Computersprache *f* *computer language*

Computerwissenschaft *f* *computing*

Container *m* *container*

Containerisierung *f* *containerization*

Containerschiff *nt* *container ship*

Control-Taste *f* *control key*

Copyright *nt* *copyright*

Corporate Identity *f* *corporate identity*

Cottage *nt* *cottage*

cpi (**Zeichen** *ntpl* **pro Inch** *m*) *cpi (characters per inch)*

CP/M *nt* *CP/M (control program/ monitor)*

CPM-Verfahren *nt* *CPM (critical path method)*

cps (**Zeichen** *ntpl* **pro Sekunde** *f*) *cps (characters per second)*

cps (**Zyklen** *mpl* **pro Sekunde** *f*) *cps (cycles per second)*

CPU *f* (**Zentraleinheit** *f*) *CPU (central processing unit)*

Cursor *m* *cursor*

cutten *to edit*

Dach *nt* *roof*

Dachboden *m* *attic; loft*

Dachfenster *nt* *skylight*

Darlehen *nt* *loan*

Darlehenskonto *nt* *loan account*

Darlehenszinssatz *m* *lending rate*

Datei *f* *file*

Dateiname *m* *filename*

Daten *ntpl* *data*

Datenbank *f* *databank; database*

Datenbankverwaltung *f* *database management*

Datenerfassung *f* *data capture*

Datensammlung *f* *data collection*

Datensatz *m* *record*

Datenschutzgesetz *nt* *data protec-*

tion law
Datensicherheit *f data security*
Datenverarbeitung *f* (**DV** *f*) *data processing (DP)*
Datum des Poststempels *nt date as postmark*
Dauerauftrag *m standing order*
Dauerton *m continuous tone; dialling tone*
Debatte *f debate*
Debetsaldo *m debit balance*
Decke *f blanket; ceiling; layer; surface; cover*
Deckladung *f deck cargo*
Deckung *f cover*
Deckungszusage *f cover note*
Defekt *m defect*
defekt *defective*
Defizit *nt deficit*
Deflation *f deflation*
deflationistisch *deflationary*
Degradierung *f degradation*
Delegation *f delegation*
delegieren *to delegate*
Delegierte(r) *f(m) delegate*
Delikt *nt tort*
Depot *nt depot*
derzeitiger Mieter *m sitting tenant*
Design *nt design; artwork*
Design Abteilung *f design department*
Designer(in) *m(f) designer*
Designteam *nt design team*
Desinflation *f disinflation*
desinvestieren *disinvest*
Desinvestition *f disinvestment*
Deskside-Computer *m deskside computer*
Desktop-Computer *m desktop computer*
Desktop-Kopierer *m desktop copier*
Desktop-Publishing *nt* (**DTP** *nt*) *desktop publishing (DTP)*
Detail *nt detail*
Devisen *fpl foreign exchange; foreign currency*
Devisenhandel *m foreign exchange (system)*
Devisenhändler(in) *m(f) foreign exchange dealer*

Devisenkontrolle *f exchange control*
Devisenmakler(in) *m(f) foreign exchange broker*
Devisenmarkt *m foreign exchange market*
Devisenterminkurs *m forward rate*
dezente Verkaufsmethode *f soft sell*
dezentralisiert *decentralized*
Diabetiker(in) *m(f) diabetic*
Diagnoseprogramm *nt diagnostic program*
Diagramm *nt diagram; chart*
Dialog *m dialogue*
Dia(positiv) *nt slide; transparency*
Diaprojektor *m slide projector*
Diebstahl *m theft*
Dienstjahre *ntpl years of service*
Dienstleistungsindustrie *f service industry; tertiary industry*
Dienstleistungssektor *m service sector; tertiary sector*
Dienstzeit *f office hours*
Diesel *nt diesel (fuel)*
Digital- *digital*
Digital-Analog-Umsetzer *m* (**DAU** *m*) *D/A converter*
Diktaphon ® *nt dictaphone* ®
Diktat *nt dictation*
diktieren *to dictate*
Schreiben *nt* **nach Diktiergerät** *nt audio-typing*
Direktabsatz *m direct marketing*
direkte Besteuerung *f direct taxation*
direkte Kosten *pl direct cost*
Direktive *f directive*
Direktlieferung *f drop shipment*
Direktor(in) *m(f) director*
Direktverkauf *m direct selling*
Direktzugriff *m direct access*
Diskette *f diskette*
Diskette *f* **mit doppelter Schreibdichte** *double-density diskette*
Diskette *f* **mit hoher Schreibdichte** *high-density diskette*
Diskettenkasten *m disk box*
Diskettenlaufwerk *nt disk drive*
Diskonthaus *nt discount house*

Diskontsatz *m bank rate*
Diskriminierung *f discrimination*
Diskussion *f discussion*
Diversifikation *f diversification*
diversifizieren *to diversify*
Dividende *f dividend*
ohne Dividende *f ex dividend*
nicht dividendenberechtigte Aktien *fpl B shares*
Dividendendeckung *f dividend cover*
docken *to dock*
Dockgebühren *fpl dock dues*
Dokument *nt document*
Dokumentarbericht *m documentary*
Dokumentarspiel *nt docudrama*
Dokumente *ntpl* **gegen Akzept** *nt documents against acceptance (D/A)*
Dokumente *ntpl* **gegen Zahlung** *f documents against payment (D/P)*
Dokumentenständer *m copy holder*
Dokumententratte *f documentary bill of exchange*
Dollarraum *m dollar area*
Dolmetscher(in) *m(f) interpreter*
Doppelbesteuerungsabkommen *nt double taxation agreement*
Doppelfenster *ntpl double glazing*
Doppelhaushälfte *f semidetached house*
doppelseitig *double-sided*
doppelseitige Anzeige *f double-page spread*
doppelte Leistung *f double indemnity*
Doppelzimmer *nt double room*
DOS *nt DOS*
Dow-Jones-Index *m Dow-Jones Average*
Dreharbeiten *fpl shooting*
Drehbank *f lathe*
die Dreiergruppe *f* **(G3** *f)* *Group of 3 (G3)*
Dritter *m third party*
Drucker *m printer*
Druckerei *f printer's*
Druckereigewerbe *nt printing industry*

DTP *nt* **(Desktop-Publishing** *nt)* *DTP (desktop publishing)*
dummes Terminal *nt dumb terminal*
Dump *m dump*
Dumping *nt dumping*
Duplikat *nt duplicate*
Durchbruch *m breakthrough*
durchgehender Zug *m through train*
Durchsatz *m throughput*
Durchschlag *m carbon copy*
durchschnittlich *average*
Durchschnittskosten *pl average cost*
Dusche *f shower (room)*
E/A *m* **(Eingabe/Ausgabe)** *I/O (input/output)*
EBU *f European Broadcasting Union (EBU)*
Echtzeit *f real time*
Eckzins *m base rate*
ECU *m* **(Europäische Währungseinheit** *m)* *ECU (European Currency Unit)*
editieren *to edit*
Effektenhandel *m dealing*
Effektenkaufabrechnung *f contract note*
EGA *m EGA (enhanced graphics adaptor)*
EG-Subvention *f EEC subsidy*
EG-Verordnungen *fpl EEC regulations*
eidesstattliche Erklärung *f affirmation; affidavit*
Eigenfinanzierung *f self-financing*
Eigenkapital *nt equity capital*
Eigentum *nt ownership; property*
Eigentumsrecht *nt right of ownership; copyright; freehold*
Eigentumsübertragung *f conveyancing*
Eigentumsurkunde *f documents of title*
Eignungsprüfung *f aptitude test*
Eilzustellung *f express delivery; special delivery*
Einbauten *mpl* **und Zubehör** *nt fixtures and fittings*
sich einchecken *to check in*

einfache Buchführung f single-entry bookkeeping
einfache Fahrkarte f one-way ticket
Einfahrzolltarif m import tariff
einfügen to insert
Einfuhrabgabe f import levy
Einführen nt importing
Einfuhrerklärung f customs entry
Einfuhrgenehmigung f import licence
Einfuhrkontingent nt import quota
Einführungsangebot nt introductory offer
Einführungskurs m induction course
Einfuhrverbot nt import ban
Einfuhrzoll m import duty
Eingabe f input
Eingabeaufforderung f prompt
Eingabedaten ntpl input (data)
Eingang m entrance
Eingangsfracht f freight inward
Eingangshalle f entrance hall; lobby
eingeben to enter; to input; to key in
eingefordertes Kapital nt called-up capital
eingefrorene Guthaben ntpl frozen assets
eingeschränkte Währung f restricted currency
eingeschriebene Sendung f recorded delivery
eingeschweißt shrink-wrapped
eingetragene Gesellschaft f registered company
eingetragener Gesellschaftssitz m registered office
eingetragenes Warenzeichen nt registered trademark
Einhaltung f compliance
Einheit f unit
Einheitssteuersatz m standard rate
einkalkulieren to allow for
einklagbar actionable
Einkommen nt income; earnings
Einkommenspolitik f incomes policy
Einkommenssteuer f income tax
Einkünfte fpl **aus Kapitalvermögen**

nt unearned income
einlegen to insert
einlösen to cash; to encash
einmaliges Verkaufsargument nt **(USP** m) unique selling point (USP)
Einnahmen fpl income; revenue; earnings
einrechnen to allow for
ein Angebot nt **einreichen für** (+acc) to tender for
einrücken to indent
Einsatzbesprechung f briefing
Einschaltquote f audience figures; viewing figures; ratings
einschätzen to assess; to evaluate; to estimate
Einschätzung f assessment; evaluation; estimation
Einschreiben nt registered post
Einschubgerät nt rack-mounted unit
Einschweißen nt shrink-wrapping
einschweißen to shrink-wrap
einseitiger Fehler m unilateral mistake
einspaltige Anzeige f single-column spread
Einspruch m **(gegen** +acc**)** appeal (against)
einstellen to recruit
Einstellung f recruitment
Einstellungsprämie f golden hello
Einstellungsuntersuchung f attitude survey
einstweilige Verfügung f injunction; writ
Eintauschwert m trade-in price
Eintragung f entry
Einwanderungsstelle f immigration
einzahlen to deposit; to pay in; to bank
Einzahlung f deposit
Einzahlungsbeleg m deposit slip
Einzahlungsbestätigung f deposit receipt
einzeilige Darstellung f single-line display
Einzelblattzuführung f single-sheet feed
Einzelfahrkarte f single (ticket)

Einzelhandelspreis m retail price; cover price

Einzelhandelspreisindex m retail price index

Einzelhandelsverkaufstelle f retail outlet

Einzelhaus nt detached house

Einzelkaufmann m, **Einzelkauffrau** f sole trader

Einzeltarifverhandlungen fpl individual bargaining

Einzelzimmer nt single room

Einzugsauftrag m direct debit

Eisen nt **und Stahl** m iron and steel

elektrische Leitungen fpl wiring

elektrische Schreibmaschine f electric typewriter

Elektrizität f electricity

Elektrogeräte ntpl electrical goods

Elektronik f electronics

elektronische Post f electronic mail

elektronischer Zahlungsverkehr m **(EZV** m**)** electronic funds transfer (EFT)

Embargo nt embargo

Emission f emission; issue

Emissionsbank f underwriter(s)

Emission f **von Gratisaktien** fpl bonus issue

Empfang m reception

Empfänger m addressee; receiver; consignee

Empfangsbereich m reception area

Empfangsbestätigung f acknowledgement (slip)

Empfangschef m receptionist

Empfangsdame f receptionist

Empfangshalle f foyer

Empfehlung f recommendation; testimonial

Empfehlungszettel m compliments slip

Endbahnhof m terminus

Endbenutzer m end user

Endlospapier nt continuous stationery

Endprodukt nt end product

Endstation f terminus

Endverbraucher(in) m(f) end user

energiebewußte Politik f energy-

saving policy

Energieindustrie f power industry

Energiesparen nt energy conservation

energiesparende Vorrichtung f energy-saving device

Engpaß m bottleneck

Entertainment nt corporate entertaining

entgiften to decontaminate

Entgiftung f decontamination

entlassen to dismiss; to lay off; to make redundant; to retire

Entlassung f dismissal; laying off; redundancy; retirement

Entlassungsabfindung f redundancy payment

Entlassungsvereinbarung f redundancy agreement

Entschädigung f compensation; indemnity

entscheiden to decide; to rule; to adjudicate

Entscheidung f decision; ruling; verdict

Entscheidungfindung f decision-making

entwanzen to debug

entwerfen to design; to draft

entwickeln to develop

Entwicklung f development

Entwicklungsgebiet nt development area

Entwicklungskosten pl development costs

Entwurf m draft; blueprint

Equity-Recht nt equity

Erbbauzins m ground rent

Erbschaftssteuer f death duty

Erdgeschoß nt ground floor

Erdölindustrie f oil industry

Erfahrung f experience

erfinden to invent

Erfinder(in) m(f) inventor

Erfindung f invention

Erfolg m success

Erfolgsautor(in) m(f) bestselling author

Erfrischungen fpl refreshments

Erfüllung f fulfilment; performance;

execution; discharge
Ergonomie f ergonomics
erhalten to conserve; to preserve;
to obtain
Erhaltung f conservation; preserva-
tion
erhöhter Schaden m aggravated
damages
sich erholen to recover; to rally
Erkerfenster nt bay window
Erlöschen nt des Risikos cessation
of risk
erreichen to reach
Ersatz m substitute; replacement
erscheinen to appear
Erscheinungsdatum nt publication
date
Ersparnisse fpl savings
Ertrag m output; outturn; return;
profit
Erträge fpl aus Anlagen fpl invest-
ment income
Ertragsanteil m royalty on sales
Ertragskonto nt revenue account
Ertragssteuer f profits tax
Erwachsenenliteratur f adult litera-
ture
Erwachsenenpublikum nt adult
audience
Erwärmung f der Erdatmosphäre f
global warming
erwarteter Gewinn m anticipated
profit
Erzählliteratur f fiction
ESPRIT ESPRIT (European Strategic
Programme for R & D in Informa-
tion Technology)
Essensmarke f luncheon voucher
Eßzimmer nt dining room
EURATOM f EURATOM
EUREKA (Europäische Behörde f für
Koordinierung in der Forschung)
EUREKA (European Research Co-
ordination Agency)
Eurobond m Eurobond
Eurobond Emission f Eurobond is-
sue
Eurocheque m Eurocheque
Eurocheque-Karte f Eurocheque
card

Eurodollar m eurodollar
Euroeinlage f Eurodeposit
Eurogeldmarkt m Eurocurrency
market
Eurokrat(in) m(f) Eurocrat
Euromarkt m Euromarket
Europa nt Europe
Europaabgeordnete(r) f(m) Euro
MP
Europäer(in) m(f) European
europäisch European
Europäische Bank f für **Wiederauf-
bau und Entwicklung** European
Bank for Reconstruction and De-
velopment (EBRD)
Europäische Freihandelsassoziation
f (**EFTA** f) European Free Trade
Association (EFTA)
Europäische Freihandelszone f
(**EFTA** f) European Free Trade
Area (EFTA)
Europäische Gemeinschaft f (**EG** f)
European Community (EC)
Europäische Gemeinschaft f für
Kohle und Stahl (EGKS f) Euro-
pean Coal and Steel Community
(ECSC)
Europäische Investitionsbank f (**EIB**
f) European Investment Bank
(EIB)
Europäische Kommission f Euro-
pean Commission
Europäische Rechnungseinheit f
European Unit of Account (EUA)
Europäischer Entwicklungsfonds m
(**EEF** m) European Development
Fund (EDF)
Europäischer Fonds m für **regionale
Entwicklung (EFRE** m) European
Regional Development Fund
(ERDF)
Europäischer Fonds m für **wäh-
rungspolitische Zusammenarbeit**
(**EFWZ** m) European Monetary
Cooperation Fund (EMCF)
Europäischer Gerichtshof m Euro-
pean Court of Justice (ECJ)
Europäische Richtlinie f European
directive
Europäischer Sozialfonds m (**ESF**

m) *European Social Fund (ESF)*
Europäischer Steuergerichtshof *m European Court of Auditors*
Europäisches Parlament *nt European Parliament (EP)*
Europäisches Währungssystem *nt* **(EWS** *nt*) *European Monetary System (EMS)*
Europäische Union *f European Union*
Europäische Währungseinheit *m* **(ECU** *m*) *European Currency Unit (ECU)*
Europäische Währungsunion *f* **(EWU** *f*) *European Monetary Union (EMU)*
Europäische Weltraumorganisation *f* **(EWO** *f*) *European Space Agency (ESA)*
Europäische Wirtschaftsgemeinschaft *f* **(EWG** *f*) *European Economic Community (EEC)*
europäisieren *Europeanize*
Europalette *f Europallet*
Europapaß *m EEC passport*
Europarat *m Council of Europe*
europaweiter Werbespot *m euro-ad*
Europfund *nt Eurosterling*
europhil *europhile*
Europort *m Europort*
Eurostrand *m Eurobeach*
Eurotunnel *m Eurotunnel*
Eurowährung *f Eurocurrency*
Eurowährungskredit *m Eurocurrency credit*
Eventualität *f eventuality; contingency*
Eventualverbindlichkeiten *fpl contingent liabilities*
Exemplar *nt copy*
existenzgefährdende Konkurrenz *f cut-throat competition*
Exklusivbericht *m exclusive (story)*
Expertensystem *nt expert system*
Export(e) *m(pl) export(s)*
Exportabteilung *f export department*
Exporteur *m exporter*
Exporthandel *m export trade*
Exporthaus *nt export house*

exportieren *to export*
Exportkampagne *f export drive*
Exportkreditabteilung *f export credit department*
Exportmanager(in) *m(f) export manager*
Exportrechnung *f export invoice*
Exportvertreter(in) *m(f) export agent*
Extragebühr *f supplement*
Extrapolation *f extrapolation*
Fabrik *f factory; plant; works*
Fabrikarbeiter(in) *m(f) factory worker*
Fabrikbesetzung *f work-in*
Facharbeiter(in) *m(f) skilled worker*
Fachpresse *f trade press*
Factoring *nt factoring*
Fähre *f ferry*
Fahrer(in) *m(f) driver*
Fahrkarte *f ticket*
Fahrkartenschalter *m ticket office*
fahrlässig *negligent*
Fahrlässigkeit *f negligence*
Fahrstuhl *m lift*
fakturieren *to bill; to invoice*
Fall *m case*
fallen *to fall; to slump*
Fälligkeitsdatum *nt due date*
Fallstudie *f case study*
falsche Darstellung *f misrepresentation*
FAO *f* **(UNO-Organisation** *f* **für Ernährung und Landwirtschaft)** *FAO (Food and Agricultural Organization)*
f.a.q. (frei Längsseite Kai *m*) *FAQ (free alongside quay)*
Farbband *nt ribbon*
Farbgrafikadapter *m CGA (colour graphics adaptor)*
Farbstoff *m colouring*
f.a.s. (frei Längsseite Schiff *nt*) *FAS (free alongside ship)*
Faseroptik *f fibre optics*
faseroptisch *fibre-optic*
Fassade *f facade*
Fax *nt fax; fax machine*
faxen *to fax*
Faxnummer *f fax number*

FCKW *m* **(Fluorochlorkohlenwasserstoff** *m*) *CFC (chlorofluorocarbon)*

f.D. **(frei Dock** *nt*) *FD (free delivered at dock)*

Feedback *nt feedback*

fehlend *lacking; absent; missing*

Fehler *m mistake; flaw*

fehlerhaft *flawed; defective; incorrect*

Fehlermeldung *f error message*

fehlertolerant *fault-tolerant*

Feinfahrantrieb *m microdrive*

Fenster *nt window*

Fensterplatz *m window seat*

Fensterumschlag *m window envelope*

Ferienarbeit *f holiday job*

Ferngespräch *nt long-distance call; trunk call*

Fernmeldewesen *nt telecommunications*

Fernschreiber *m telex machine*

Fernsehanstalt *f TV company*

Fernsehapparat *m television*

Fernsehen *nt television; broadcasting*

Fernsehfilm *m television film*

Fernsehgesellschaft *f television company*

Fernsehmonitor *m television monitor*

Fernsehserie *f television series; television serial*

Fernsehtelefon *nt videophone*

Fernsprechauskunft *f directory enquiries*

Fertigstellung *f completion*

Fertigungskontrolle *f production control*

Fertigungsstraße *f production line*

Fertigwaren *fpl finished goods; manufactured goods*

feste Anlagen *fpl fixed assets*

feste Buchung *f firm booking*

Festplatte *f hard disk*

Festpreis *m firm price*

Festpreisvertrag *m fixed-price contract*

feststehende Belastung *f fixed charge*

Fettdruck *m bold type*

Feuerleiter *f fire escape*

Feuerschaden *m fire damage*

Feuertreppe *f fire escape*

Feuer- und Diebstahlversicherungspolice *f fire and theft insurance policy*

Feuerversicherung *f fire insurance*

Feuerwehr *f fire brigade*

Film *m film*

Film Crew *f film crew*

filmen *to film*

Filmindustrie *f film industry*

Filmrechte *ntpl film rights*

Filter *m filter*

Filzstift *m felt pen*

Finanzamt *nt tax office*

Finanzbeamter *m*, **Finanzbeamtin** *f tax collector*

Finanzbuchhalter(in) *m(f) financial accountant*

Finanzdirektor(in) *m(f) finance director*

finanzielles Risiko *nt financial risk*

Finanzier *m financier*

Finanzierung *f financing*

Finanz(ierungs)gesellschaft *f finance company*

Finanzmanagement *nt financial management*

Finanzwelt *f (world of) finance*

Finanzwesen *nt finance*

fingierte Entlassung *f constructive dismissal*

Firma *f firm; company*

Firmenimage *nt corporate image*

Firmenlogo *nt corporate logo*

Firmenwerbung *f corporate advertising*

Fiskalpolitik *f fiscal policy*

Fixkosten *pl fixed cost*

Flachordner *m box file*

flau *sluggish*

Fließband *nt assembly line; production line; conveyor belt*

Fließbandproduktion *f assembly-line production; flow-line production*

Flip-Chart *f flip-chart*

Floppy-Disk *f floppy disk*

Flug *m* *flight*
Flughafen *m* *airport*
Flughafenbus *m* *airport bus*
Flughafengebühr *f* *airport tax*
Flughafenpolizei *f* *airport police*
Flugpassagier *m* *airline passenger*
Flugsteig *m* *gate*
Flugtüchtigkeit *f* *airworthiness*
Flugzeit *f* *flying time*
Flugzeug *nt* *aeroplane*
Flur *m* *corridor; hall; landing*
Flußdiagramm *nt* *flowchart*
f.o.b. (frei an Bord *m***)** *FOB (free on board)*
Föderalismus *m* *federalism*
föderalistisch *federal*
Föderation *f* *federation*
Fön ® *m* *hairdryer*
Fördergebiet *nt* *development area*
Förderung *f* *support; promotion; development; mining*
Forderungen *fpl* *accounts receivable; demands; claims*
Formalität *f* *formality*
Formatieren *nt* *formatting*
formatieren *to format*
Formatvorlage *f* *style sheet*
Forscher(in) *m(f)* *researcher*
Forschung *f* *research*
Forschungsabteilung *f* *research department*
Forschungsbudget *nt* *research budget*
Forschungslabor *nt* *research laboratory*
Forschungsprogramm *nt* *research programme*
Forschung *f* **und Entwicklung** *f* **(FuE** *f***)** *research and development (R & D)*
fortschreiten *to progress*
Fortschritt *m* *progress*
Fortsetzung *f* *sequel*
in Fortsetzungen *fpl* **veröffentlichen** *serialize*
fossile Brennstoffe *mpl* *fossil fuels*
Fotoapparat *m* *camera*
Fotogelegenheit *f* *photo opportunity*
Fotograf(in) *m(f)* *photographer*

Fotografie *f* *photograph*
fotografieren *to photograph*
Fotokopie *f* *photocopy*
fotokopieren *to photocopy*
Fotokopiergerät *nt* *photocopier*
Fototermin *m* *photo call*
Fracht *f* *freight; cargo*
Frachtbrief *m* *consignment note*
frachtfrei *carriage free or paid*
Fracht *f* **gegen Nachnahme** *f* *freight forward*
Frachtkosten *pl* *freight charges*
Frachtversicherung *f* *freight insurance*
Fracht *f* **zahlt Empfänger** *carriage forward*
Franchise *f* *franchise*
Franchisegeber(in) *m(f)* *franchiser*
Franchisenehmer(in) *m(f)* *franchisee*
Franchisevereinbarung *f* *franchise agreement*
Frankiermaschine *f* *franking machine*
frankierter Rückumschlag *m* *sae (stamped addressed envelope)*
franko *franco*
freiberuflich *freelance*
freiberuflich arbeiten *to (work) freelance*
freiberuflicher Mitarbeiter *m*, **freiberufliche Mitarbeiterin** *f* *freelance worker*
freie Marktwirtschaft *f* *free enterprise*
freier Grundbesitz *m* *freehold property*
freie Stelle *f* *vacancy*
Freihandel *m* *free trade*
Freistellung *f* *release*
Freistellungsklausel *f* *exemption clause*
Freiumschlag *m* *prepaid envelope*
freiwillige Abgaben *fpl* *voluntary deductions*
freiwillige Liquidation *f* *voluntary liquidation*
Freizeichnungsklausel *f* *exclusion clause*
Fremdenverkehrsindustrie *f* *tourist*

industry

Fremdkapital nt loan capital

Fremdwährungswechsel m foreign bill

Friseur(-euse) m(f) hairdresser

Frist f deadline

Fristablauf m deadline; lapse of time

Frühstück nt breakfast

Frühwarnsystem nt early warning system

FT-Index m FT Index

FuE f (**Forschung** f **und Entwicklung** f) R & D (research and development)

führen to lead; to run; to manage; to stock

Führerschein m driving licence

Führungsebene f managerial level

Führungskraft f executive

Führungsstil m management style

Fundament nt foundations

Fundbüro nt lost property office

die Fünfergruppe f (**G5** f) Group of 5 (G5)

Funkrufempfänger m pager

Funktelefon nt cellular telephone

Funktionstaste f function key; hot key

Fusion f merger; amalgamation; fusion

fusionieren to merge; to amalgamate

Fußboden m floor

Gag m gag; gimmick

galoppierende Inflation f galloping inflation; hyperinflation

Gang m corridor; aisle; progress

in Gang in progress

Garage f garage

Garant m guarantor; underwriter

Garantie f guarantee; warranty

garantieren to guarantee; to underwrite

Garbage m garbage

Garten m garden

Gas nt gas

Gästebuch nt register; visitor's book

Gattungssachen fpl unascertained goods

Gebäude nt building

Gebäudeversicherung f house insurance; buildings insurance

geben to give; to allow

Gebrauchsgüter ntpl consumer durables

gebraucht used; second-hand

Gebühr f fee

Gefälligkeitswechsel m accommodation bill

Gefälligkeitszeichner(in) m(f) accommodation party

Gegenakkreditiv nt back-to-back loan

Gegenangebot nt counter-offer

Gegenanspruch m counter-claim

Gegenleistung f quid pro quo

Gegenpartei f other party; opposing party

Gegensprechanlage f intercom

gegenzeichnen to countersign

Gehalt nt salary; pay

Gehaltserhöhung f salary increase

Gehaltsüberprüfung f salary review

Geheimnummer f ex-directory number

geistiges Eigentum nt intellectual property

Gelbe Seiten fpl Yellow Pages ®

Geld nt money

Geldautomat m cash dispenser; automated telling machine (ATM)

Geldautomatenkarte f cash card

Gelderwerb m money-making

Geldgeber(in) m(f) backer

Geldmarkt m money market

Geldschein m banknote

Geldvolumen nt money supply

Gelegenheitsarbeiter(in) m(f) casual worker

gelenkte Wirtschaft f controlled economy

Gemeindesteuer f council tax

Gemeinkosten pl overheads

gemeinnützig non-profit-making

gemeinsame Agrarpolitik f (**GAP** f) Common Agricultural Policy (CAP)

Gemeinsamer Außenzoll m Com-

mon External Tariff (CET)

Gemeinsamer Fonds *m* **für Bedarfsgüter** *Common Fund for Commodities (CFC)*

gemeinsamer Irrtum *m* *common mistake*

Gemeinsamer Markt *m* *Common Market*

gemeinsames Konto *nt* *joint account*

gemeinsam genutzte Systemeinrichtung *f* *shared facility*

Gemeinschaftsbesitz *m* *collective ownership*

Gemeinschaftshaushalt *m* *Common Budget*

Gemeinschaftsrecht *nt* *community law*

gemischte Lebensversicherung *f* *endowment assurance*

gemischte Wirtschaftsform *f* *mixed economy*

Generaldirektion *f* **(DG)** *Directorate General (DG)*

Generalstaatsanwalt *m* *public prosecutor; district attorney*

Generalstreik *m* *general strike*

Genossenschaft *f* *cooperative*

Gentleman's Agreement *nt* *gentleman's agreement*

Gepäckaufbewahrung *f* *left-luggage office or counter*

Gepäckausgabe *f* *baggage reclaim*

Gepäckfach *nt* *luggage locker*

Gepäckträger *m* *porter*

geplant *projected*

geplantes Veralten *nt* *built-in obsolescence*

geräumig *spacious*

gerecht *just; legitimate; equitable*

Gericht *nt* *court; dish*

gerichtliche Entscheidung *f* *adjudication*

Gerichtsbarkeit *f* *jurisdiction*

Gerichtshof *m* *law court*

Gerichtsurteil *nt* *judgement*

Geschädigte(r) *f(m)* *claimant*

Geschäft *nt* *business; shop; deal*

Geschäftsadresse *f* *business address*

Geschäfts(brief)papier *nt* *letterhead paper*

Geschäftsfrau *f* *businesswoman*

geschäftsführender Ausschuß *m* *management committee*

Geschäftsführer(in) *m(f)* *manager(ess); general manager(ess); managing director (MD)*

Geschäftsjahr *nt* *financial year*

Geschäftskostenaufteilung *f* *allocation of overheads*

Geschäftsleute *pl* *business people*

Geschäftsmann *m* *businessman*

Geschäftsordnungspunkt *m* *point of order*

Geschäftsreise *f* *business trip*

Geschenkgutschein *m* *gift voucher*

Geschwindigkeitsbegrenzung *f* *speed limit*

Gesellschaft *f* *company; firm*

Gesellschafter(in) *m(f)* *partner*

Gesellschaft *f* **mit beschränkter Haftung (GmbH** *f***)** *private limited company*

Gesellschaftsgründung *f* *flotation*

Gesellschaftsraum *m* *lounge*

Gesellschaftsrecht *nt* *company law*

Gesellschaftsvertrag *m* *articles of association*

Gesetz *nt* *law; statute*

Gesetzeslücke *f* *loophole*

Gesetzgebung *f* *legislation*

gesetzlich *lawful; legal; statutory*

gesetzliche Abzüge *mpl* *statutory deductions*

gesichert *secure(d)*

gesicherter Gläubiger *m* *secured creditor*

gestaffelte Sozialrente *f* *graduated pension*

Gesundheit *f* *health*

Gesundheitsrisiko *nt* *health hazard*

gesungener Werbeslogan *m* *jingle*

getönte Scheibe(n) *f(pl)* *tinted window*

Gewährleistung *f* *guarantee; warranty*

Gewahrsamsinhaber(in) *m(f)* *bailee*

gewerblich *industrial; commercial*

Gewerkschaft *f* *trade union*

gewerkschaftliche Vertrauensperson f shop steward
gewerkschaftlich organisierter Streik m official strike
Gewerkschaftsabkommen nt trade union agreement
Gewerkschaftsbeitrag m union dues
Gewinn m earnings; profit; gain; prize
Gewinnaufschlag m mark-up; profit margin
Gewinnbeteiligung f profit-sharing
Gewinnbeteiligungsplan m profit-sharing scheme
gewinnbringend money-making; profitable
Gewinn m **je Aktie** f earnings per share
Gewinnschwellen-Diagramm nt break-even chart
Gewinnspanne f profit margin
Gewinn-und-Verlustrechnung f income and expenditure account; profit and loss account
Gewinnverteilungskonto nt appropriation account
Gewohnheitsrecht nt common law
Gießerei f foundry
giftig toxic
Giftigkeit f toxicity
Gigabyte nt gigabyte
Gigaflops pl gigaflops
GIGO GIGO (garbage in garbage out)
Girokonto nt current account
Gläubiger(in) m(f) creditor
gleichberechtigt single status
gleicher Lohn m equal pay
Gleichheit f equality
Gleitzeit f flexitime
Globalpolice f comprehensive policy
Goldreserven fpl gold reserves
Goldstandard m gold standard
graphische Darstellung f graphics
Gratisaktie f bonus share
Grenzkosten pl marginal cost(s)
grobe Schätzung f rough estimate; guesstimate

Großanzeigenwerbung f display advertising
Großbuchstabe m capital letter
Größenvorteile mpl economies of scale
Großhandelspreis m trade price
Großraumbüro nt open-plan office
Großrechner m mainframe
großzügiges Abfindungsversprechen nt **für den Fall einer Übernahme** golden parachute
grün green
Grundlohn m basic wage
Grundsatz m standard; principle
Grundstoffe mpl primary products
Grundstückserschließung f property development
Grundstückserschließungsunternehmen nt property developer
Grundstücksverwalter(in) m(f) property manager
Grundstücksverwaltung f property management
Gründungsbericht m statutory report
Gründungsversammlung f statutory meeting
grünes Pfund nt green pound
grüne Versicherungskarte f green card
Gut nt property; estate
Gutachten nt survey
Gutachter(in) m(f) surveyor
gut ausgestattet fully-equipped
Güter ntpl goods; freight
Güter ntpl **des täglichen Bedarfs** m convenience goods
Güterkraftverkehr m road haulage
Güterzug m freight train; goods train
gutgläubig bona fide; trusting
Guthaben nt credit
gutschreiben to credit
Gutschrift f credit note
Gutsverwalter(in) m(f) estate manager
Hab nt **und Gut** nt goods and chattels
Hacken nt hacking
Hafenanlagen fpl dock(s)

Hafengebühren *fpl harbour dues*
haftbar *liable*
Haftbefehl *m warrant*
Haftpflichtversicherung *f third-party insurance; liability insurance*
Haftung *f liability*
Haftungsfreistellungsklausel *f indemnity clause*
halbautomatisch *semi-automated*
halbjährlich *half-yearly*
Halbpension *f half board*
Halle *f hall*
Haltbarkeitsdatum *nt sell-by date*
Handel *m commerce; trade*
handeln mit *to deal in*
Handelsbank *f commercial bank*
Handelsbilanz *f balance of trade*
Handelsdelegation *f trade mission*
Handelskammer *f Chamber of Commerce*
Handelsmesse *f trade fair*
Handelsministerium *nt Board of Trade; Department of Commerce*
Handelsrecht *nt commercial law*
Handelsschiff *nt merchantman*
Handelsschranke *f trade barrier*
Handelsvertreterversammlung *f sales meeting*
Handelsware *f merchandise*
Handgepäck *nt hand luggage*
handgeschrieben *handwritten*
Händler(in) *m(f) dealer*
Händlerrabatt *m trade discount*
Hängemappe *f suspension file*
Hardware *f hardware*
harter ECU *m hard ECU*
harte Währung *f hard currency*
Hauptbuch *nt ledger*
Hauptredner(in) *m(f) keynote speaker*
Hauptsendezeit *f prime time*
Hauptspeicher *m main memory*
Haus *nt house*
Haushalt *m budget; household; housekeeping*
Haushaltskontrolle *f budgetary control*
Haushaltsperiode *f budget period*
Haushaltsplan *m budget*
den Haushaltsplan *m* **aufstellen** *to budget*
Hausierer(in) *m(f) door-to-door salesman/woman*
hausinterne Mitteilung *f internal memo*
Hausmarke *f own brand; proprietary brand*
Hausratversicherung *f (home) contents insurance*
Hausse *f boom; bull market*
haussierend *bullish*
Hausstil *m house style*
Havarie *f average*
Havarie-Grosse-Schaden *m general average loss*
Havarieklausel *f average clause*
Hefter *m stapler*
Heimarbeiter(in) *m(f) homeworker*
Heizkörper *m radiator*
herausgeben *to issue; to publish; to edit*
Herbizid *nt herbicide*
Herkunftsland *nt country of origin*
herstellen *to manufacture*
Hersteller *m manufacturer*
Herstellung *f manufacture; manufacturing*
Herstellungskosten *pl manufacturing costs*
Herstellungssektor *m manufacturing sector*
Herstellungszyklus *m manufacturing cycle*
Hilfe-Menü *nt help menu*
Hilfsmittel *nt aid*
Hilfsprogramme *ntpl utility software*
Hinterleger(in) *m(f) bailor*
Hinterlegungsstelle *f depository*
hochauflösend *high resolution*
Hochglanzmagazin *nt glossy magazine*
Hochkonjunktur *f boom*
Höchsttarif *m peak rate*
höchstzulässige Produktionsausschußquote *f acceptable quality level*
Hoch- und Tiefbau *m civil engineering*
Höhe *f* **des Lagerbestands** *m stock level*

höhere Gewalt *f act of God*
höhere-Gewalt-Klausel *f force majeure clause*
Holdinggesellschaft *f holding company*
Holzindustrie *f timber industry*
Honorar *nt fees*
Honorar *nt* **für Gutachten** *nt survey fee*
horizontale Integration *f horizontal integration*
Hotel *nt hotel*
Hotel- und Gaststättengewerbe *nt catering (industry)*
HS Nummer *f HS number*
Human Relations *pl human relations*
Hybridsystem *nt hybrid system*
Hypothek *f mortgage*
hypothekarisch belasten *to mortgage*
Hypothekengläubiger(in) *m(f) mortgagee*
Hypothek *f* **mit Lebensversicherung** *f endowment mortgage*
Ikon *nt icon*
illegal *illegal; illegally*
Illegalität *f illegality*
Illustration *f illustration*
Image *nt image*
Immobilie *f property*
Immobilien *fpl real estate; properties*
Immobilienmakler(in) *m(f) estate agent*
Immobilienmarkt *m property market*
Impfschein *m vaccination certificate*
Impfung *f vaccination*
Import(e) *m(pl) import(s)*
Importabgabe *f import surcharge*
Importeur *m importer*
Import-Export-Handel *m import-export*
importieren *to import*
Impulskauf *m impulse purchase*
Impulskaufen *nt impulse buying*
Incoterms *pl Incoterms*
Indemnitätsbrief *m letter of indemnity*

indirekte Besteuerung *f indirect taxation*
indirekte Nachfrage *f indirect demand*
Indossant *m endorser*
Indossat *m endorsee*
indossieren *to endorse*
Induktion *f induction*
Industrie *f industry*
Industriedesign *nt industrial design*
Industriegebiet *nt industrial estate*
Industrielle(r) *f(m) industrialist*
industrielle Kapazität *f industrial capacity*
Industrieprodukte *ntpl industrial goods*
Industriespionage *f industrial espionage*
industrieweite Abmachung *f industry-wide agreement*
Inflation *f inflation*
inflationsbereinigte Bilanzierung *f current cost accounting*
Informatik *f informatics; information technology; computing; computer science*
Informatiker(in) *m(f) computer scientist*
Informationsabruf *m information retrieval*
Informationsindustrie *f information industry*
Informationstechnik *f IT (information technology)*
Infrastruktur *f infrastructure*
Inhaber(in) *m(f) owner; holder; bearer*
Inhaber(in) *m(f)* **eines Europapasses** *EEC passport-holder*
Inhaberobligation *f bearer bond*
Inhaberwechsel *m bearer bill*
Inhaltsvermerk *m docket*
Inhaltsverzeichnis *nt directory*
Inkassobank *f collecting bank*
Inkassobüro *nt debt collection agency*
Inklusivpreis *m all-in price; all-in rate*
Inkompetenz *f incompetence; inefficiency*

Inkrafttreten *nt* **der Kündigung** *f* termination date
Inland- *home; domestic; inland*
Inlandsabsatz *m* domestic sales; home sales
Inlandsflug *m* domestic flight
Innenausstatter(in) *m(f)* interior decorator
Innenausstattung *f* interior decoration
innerbetriebliche Ausbildung *f* on-the-job training
Innere *nt* interior
innergemeinschaftlicher Handel *m* intra-community trade
Innovation *f* innovation
innovativ innovative
inoffizieller Markt *m* unofficial market
Insektizid *nt* insecticide
Inserent(in) *m(f)* advertiser
Insiderhandel *m* insider dealing
Insolvenz *f* insolvency
installieren to install
instruieren to brief
Instruktionen *fpl* instructions; brief
integriertes Buchführungspaket *nt* integrated accounting package
Integrierte Verschmutzungskontrolle *f* Integrated Pollution Control (IPC)
intelligentes Terminal *nt* intelligent terminal
Intensivtest *m* soak test
internationale Abteilung *f* international division
Internationale Arbeitsorganisation *f* (IAO *f*) International Labour Organization (ILO)
Internationale Atomenergie-Organisation *f* (IAEO *f*) International Atomic Energy Agency (IAEA)
Internationale Bank *f* **für Wiederaufbau und Entwicklung** (IBRD *f*) International Bank for Reconstruction and Development (IBRD)
Internationale Entwicklungsorganisation *f* International Develop-

ment Association (IDA)
Internationale Fernmelde-Union *f* (IFU *f*) International Telecommunications Union (ITU)
Internationale Finanz-Corporation *f* (IFC *f*) International Finance Corporation (IFC)
Internationale Handelskammer *f* (IHK *f*) International Chamber of Commerce (ICC)
Internationale Handelsorganisation *f* International Trade Organization (ITO)
internationaler Antwortschein *m* international reply coupon
Internationaler Fonds *m* **für Agrarentwicklung** International Fund for Agricultural Development (IFAD)
Internationaler Gerichtshof *m* (IGH *m*) International Court of Justice (ICJ)
Internationaler Währungsfonds *m* (IWF *m*) International Monetary Fund (IMF)
internationales Recht *nt* international law
Inventar *nt* inventory
Inventur *f* stocktaking
investieren (in) to invest (in)
Investition *f* investment
Investitionsplan *m* capital budget
Investitionszuschuß *m* investment grant
Investmentbank *f* investment bank
Investmentfonds *m* unit trust
Investmentgesellschaft *f* investment company
Investmenttrust *m* investment trust
Investor(in) *m(f)* investor
ISBN *f* ISBN (international standard book number)
Jahresbericht *m* annual report; annual return
Jahreszinssatz *m* annual percentage rate (APR)
jährliche Zahlung *f* annuity
JHV *f* (**Jahreshauptversammlung** *f*) AGM (annual general meeting)
Joint-venture *nt* joint venture

Journal *nt daybook*
Journalist(in) *m(f) journalist*
Joystick *m joystick*
Jugendliteratur *f literature for young people*
junges Publikum *nt young audience*
juristische Person *f corporation*
Just-in-time Produktion *f just-in-time manufacturing*
Justizminister *m minister of justice; Attorney-General*
Kabelfernsehen *nt cable television*
ab Kai *m ex dock*
Kalkulation *f calculation; costing*
Kalkulationstabelle *f spreadsheet*
Kalkulator(in) *m(f) cost accountant*
Kamera *f film camera*
Kameramann *m cameraman*
Kamin *m fireplace; chimney*
Kanalisation *f mains sewage*
Kanaltunnel *m Channel Tunnel*
Kapital *nt capital*
Kapitalanlage *f capital investment*
Kapitalaufwand *m capital expenditure*
Kapitalbildung *f capital formation*
Kapitalertragssteuer *f capital gains tax (CGT)*
Kapitalgewinn *m capital gains*
Kapitalgüter *ntpl capital goods*
kapitalintensiv *capital-intensive*
Kapitalkosten *pl capital charges*
Kapitalstruktur *f capital structure*
Kapitalverkehr *m capital movement*
Kapitalverkehrsbilanz *f capital account*
Kapitalverkehrssteuer *f capital transfer tax*
Kapitalvermögen *nt capital assets*
Kapitalverzinsung *f return on capital*
Kargo *m cargo*
Karte *f map; card*
Kartei *f card index*
Kartell *nt cartel*
Kartellamt *nt monopolies commission*
Kartellgesetzgebung *f anti-trust legislation*
Kartentelefon *nt cardphone*

Karton *m carton*
in Kartons verpackt *cartonned*
Kassapreis *m spot price*
Kasse *f tin; cashdesk; check-out*
Kassenbestand *m balance in hand*
Kassenbuch *nt cashbook*
Kassenkonto *nt cash account*
Kassette *f cassette; cartridge*
Kassettenrecorder *m cassette player*
Kassierer(in) *m(f) cashier*
Katalog *m catalogue*
kaufen *to buy*
Käufer(in) *m(f) buyer*
Käufermarkt *m buyer's market*
Kaufoption *f call option*
Kaufpreis *m purchase price*
Kaufübernahme *f durch das Management management buyout*
Kaufverhalten *nt buying behaviour*
Kaufvertrag *m contract of sale*
Kaufvertrag *m unter Eigentumsvorbehalt m conditional sale agreement*
Kaution *f bail; fidelity bond*
Keller *m cellar*
Kennung *f answer-back code*
Keramikfabrik *f pottery*
Kettenladen *m chain store*
KI *f (künstliche Intelligenz f) AI (artificial intelligence)*
Kilobyte *nt kilobyte*
Kinderbuch *nt children's book*
Kino *nt cinema*
Kiste *f crate*
Kläger(in) *m(f) complainant; plaintiff*
Klappentext *m blurb*
Klausel *f clause*
Klebeumbruch *m paste-up*
Kleinanzeigen *fpl classified advertisements*
Kleingedrucktes *nt small print*
Klient(in) *m(f) client; principal*
Klimaanlage *f air conditioning*
klimatisiert *air-conditioned*
Kodizill *nt codicil*
kollaboratives Projekt *nt collaborative project*
kollationieren *to collate*

kommerziell *commercial*
Kommission *f commission*
Kommissionswaren *fpl goods on consignment*
Kommunikationskanäle *mpl channels of communication*
Komödie *f comedy; theatre*
kompatibel *compatible*
nicht kompatibel *incompatible*
Kompromiß *m compromise*
einen Kompromiß *m* **schließen** *to compromise*
Konferenz *f conference*
Konferenzräumlichkeiten *fpl conference facilities*
Konferenzsaal *m conference hall*
Konferenzschaltung *f conference call*
Konferenzzentrum *nt conference centre*
Konferenzzimmer *nt conference room*
Konglomerat *nt conglomerate*
Konjunkturrückgang *m slowdown in the economy*
Konkurrenz *f competition*
konkurrenzfähiger Preis *m competitive price*
Konkurshandlung *f act of bankruptcy*
Konkursschuldner(in) *m(f) bankrupt*
Konkursverwalter(in) *m(f) official receiver*
Konkursverwaltung *f receivership*
Konnossement *nt bill of lading*
Konservenfabrik *f cannery*
Konsole *f console*
konsolidierte Bilanz *f consolidated balance sheet*
Konsolidierung *f consolidation*
Konsols *mpl consols*
Konsortium *nt consortium*
konstruieren *to construct; to construe; to devise*
Konsulatsfaktur *f consular invoice*
Konsultation *f consultation*
Konsumdenken *nt consumerism*
Konsumgüter *ntpl consumer goods*
Kontaktversuch *m attempt to make contact*

Kontinent *m Continent*
kontinental *continental*
Konto *nt account*
Kontoauszug *m bank statement; statement of account*
Konto *m* **mit hohem Zinssatz** *m high-interest account*
Kontonummer *f account number*
Kontostand *m balance*
Kontrollgruppe *f control group*
Kontrollsystem *nt control system*
Kontroverse *f dispute*
konvertierbarer Anleihestock *m convertible loan stock*
konvertierbare Währung *f convertible currency*
frei konvertierbare Währung *f free currency*
nicht-konvertierbare Währung *f non-convertible currency*
Konzept *nt concept*
Konzernabschluß *m consolidated accounts*
Konzession *f concession; franchise*
Konzession *f* **entziehen** *disenfranchise*
Konzessionär(in) *m(f) concessionaire*
konzessionieren *to franchise*
konzessionierter Alkoholhandel *m licensed trade*
Kopfhörer *mpl headphones*
Kopfjäger(in) *m(f) headhunter*
Kopie *f copy*
kopieren *to copy*
Kopierladen *m copy shop*
Kopierpapier *nt copy paper*
Kopierschutzstecker *m dongle*
Körperschaftssteuer *f corporation tax*
Korrekturband *nt correction ribbon/tape*
Korrekturflüssigkeit *f correcting fluid*
Korrespondenzqualität *f letter quality*
korrumpieren *to corrupt*
Korrumpierung *f corruption*
korrupt *corrupt*
Kosten *pl cost(s); expenses; outlay*

kosten *to cost*
Kosten *pl* **berechnen** *to cost*
kostendeckend arbeiten *to break even*
Kostenkontrolle *f cost control*
Kostennutzenanalyse *f cost-benefit analysis*
Kosten *pl* **pro Arbeitskraft pro Jahr** *man-year costs*
Kosten *pl* **pro Einheit** *f unit cost*
Kostenrechnung *f cost accounting*
Kostenrentabilität *f cost-effectiveness*
kostentreibende Inflation *f cost-push inflation*
Kosten *pl* **und Fracht** *f cost and freight (C & F)*
Kostenvoranschlag *m estimate; quotation; quote*
kostenwirksam *cost-effective*
Kraftfahrzeugversicherung *f car insurance; motor insurance*
Krankengeld *nt sick pay*
Krankenhaus *nt hospital*
Krankenversicherung *f medical insurance; health insurance*
Krankenwagen *m ambulance*
Kreativabteilung *f creative department*
Kredit *m credit; loan*
Kreditaufnahme *f borrowing*
Kredit *m* **aufnehmen** *to borrow*
Kreditauskunft *f trade reference*
Kreditauskunftei *f credit agency*
Kreditbeschränkung *f credit squeeze*
Kreditgrenze *f credit limit*
Kreditkarte *f credit card*
Kreditkonto *nt credit account*
Kreditkontrolle *f credit control*
Kreditmöglichkeiten *fpl credit facilities*
Kreditnehmer(in) *m(f) borrower*
Kreditsaldo *m credit balance*
Kreditwürdigkeit *f creditworthiness*
Kreisdiagramm *nt pie chart*
Krisenmanagement *nt crisis management*
kritische Pfadanalyse *f critical path analysis*

Küche *f kitchen*
Kulanzzahlung *f ex gratia payment*
Kunde *m,* **Kundin** *f customer; client; account*
Kundenbetreuer(in) *m(f) account executive*
Kundendienst *m customer services department; after-sales service*
Kundendienstabteilung *f customer services department*
Kundenkredit *m customer credit*
Kundenprofil *nt customer profile*
kundenspezifisch *custom-built*
kundenspezifische Software *f bespoke software*
Kundenwerber(in) *m(f) canvasser; advertiser*
Kundenwerbung *f canvassing*
Kündigung *f* **eines Arbeitsvertrages** *m termination of employment*
Kündigungsfrist *f notice*
Kündigungsschutz *m security of tenure*
künstlich *man-made; artificial*
künstliche Intelligenz *f (KI f) artificial intelligence (AI)*
Kurier *m courier*
Kurierdienst *m courier service*
kursiv *italic*
kursive Antiqua *f sloped roman*
Kurzarbeit *f short time*
kürzen *to cut back*
Kurzfilm *m short film*
kurzfristig *short-term*
kurzfristiger Schatzwechsel *m treasury bill*
kurzfristige Verbindlichkeiten *fpl current liabilities*
Kurzläufer *mpl shorts*
Kürzung *f cutback*
Kybernetik *f cybernetics*
Labor *nt laboratory*
Laborleiter(in) *m(f) laboratory manager*
Labortechniker(in) *m(f) laboratory technician*
Ladedock *nt loading dock*
laden *to load; to download; to boot (up)*
Ladeplatz *m loading bay*

Ladeschein *m certificate of shipment*
Ladeverzeichnis *nt ship's manifest*
Ladung *f load(ing); shipment*
Lagebericht *m status report*
auf Lager *nt in stock*
Lagerbestand *m stock*
Lagercode *m stock code*
Lagerfachkarte *f bin card/tag*
Lagerhalter(in) *m(f) stock controller*
Lagerhaltung *f stock management*
Lager(haus) *nt warehouse*
Lagerkapazität *f warehouse capacity*
Lagerkontrolle *f stock control*
Lagerkosten *pl warehousing costs*
Lagerliste *f stocklist*
Lagerschein *m warrant*
Lagerumschlag *m stock turnover*
LAN *nt LAN (local area network)*
lancieren *to launch*
Lancierung *f launch*
Land *nt land*
landen *to land*
Landkarte *f map*
Landung *f landing*
Landwirtschaft *f agribusiness*
landwirtschaftlich genutztes Grundstück *nt agricultural land*
langfristig *long-term*
Laptop *m laptop*
Lärmbelästigung *f noise pollution*
Laserdrucker *m laser printer*
Laserplatte *f laser disk*
Lastschriftanzeige *f debit note*
Lastwagen *m lorry; truck*
Laufbahnentwicklung *f career development*
laufende Kosten *pl running costs*
Laufwerk *nt drive*
Laufwerk *nt für Worm worm drive*
Laufzeit *f run time; term; operational life; period*
Laufzeit *f eines Kredits credit period*
Lautsprecheranlage *f PA system*
LCD *nt LCD (liquid crystal display)*
Lebenserwartung *f life expectancy*
Lebenshaltungskostenindex *m cost of living index*

Lebenslauf *m CV (curriculum vitae)*
Lebensstandard *m standard of living*
Lebensstil *m lifestyle*
Lebensversicherung *f life insurance*
Lebensversicherung *f auf den Todesfall m whole-life insurance*
Lebensversicherungspolice *f endowment policy*
Leck *nt leakage*
Leerlaufkapazität *f idle capacity*
Leerlaufzeit *f idle time*
Leertaste *f space bar*
Legalität *f legality*
Lehre *f apprenticeship*
Leibrente *f life annuity*
Leichtindustrie *f light industry*
leicht liquidierbares Vermögen *nt near-money*
leihen *to lend; to loan*
sich *(dat)* **leihen** *to borrow*
Leinwand *f screen*
Leistungsbesprechung *f performance review*
Leistungsbeurteilung *f appraisal*
Leistungsbewertung *f evaluation*
leistungsbezogener Lohn *m performance-related pay*
Leistungsfähigkeit *f efficiency*
Leistungslohnsatz *m piece rate*
Leistungslohnsystem *nt payment-by-results system*
Leistungstest *m proficiency test*
Leistungszulage *f merit pay*
leiten *to manage; to lead; to conduct*
leitender Angestellter *m,* **leitende Angestellte** *f line manager*
leitender Direktor *m,* **leitende Direktorin** *f executive director*
leitendes Personal *nt managerial staff*
Leiter(in) *m(f)* **der Finanzabteilung** *m(f) financial controller*
Leiter(in) *m(f)* **der Forschungsabteilung** *f research manager*
Leiter(in) *m(f)* **für Marktentwicklung** *f market development manager*
Leitung *f management; running;*

pipe; wire
Leitz-Ordner ® *m lever arch file*
Leserzahlen *fpl audience figures; number of readers*
letzte Zahlungsaufforderung *f final demand*
Licht *nt light*
Lichtstift *m light pen*
Lieferant(in) *m(f) supplier*
lieferfähiger Zustand *m deliverable state*
liefern *to deliver*
Lieferpreis *m delivered price*
Lieferschein *m delivery note*
Lieferung *f delivery*
Lieferverzögerung *f late delivery*
Lieferwagen *m van*
Lieferzeit *f delivery time; lead time*
Liegegeld *nt demurrage*
Liegewagenplatz *m couchette*
Liegezeit *f lay days*
Linienflug *m scheduled flight*
linksbündig ausrichten *to justify left*
Liquidation *f liquidation; winding up*
Liquidationsquote *f liquidity ratio*
Liquidationswert *m break-up value*
Liquidator *m liquidator*
liquidieren *to liquidate; to wind up*
Liquidität *f liquidity*
Listenpreis *m list price*
literarischer Agent *m literary agent*
Lizenzabkommen *nt licensing agreement*
LKW-Transportunternehmen *nt trucking company*
Lloyd's Seeversicherungszertifikat *nt Lloyd's Certificate of Marine Insurance*
Locher *m paper punch*
Lockangebot *nt loss leader*
Logik *f logic*
Logo *nt logo*
Lohn *m salary; wage*
Lohngefälle *nt wage differential*
Lohnkosten *pl labour costs*
Lohnliste *f payroll*
Lohnnebenleistungen *fpl fringe benefit*
Lohnpolitik *f wages policy*

Lohn-Preis-Spirale *f wage-price spiral*
Lohnschwellenvereinbarung *f threshold agreement*
Lohnsteuer *f income tax*
Lohnstopp *m wage freeze*
Lohnstreifen *m pay slip*
Lokopreis *m spot price*
Los *nt batch*
löschen *to delete; to erase*
Luftfahrtindustrie *f aeronautical industry*
Luftfracht *f air freight; air cargo*
Luftfrachtbrief *m air consignment note; air waybill*
Luftkissenboot *nt hovercraft*
Luftpost *f airmail*
Luftverschmutzung *f air pollution*
Luxussteuer *f luxury tax*
Magnetband *nt magnetic tape*
Magnetplatte *f magnetic disk*
Mahnung *f reminder*
Mailbox *f mailbox*
Makler(in) *m(f) broker; jobber*
Maklerbüro *nt estate agency*
Maklergebühr *f brokerage*
Makroökonomie *f macroeconomics*
Management *nt management*
Management *nt durch Krisen fpl management by crisis*
Management-Infor›DH‹ma›DH‹tions-System *nt (MIS nt) man›DH‹age›DH‹ment information system (MIS)*
Managementkurs *m management course*
Management Team *nt management team*
Manager(in) *m(f) manager(ess)*
Manager(in) *m(f) für Marktentwicklung f market development manager*
Manager(in) *m(f) für neue Kunden new business manager*
Mandat *nt mandate*
Mängelausschluß *m caveat emptor*
Manifest *nt manifest*
Mansarde *f attic room*
Mantelfirma *f shell company*
Marginalmarkt *m fringe market*

Marke *f brand*
Markenakzeptanz *f brand acceptance*
Markenartikel *mpl proprietary goods*
Markenbewußtsein *nt brand awareness*
Markenimage *nt brand image*
Markentreue *f brand loyalty*
Marketing *nt marketing; marketing department*
Marketing-Direktor(in) *m(f) marketing director*
Marketing-Informationen *fpl marketing intelligence*
Marketing-Kampagne *f marketing campaign*
Marketing-Konzept *nt marketing concept*
Marketing-Manager(in) *m(f) marketing manager*
Marketing-Mix *nt marketing mix*
Marketing-Plan *m marketing plan*
Marketing-Strategie *f marketing strategy*
Markt *m market*
Marktanalyse *f market analysis*
Marktanteil *m market share*
Marktbedarf *m market demand*
Marktdurchdringung *f market penetration*
Marktentwicklung *f market trends*
Marktforschung *f market research*
Marktführer *m market leader*
marktgängig *marketable*
Marktkräfte *fpl market forces*
Marktlücke *f gap in the market; niche*
Marktmanipulation *f market rigging*
Marktpotential *nt market potential*
Marktpreis *m market price*
Marktprofil *nt market profile*
Markttest *m market test; market trial*
Marktwert *m market value*
Marktwirtschaft *f market economy*
Maschine *f machine*
Maschinen *fpl machines; plant*
maschinengeschrieben *typewritten*
Maschinenhalle *f machine shop*

maschinenlesbar *machine-readable*
maschinenunterstützte Übersetzung *f MAT (machine-assisted translation)*
Maschinist(in) *m(f) machinist*
für die Massen *fpl mass-market*
Massenartikel *mpl mass-produced items*
Massenfrachtgut *nt bulk cargo*
für den Massenmarkt *m mass-market; down-market*
Massenmedien *ntpl mass media*
Massenproduktion *f mass production*
Maßstab *m standard; scale; benchmark*
Material *nt materials*
Matrixdrucker *m dot matrix printer*
Mauer *f (outside) wall*
Maus *f mouse*
MdEP *nt (Mitglied nt des Europäischen Parlaments) MEP (Member of the European Parliament)*
Medien *ntpl media*
Medienanalyse *f media analysis*
Medienforschung *f media research*
Medieninteresse *nt media interest*
Medienplaner(in) *m(f) media planner*
Megabyte *nt (MB) megabyte (Mb)*
Mehrbenutzersystem *nt multi-user system*
Mehrfachpackung *f im Einführungsangebot nt banded pack*
Mehrheitsbeteiligung *f majority shareholding $*
Mehrwertsteuerbefreiung *f zero-rating*
Mengeneinkauf *m bulk buying*
Mengenrabatt *m quantity discount; volume discount*
Menü *nt menu*
Merchandising *nt merchandising*
Merchant Bank *f merchant bank*
Merchant Banker *m merchant banker*
Merkmal *nt feature*
Messe *f trade fair*
Metallurgie *f metallurgy*
Microfiche-Leser *m microfiche read-*

er
Miete *f rent*
mieten *to hire; to rent*
Mieter(in) *m(f) tenant*
Mietpreis *m hire price*
Mietverhältnis *nt tenancy*
Mietvertrag *m contract of hire*
Mikrochip *m microchip*
Mikrocomputer *m microcomputer*
Mikrofiche *m or nt microfiche*
Mikrofilm *m microfilm*
Mikrofilm-Leser *m microfilm reader*
Mikrofon *nt microphone*
Mikrometer *nt micrometer*
Mikroökonomie *f microeconomics*
Mikroprozessor *m* (**MP** *m*) *microprocessor (MP)*
Mikrosekunde *f microsecond*
Millisekunde *f millisecond*
Minderheitsaktionär(in) *m(f) minority shareholder*
Minderheitsbeteiligung *f minority shareholding*
minderwertig *substandard*
Mindesbestellung *f minimum order*
Mindestlohn *m minimum wage*
minimieren *to minimize*
Ministerrat *m Council of Ministers*
mips (**Millionen Anweisungen** *fpl* **pro Sekunde** *f*) *mips (millions of intructions per second)*
Mischen *nt mixing; blending; merge*
mischen *to mix; to blend; to merge*
MIS *nt* (**Management-Informationssystem** *nt*) *MIS (management information system)*
Miteigentum *nt co-ownership*
Mitgliedstaat *m Member State*
Mitteilung *f memorandum*
mittelmäßig *mid-market*
mittleres Management *nt middle management*
mobiles Datensystem *nt mobile data system*
Mobilität *f* **der Arbeitskräfte** *fpl mobility of labour*
möbliert *furnished*
Modeindustrie *f fashion industry*

Modell *nt model; mock-up*
Modem *nt modem*
modern *modern; up-to-date*
modernisieren *to modernize*
Modul *nt module*
monatlich *monthly*
Monatsrate *f monthly instalment*
Monatszeitschrift *f monthly (magazine)*
Monetarismus *m monetarism*
Monetarist(in) *m(f) monetarist*
Monitor *m monitor*
Monopol *nt monopoly*
Montagewerk *nt assembly plant*
Monteur(in) *m(f) fitter*
Moratorium *nt moratorium*
Morgen *m morning; acre*
Morgensitzung *f morning session*
Motivation *f motivation*
motivieren *to motivate*
Müllbeseitigung *f waste disposal*
Mülldeponie *f rubbish dump; garbage dump*
Multitasking *nt multi-tasking*
Münzfernsprecher *m payphone*
Musikindustrie *f music industry*
Muster *nt sample*
Muttergesellschaft *f parent company*
Mutterschaftsgeld *nt maternity benefit*
Mutterschaftsurlaub *m maternity leave*
mutwilliger Schaden *m malicious damage*
MwSt *f* (**Mehrwertsteuer** *f*) *VAT (value-added tax)*
Nachbar(in) *m(f) neighbour*
Nachbestellung *f repeat order*
Nachfaßbesuch *m follow-up call*
Nachfassen *nt follow-up*
nachfassen *to follow up*
Nachfrage *f demand*
Nachfrageinflation *f demand-pull inflation*
Nachfragemarkt *m growth market*
Nachfragemonopol *nt monopsony*
Nachfrageverlagerung *f shift in demand*
Nachfragevorausschau *f demand*

forecasting

Nachmittagssitzung *f afternoon session*

per Nachnahme *f cash on delivery (COD)*

Nachschlagewerk *nt reference book*

Nachspeise *f supper*

nachstehend *undermentionned*

Nachtisch *m supper*

Nachtportier *m night porter*

Nachtsafe *m night safe*

Nachtschicht *f night shift*

Nachzahlung *f back pay*

Nahrungsmittelindustrie *f food industry*

Nahrungsmittelverarbeitung *f food processing*

Nanosekunde *f nanosecond*

natürliche Personalreduzierung *f natural wastage*

natürliche Ressourcen *fpl natural resources*

Nebenanschluß *m extension*

nebeneinanderliegend *adjacent*

Nebenkosten *pl incidental expenses*

Nebenprodukt *nt by-product; spin-off*

negoziierende Bank *f negotiating bank*

nennen *to name; to call; to quote*

Nennwert *m denomination; par value*

Nettogewinn *m net profit*

Nettolohn *m net pay; take-home pay*

Nettoverlust *m net loss*

Netzwerk *nt network*

neu *new; recent*

Neuerer *m innovator*

neu für alt *new for old*

Neugier weckende Werbung *f teaser*

neu laden *to reboot*

Neuverteilung *f reallocation*

Niche-Marketing *nt niche marketing*

Nichtanerkennung *f repudiation*

Nichtangabe *f non-disclosure*

Nichtannahme *f non-acceptance*

Nichterfüllung *f non-performance*

Nichterscheinen *nt am Arbeitsplatz*

m absenteeism

nichtig *void*

Nichtlieferung *f non-delivery*

Nichtraucherabteil *nt non-smoking compartment*

Nichtraucherzimmer *nt non-smoking room*

nichtschuldige Partei *f innocent party*

Nichtzahlung *f non-payment*

Niederhaltung *f von Löhnen mpl wage restraint*

Niederlassung *f branch; registered office; setting up*

Norm *f norm; standard*

Notausgang *m emergency exit; fire exit*

Notenbank *f central bank*

Notiz *f note*

Notruftelefon *nt emergency telephone*

null und nichtig *null and void*

Nummernkonto *nt numbered account*

Nutzlast *f payload*

obengennant *above-mentioned*

im oberen Stock *m upstairs*

Obligation *f obligation; debenture*

obligatorisch *obligatory; mandatory*

öffentliche Arbeiten *fpl public works*

öffentliche Dienstleistungen *fpl public services; utilities*

öffentlicher Feiertag *m bank holiday*

öffentlicher Sektor *m public sector*

Öffentlichkeit *f public; the general public*

off-line *off line; off-line*

Ökologe *m,* **Ökologin** *f ecologist*

Ökologie *f ecology*

ökologisch *ecological*

Öl *nt oil*

Oligopol *nt oligopoly*

on-line *on line; on-line*

Optimum *nt optimum*

Option *f option*

optischer Klarschriftleser *m optical character reader*

optische Zeichenerkennung *f* **(OCR)** *optical character recognition (OCR)*

Organisation *f organization; housekeeping*

Organisation *f* **der arabischen erdölexportierenden Länder (OAPEC** *f***)** *Organization of Arab Petroleum Exporting Countries (OAPEC)*

Organisation *f* **der erdölexportierenden Länder (OPEC** *f***)** *Organization of Petroleum Exporting Countries (OPEC)*

Organisation *f* **für industrielle Entwicklung der Vereinten Nationen (UNIDO** *f***)** *UN Industrial Development Organization (UNIDO)*

Organisation *f* **für wirtschaftliche Zusammenarbeit und Entwicklung (OECD** *f***)** *Organization for Economic Cooperation and Devel- opment (OECD)*

Organisationsplan *m organization chart*

Ortsgespräch *nt local call*

Output *nt output*

Overheadprojektor *m overhead projector*

ozonfreundlich *ozone-friendly*

ozonsicher *ozone-safe*

Pachtbesitz *m leasehold (property)*

pachten *to lease*

Pachtvertrag *m lease*

Päckchen *nt parcel; package*

Paket *nt parcel; package; pack; packet; bundle*

Paketpost *f parcel post*

Paketschnürmaschine *f packet tying machine*

Palette *f pallet*

palettieren *to palletize*

palettierte Kartons *mpl palletized cartons*

Palettisierung *f palletization*

pan-europäisch *pan-European*

Panne *f breakdown*

Panoramafenster *nt picture window*

Papiergeld *nt paper money*

papierloses Büro *nt paperless office*

Papierschneidemaschine *f guillotine*

Papiervorschub *m form feeder*

Paragraph *m paragraph; article*

Parameter *m parameter*

über pari *above par*

unter pari *below par*

Parkhaus *nt multi-storey car park*

Parkmöglichkeiten *fpl parking facilities*

Parkplatz *m car park; parking space*

Partnerschaft *f partnership*

Passiva *pl liabilities*

passive Handelsbilanz *f adverse trade balance*

Paßkontrolle *f passport control*

Paßwort *nt password*

Patent *nt patent*

Patentamt *nt patent office*

patentieren lassen *to patent*

Patentrechte *ntpl patent rights*

Patenturkunde *f letters patent*

Pauschalpolice *f blanket policy*

Pauschalregulierung *f lump sum settlement*

Pauschalsatz *m flat rate*

PC *m* **(Personalcomputer)** *PC (personal computer)*

Pendelflugdienst *m shuttle service*

Pensionierung *f retirement*

Penthouse *nt penthouse*

Peripheriegerät *nt peripheral*

Personal *nt personnel; staff*

Personalabteilung *f personnel department*

Personalausbildung *f staff training*

mit Personal besetzen *to staff*

Personalchef(in) *m(f) personnel manager*

Personaldarlehen *nt personal loan*

Personalführung *f personnel management; man management*

Personalmangel *m undermanning*

Personalplanung *f manpower planning*

Personengesellschaft *f partnership*

persönlicher Assistent *m*, **persönliche Assistentin** *f personal assistant (PA)*

persönlicher Steuerfreibetrag *m personal allowance*

persönlicher Verkauf *m personal*

selling
Pestizid *nt pesticide*
petrochemische Industrie *f petroleum industry*
Petrodollar *m petrodollar*
Pfand *nt pledge; security; forfeit*
Pfändung *f attachment*
Pharmaindustrie *f pharmaceutical industry; pharmaceuticals*
Phase *f phase*
Phonotypistin *f audio-typist*
Phosphat *nt phosphate*
Pilotanlage *f pilot plant*
Pilotprojekt *nt pilot project; pilot scheme*
Pixel *nt pixel*
Plagiat *nt plagiarism*
Plakat *nt poster*
Plan *m plan*
planen *to plan; to project; to schedule*
Planung *f planning; scheduling*
Planung *f* **für Eventualfälle** *contingency planning*
Planungsstab *m think tank*
Planwirtschaft *f planned economy*
Platte *f record; panel; sheet*
Plattenkapazität *f disk capacity*
Platzhalter *m wildcard*
Plotter *m plotter*
Podest *nt podium*
Point of Sale *m* **(P.O.S.)** *point of sale (POS)*
Police *f policy*
Politik *f politics; policy*
Polizei *f police*
Polizeiwache *f police station*
Polizist(in) *m/f policeman/woman*
Portable *nt portable (computer)*
Portefeuille *nt portfolio*
Portier *m porter; doorman*
portofrei *post free; post paid*
Portokasse *f petty cash*
Porto *nt* **und Verpackung** *f postage and packing*
Postabfertigungsraum *m mailroom*
Postamt *nt post office*
Postanweisung *f postal order*
Post *f* **auf dem Landweg/Seeweg** *surface mail*

Postfach *nt PO Box; post box*
postlagernd *poste restante*
Postleitzahl *f post code*
Poststempel *m postmark*
Postwurfsendungen *fpl junk mail*
Postwurfwerbung *f direct-mail advertising*
potentieller Kunde *m,* **potentielle Kundin** *f potential customer*
PR *f PR*
Praktikum *nt (work) placement*
Prämie *f premium*
Prämienzuschlag *m loading*
PR Arbeit *f PR exercise*
Präsentation *f presentation*
Präsident(in) *m(f) president; chairman/woman*
Präzedenzfall *m precedent*
Preis *m price*
Preis *m* **ausschließlich Zollgutlagerung** *f in-bond price*
Preis *m* **bei Barzahlung** *f cash price*
Preisbindung *f price-fixing*
Preisbindung *f* **der zweiten Hand** *resale price maintenance*
Preisbindungsabkommen *nt price maintenance agreement; fair-trade agreement*
Preis *m* **einschließlich Zoll** *duty-paid price*
preisempfindlich *price-sensitive*
Preiserhöhung *f price increase; mark-up*
Preisgestaltungspolitik *f pricing policy*
Preisklasse *f price range*
Preiskontrolle *f price control*
Preiskrieg *m price war*
Preisliste *f price list*
Preisnachlaß *m discount; allowance*
Preis *m* **pro Einheit** *f unit price*
Preisschild *nt price tag*
Preissenkung *f price-cutting*
Preis- und Einkommenspolitik *f prices and incomes policy*
Premiere *f première; preview*
Presse *f press*
Presseagent(in) *m(f) press agent*
Pressekonferenz *f press conference*
Pressesprecher(in) *m(f) press offic-*

er; *public relations officer (PRO)*
Pressetermin *m press call*
Presseverlautbarung *f press release*
PR Frau *f PR woman*
prima facie *prima facie*
Primärerhebung *f field research*
privat *private*
Privatbesitz *m private property; private ownership*
in Privatbesitz *m privately-owned*
privater Sektor *m private sector*
Privatgesellschaft *f private company*
privatisieren *to privatize*
Privatisierung *f privatization*
PR Leute *pl PR people*
PR Mann *m PR man*
Probe *f test; sample*
Probe(packung) *f give-away*
Probezeit *f trial period; probationary period*
Produkt *nt product*
Produktdesign *nt product design*
Produktentwicklung *f product development*
Produkthaftpflichtversicherung *f product liability insurance*
Produktion *f production*
Produktionsgesellschaft *f production company*
Produktionskontrolle *f production control*
Produktionsmanager(in) *m(f) production manager*
Produktionsplanung *f production planning*
Produktionsproblem *nt production problem*
Produktivität *f productivity*
Produktmanager(in) *m(f) product manager; brand manager*
Produktpalette *f product range*
Produzent(in) *m(f) producer*
produzieren *to produce; to output*
Pro-forma-Rechnung *f pro-forma invoice*
Programm *nt programme; program*
Programmieren *nt programming*
programmieren *to program*
Programmierer(in) *m(f) computer programmer*
Programmierfehler *m bug*
Programmiersprache *f programming language*
Programmunterbrechung *f für Werbung commercial break*
Progressivbesteuerung *f progressive taxation*
Projekt *nt project*
Projektion *f projection*
Projektleiter(in) *m(f) project manager*
Projektor *m projector*
Prompt *m prompt*
Prospekt *m prospectus; brochure; leaflet*
Protektionismus *m protectionism*
Protokoll *nt protocol; minutes*
Protokollbuch *nt minute book*
protokollieren *to take the minutes; to minute; to log*
Prototyp *m prototype*
Provision *f commission; bank charges; turn*
Prozeß *m process; lawsuit; trial; action*
Prozessor *m processor*
prüfen *to examine; to check; to audit*
Publicity *f publicity*
Publicity-Veranstaltung *f publicity event*
Public Relations *fpl public relations*
Public Relations Berater(in) *m(f) public relations consultant*
Public Relations Firma *f public relations firm*
Public Relations Veranstaltung *f public relations event*
Publikum *nt public; audience*
Publikumsforschung *f audience research*
Publizieren *nt publication*
Puffer *m buffer*
Pult *nt lectern*
Pumpe *f pump*
Qualifikation *f qualification*
Qualitätsingenieur(in) *m(f) quality controller*
Qualitätssicherung *f quality assur-*

ance; quality control
Quelle *f source*
Quittung *f receipt*
Rabatt *m discount*
Radiergummi *m eraser*
Radio *nt radio*
Radioaktivität *f radioactivity*
Raffinerie *f refinery*
RAM *m RAM (random access memory)*
Rand *m margin*
Rate *f instalment*
Ratenkauf *m hire purchase*
ratifizieren *to ratify*
Ratifizierung *f ratification*
rationalisieren *to rationalize*
Rationalisierung *f rationalization*
Raubkopie *f pirate copy*
eine Raubkopie *f* **herstellen** *to pirate*
Rauch *m smoke*
Raucherabteil *nt smoking compartment*
Räumungsverkauf *m clearance sale*
rebooten *to reboot*
Rechner *m calculator*
rechnerischer Gewinn *m paper profit*
Rechnung *f bill; invoice*
Rechnungswesen *nt accountancy*
Recht *nt right*
Rechtfertigung *f justification*
rechtliche Voraussetzung *f legal requirement*
Rechtsabteilung *f legal department*
Rechtsanwalt *m*, **Rechtsanwältin** *f lawyer*
rechtsbündig ausrichten *to justify right*
Rechtschreibprüfung *f spellchecker*
Rechtsstreit *m litigation*
rechtsverbindlich *legally binding*
recyceln *to recycle*
recycelt *recycled*
Recycling-Anlage *f recycling plant*
Recyclingpapier *nt recycled paper*
Rede *f speech; talk*
reden *to speak; to talk*
Redner(in) *m(f) speaker*
Reederei *f shipping company*

Referenz *f reference; referee*
Reflation *f reflation*
Regal *nt cupboard*
Regelung *f regulation; settlement; ruling*
Regionalentwicklungszuschuß *m regional development grant*
regulieren *to regulate; to settle; to adjust*
regulierter Markt *m captive market*
Regulierung *f adjustment*
Reichweite *f reach*
Reifenpanne *f puncture; punctured tyre; flat tyre*
Reihenhaus *nt terraced house*
reine Forschung *f pure research*
reiner Wechsel *m clean bill of exchange*
reines Konnossement *nt clean bill of lading*
Reinigungsdienst *m dry-cleaning service; valet service*
Reinvermögen *nt net assets*
Reisebüro *nt travel agency*
Reisebus *m coach*
Reiseführer *m guide; guidebook*
Reiseindustrie *f travel industry*
Reisepaß *m passport*
Reiseroute *f itinerary*
Reisescheck *m traveller's cheque*
Reiseversicherung *f travel insurance*
Reißwolf *m shredder*
Reklametafel *f billboard*
Reklamewand *f hoarding*
Rendite *f rate of return*
renoviert *renovated; refurbished*
Renovierung *f renovation; refurbishment*
rentabel *profitable; profit-making*
Rentabilität *f profitability*
Rentabilitätsstudie *f profitability study; feasibility study*
Rentenfonds *m pension fund*
Rentenversicherung *f pension; pension scheme*
Report *m report; exposé; contango*
reprivatisieren *to denationalize*
Reprivatisierung *f denationalization*
Reserven *fpl reserves*

Reservewährung *f reserve currency*
reservieren *to reserve*
Reservierung *f reservation*
Ressourcen *pl resources*
Restposten *m broken lot*
Retouren *fpl returns*
Revolving-Kredit *m revolving credit*
rezensieren *to review*
Rezension *f review*
Rezensionsexemplar *nt review copy*
Rezept *nt prescription; remedy; recipe*
Rezession *f recession*
R-Gespräch *nt reverse-charge call; transfer charge call*
Richter(in) *m(f) magistrate; judge*
Richtigstellung *f rectification*
Richtlinie *f guideline*
Ringbuch *nt ring binder*
RISC *m RISC (reduced instruction set computer)*
Risiko *nt risk; venture*
Risikobeginn *m commencement of risk*
Risikokapital *nt risk capital; venture capital*
Risikolebensversicherung *f term insurance*
Roboter *m robot*
Robotertechnik *f robotics*
Rohstoffe *mpl raw materials*
Roll- und Verpackungsmaschine *f rolling and wrapping machine*
ROM *m ROM (read-only memory)*
Rückantwortekarte *f reply-paid postcard*
rückdatieren *to backdate*
Rückfahrkarte *f return ticket*
Rückflug *m return flight*
Rückflugschein *m return air ticket*
Rückforderung *f return order*
rückkaufen *to repurchase; to surrender*
Rückkaufswert *m cash surrender value*
Rücklage *f reserves*
rückläufiger Markt *m falling market*
rückläufige Tendenz *f downward trend*
Rückstand *m backlog; residue*

Rückstände *mpl arrears*
Rückstellung *f provision*
Rücktrittsklausel *f cancellation clause*
rückvermieten *to lease back*
Rückvermietung *f leaseback*
Rückvermietungsabkommen *nt leaseback arrangement*
rückversichern *to reinsure*
Rückversicherung *f reinsurance*
Rückversicherungspool *m reinsurance pool*
Rückwand *f rear*
rückzahlbar *redeemable*
Rufzeichen *nt ringing tone*
Ruhestand *m retirement*
in den Ruhestand *m* **treten** *to retire*
Rundfunk *m radio*
Rundschreiben *nt circular*
Saal *m hall*
Sachbezuge *m benefit*
Sachleistung *f benefit-in-kind; payment in kind*
Sachliteratur *f non-fiction*
Safe *m or nt safe*
saisonbereinigte Zahlen *fpl seasonally-adjusted figures*
Sammelantrag *m composite motion*
sanieren *to redevelop*
Sanierung *f redevelopment*
sanitäre Installation *f sanitary facilities; plumbing*
Sanitätswache *f first aid post*
Sanktionen *fpl sanctions*
Satellit *m satellite*
Satellitenantenne *f satellite dish*
Satellitenfernsehen *nt satellite television*
Sättigungsreichweite *f blanket coverage*
Satzung *f by(e-)law*
saubere Luft *f clean air*
saubere Technologie *f clean technology*
säubern *to clean up*
Säuberungskampagne *f clean-up campaign*
Säulendiagramm *nt histogram*
Schablone *f template*

Schaden *m damage*
Schadenersatz *m damages*
Schadenfreiheitsrabatt *m no-claims bonus*
Schadensabschätzer(in) *m(f) assessor*
Schadensabteilung *f claims department*
Schadenselbstbeteiligungsklausel *f excess clause*
Schadensersatz *m damages*
Schadensfeststellung *f assessment (of damages)*
Schadensminderung *f mitigation of loss*
Schadenssachverständige(r) *f(m) adjuster*
Schadensuntersuchung *f damage survey*
Schadensversicherung *f indemnity insurance*
Schadenteilungsabkommen *nt knock-for-knock agreement*
schädlich *damaging*
Schadstoff *m noxious substance; pollutant*
Schaffner(in) *m(f) guard*
Schallplatte *f record*
Schalterbeamten *m/fpl counter staff*
Schalterbeamter *m,* **Schalterbeamtin** *f cashier; teller; counter clerk*
Schattenwirtschaft *f black economy*
schätzen *to assess; to estimate*
Schätzer(in) *m(f) estimator*
Schaubild *nt graph*
Schaufensterplakat *nt showcard*
Schauspieler(in) *m(f) actor*
Scheck *m cheque*
Scheckkarte *f cheque (guarantee) card*
Schichtarbeit *f shiftwork*
Schichtarbeiter(in) *m(f) shiftworker*
Schiedsklausel *f arbitration clause*
Schiedsrichter(in) *m(f) arbitrator*
Schiedsverfahren *nt arbitration*
frei Schiene *f FOR (free on rail)*
Schiff *nt ship; vessel*
ab Schiff *nt ex ship*
Schiffsbau *m shipbuilding*

Schiffsbesichtigung *f marine survey*
Schiffseigner *m shipowner*
Schiffsmeldung *f ship's report*
Schiffszettel *m shipping note*
Schlafwagen *m sleeping car*
Schlafzimmer *nt bedroom*
Schleuderpreis *m cut-price*
Schlichtung *f conciliation*
schließen *to close; to shut down*
Schließfach *nt locker*
Sc'ılüssel *m key*
Schlußkurs *m closing price*
Schneidemaschine *f cutting machine*
Schnellzug *m express train*
Schnittstelle *f interface*
schnurloses Telefon *nt cordless telephone*
Schreibarbeit *f paperwork*
Schreibdienste *mpl secretarial services*
schreibgeschützt *write-protected*
Schreibkraft *f typist*
Schreibkräfte *fpl clerical staff*
Schreibmaschine *f typewriter*
Schreibpapier *nt notepaper; writing paper*
Schreibtisch *m desk*
Schreibtischlampe *f desk light*
Schreibunterlage *f desk pad*
Schreibwaren *fpl stationery*
Schreibzentrale *f typing pool*
Schrift *f (hand)writing; script; font; typeface*
Schriftart *f font; typeface*
schriftliches Übernahmeangebot *nt offer document*
Schrumpfverpackung *f shrink-wrapping*
Schuld *f debt; guilt; blame; fault*
schuldige Partei *f guilty party*
Schuldner(in) *m(f) debtor*
Schuldrecht *nt contract law*
Schuldschein *m promissory note*
Schundliteratur *f pulp fiction*
Schuttabladen *nt dumping*
schützen *to protect*
Schwamm *m (board) eraser*
schwanken *to fluctuate*
Schwankung *f fluctuation*

Schwarzarbeit *f moonlighting*
schwarze Liste *f blacklist*
auf die Schwarze Liste setzen *to blacklist*
Schwarzmarkt *m black market*
schwebende Belastung *f floating charge*
Schwerindustrie *f heavy industry*
Schwestergesellschaft *f affiliated company*
Schwimmbad *nt swimming pool*
SCSI *f SCSI (small computer system interface)*
Seehafenspediteur *m shipping agent*
Seerecht *nt maritime law*
Seerechtsanwalt *m*, **Seerechtsanwältin** *f maritime lawyer*
Seetüchtigkeit *f seaworthiness*
Seeversicherung *f marine insurance*
Seitenformatierung *f pagination*
Sekretär(in) *m (f) secretary*
selbständig *independent; self-employed*
Seminar *nt seminar*
senden *to send; to broadcast*
Sendezeit *f time slot*
Sendung *f programme; consignment; broadcast*
Sequestration *f sequestration*
Serie *f series*
Serienproduktion *f batch production*
Service-Center *nt service centre*
Shareware *f shareware*
Sicherheit *f collateral; security; safety*
Sicherheit *f des Arbeitsplatzes m job security*
Sicherheitsbeamter *m*, **Sicherheitsbeamtin** *f safety officer*
Sicherheitsbestimmungen *fpl safety standards*
Sicherheitsgurt *m safety belt; seatbelt*
sichern *to protect; to secure; to back up*
Sicherungsdiskette *f back-up disk*
Sicherungskopie *f back-up (copy)*
Sicherungsrecht *nt charge*

sichtbare Ausfuhren *fpl visible exports*
sichtbare Einfuhren *fpl visible imports*
Sichtsprechanlage *f video entry system*
die Siebenergruppe *f (G7 f) Group of 7 (G7)*
Siedlung *f residential estate*
Simulation *f simulation*
Sit-in *nt sit-in*
Sitz *m seat*
Skonto *nt or m cash discount*
Slogan *m slogan*
Softcopy *f soft copy*
Software *f software*
Softwareentwicklung *f software engineering*
Softwarehaus *nt software house*
Software-Ingenieur(in) *m (f) software engineer*
Softwarepaket *nt software package*
Soll *nt debit*
solvent *solvent*
Solvenz *f solvency*
Sonderangebot *nt special offer; bargain*
Sonderpreis *m bargain price; offer price*
Sonderziehungsrechte *ntpl (SZR ntpl) special drawing rights (SDR)*
Sonntagsbeilage *f Sunday supplement*
Sonntagszeitung *f Sunday newspaper*
Sonstiges *AOCB (any other competent business)*
sortieren *to sort*
Souterrain *nt basement*
Sozialversicherung *f national insurance*
Sozialversicherungsbeiträge *mpl national insurance contributions*
sozialwirtschaftlich *socio-economic*
Sparbuch *nt bankbook*
sparen *to save; to economize*
Sparkasse *f savings bank*
Sparkonto *nt savings account; deposit account*
Spätschicht *f late shift; back shift*

Spediteur *m* shipper; carrier; freight forwarder; forwarding agent

Spedition *f* carriage; shipping agency; freight forwarding; forwarding agency

Speicher *m* memory; storage

Speicherabzug *m* dump

Speicherschreibmaschine *f* memory typewriter

Speisesaal *m* dining room

Speisewagen *m* dining car; restaurant car

Spekulant(in) *m(f)* speculator; stag

Spekulation *f* speculation

spekulieren to speculate

Sperren *nt* ban; embargo; arrestment

Sperrkonto *nt* frozen account

Spesen *pl* expenses

Spesenkonto *nt* expense account

Spezialisierung *f* specialization

Speziessachen *fpl* ascertained goods

Spielfilm *m* feature film

mit Spielfilmlänge *f* feature-length

Spielfilmserie *f* drama series

sponsern to sponsor

Sponsor(in) *m(f)* sponsor

Sprache *f* language; speech

Spracherkennung *f* speech recognition

Spracherzeugung *f* speech generation

Sprachsynthese *f* speech synthesis

Sprecher(in) *m(f)* spokesman/woman

Spur *f* track

staatlicher Eingriff *m* government intervention

Staatsangehörige(r) *f(m)* citizen; national

Staatsanleihe *f* government stock

Staatsanwalt *m*, **Staatsanwältin** *f* prosecuting counsel

staatseigen state-owned

Staatseigentum *nt* state ownership; public ownership

Staatspapiere *ntpl* gilt-edged securities

Staatssektor *m* state sector

Stabilisierung *f* stabilization

Stadtmitte *f* city centre; town centre

Stadtplan *m* street map

Stagflation *f* stagflation

Stagnation *f* stagnation

Stahl *m* steel

Stahlindustrie *f* steel industry

Stahlwerk *nt* steelworks

Stammaktie *f* ordinary share

Stammaktien *fpl* common stock; ordinary shares

Stand *m* stand; state; level

Stand-alone-Gerät *nt* stand-alone

Standard *m* standard

Standard- default

Standardisierung *f* standardization

Standardkosten *pl* standard cost

Standardtarif *m* standard rate

Standesordnung *f* code of practice

Start *m* take-off; start

starten to take off; to start

statischer Markt *m* static market

stechen to clock in/on; to clock off/out

Stechkarte *f* time card; time sheet; job card

Stechuhr *f* time clock

Steckdose *f* power point

steigend rising; buoyant

steigende Tendenz *f* upward trend

Stelle *f* place; post; job

stellvertretender Direktor *m*, **stellvertretende Direktorin** *f* associate director; deputy chief executive

stellvertretender Geschäftsführer *m*, **stellvertretende Geschäftsführerin** *f* assistant manager(ess)

stellvertretender Manager *m*, **stellvertretende Managerin** *f* acting manager(ess)

stellvertretender Vorsitz *m* vice-chair(person)

stellvertretender Vorsitzender *m*, **stellvertretende Vorsitzende** *f* vice-chairman, vice-chairwoman

Stempelgebühr *f* stamp duty

stempeln to clock in/on; to clock off/out

Steppdecke *f quilt*
Steuer *f tax*
Steuerbefreiung *f tax exemption*
Steuerberater(in) *m(f) tax accountant; tax consultant*
Steuerbescheid *m tax bill*
Steuereinheit *f control unit*
Steuererhebung *f tax collection*
Steuererhöhung *f tax increase*
Steuererklärung *f tax return*
steuerfrei *tax-free; free of tax; non-taxable*
Steuerfreibetrag *m tax allowance*
steuerfreie Periode *f tax holiday*
Steuergutschrift *f tax credit*
Steuerhinterziehung *f tax evasion*
Steuerjahr *nt tax year; fiscal year*
Steuerkennziffer *f tax code*
Steuerklasse *f tax bracket*
Steuerlücke *f tax loophole*
Steuermaßnahmen *fpl fiscal measures*
nach Steuern *after tax*
vor Steuern *before tax; pre-tax*
Steuerparadies *nt tax haven*
steuerpflichtig *taxable*
Steuerrücklage *f tax reserve*
Steuerrückstand *m back duty*
Steuerrückvergütung *f tax rebate*
Steuersenkung *f tax cut*
Steuertabelle *f tax tables; tax schedule*
Steuerumgehung *f tax avoidance*
Steuervergünstigung *f tax concession; tax relief*
Steuerverlust *m tax loss*
Steuervorteil *m tax advantage; tax benefit*
Steward *m steward*
Stewardeß *f stewardess*
Stichtag *m deadline*
stiller Gesellschafter *m*, **stille Gesellschafterin** *f silent partner; sleeping partner*
stiller Teilhaber *m*, **stille Teilhaberin** *f silent partner; sleeping partner*
stimmrechtslose Aktien *fpl A shares; non-voting shares*
Stock *m floor; storey*
Stockwerk *nt storey*

storniert *cancelled*
Stornierung *f cancellation*
Störung *f fault; hiccup; disruption; disturbance*
stoßfest *shockproof*
Stoßwirkung *f impact*
Strafklausel *f penalty clause*
Strafrecht *nt criminal law*
strafrechtlich verfolgen *to prosecute*
Strategie *f strategy*
Streik *m strike*
streiken *to strike*
Streikende(r) *f(m) striker*
Streikposten *m picket*
streng vertraulich *private and confidential*
Streuplaner(in) *m(f) media buyer*
Strichcode *m bar code*
Stück *nt piece; unit; play*
Stückpreis *m unit price*
Student(in) *m(f) student*
Studie *f study*
Sturmschaden *m storm damage*
Sturmversicherung *f storm insurance*
Sturz *m slump*
Stützungskäufe *mpl support buying*
Subrogation *f subrogation*
Subunternehmervertrag *m subcontract*
Subvention *f subsidy*
subventionieren *to subsidize*
Suchen *nt* **und Ersetzen** *nt search and replace*
Suite *f suite*
Superkargo *m supercargo*
Syntaxfehler *m syntax error*
System *nt system*
Systemanalyse *f systems analysis*
Systemanalytiker(in) *m(f) systems analyst*
Systembediener(in) *m(f) system operator*
Tabakindustrie *f tobacco industry*
Tachograph *m tachograph*
Tafel *f (black)board*
Tag *m* **der offenen Tür** *open day; open house*
Tagesordnung *f agenda*

GERMAN–ENGLISH GLOSSARY

Tageszeitung *f daily (newspaper)*
täglich *daily*
Tagschicht *f day shift*
Tagung *f convention; conference; sitting*
Tankstelle *f service station*
Tantiemen *fpl royalties*
Tapete *f wallpaper*
neu tapeziert *redecorated*
Target-Marketing *nt target marketing*
Tarifverhandlungen *fpl wage negotiations; collective bargaining*
Tastatur *f keyboard*
Taste *f key*
Tastenfeld *nt keypad*
tätiger Gesellschafter *m*, **tätige Gesellschafterin** *f active partner*
Tätigkeitsbericht *m progress report*
tauschen *to exchange; to barter*
Tauschhandel *m barter*
Taxi *nt taxi*
Taxifahrer(in) *m(f) taxi driver*
Taxistand *m taxi rank*
Technik *f engineering*
Technologie *f technology*
technologisch *technological*
teileingezahlte Aktie *f partly-paid share*
Teilhaber(in) *m(f) partner*
teilnehmen *to take part; to attend*
Teilzahlung *f part payment*
Teilzahlungs(kauf)vertrag *m hire-purchase agreement*
Teilzeitbeschäftigte(r) *f(m) part-timer*
Telefon *nt telephone*
Telefonbuch *nt telephone directory*
Telefonist(in) *m(f) switchboard operator*
Telefonkarte *f phonecard*
Telefonverkauf *m telesales*
Telefonzelle *f (tele)phone box*
Telekonferenzschaltung *f teleconferencing*
Telemarketing *nt telemarketing*
Telex *nt telex; telex machine*
ein Telex schicken *(+dat) to telex (somebody)*
telexen *to telex*

Telexverzeichnis *nt telex directory*
Tendenz *f trend; tendency*
Teppich *m carpet*
Teppichboden *m wall-to-wall carpeting*
Terminabschluß *m forward contract*
Terminal *nt terminal*
Termindevisen *pl forward exchange*
Termingeschäfte *ntpl futures*
Terminjäger *m progress chaser*
Terminkontrakt *m forward contract*
Terminverkauf *m forward sales*
tertiärer Sektor *m tertiary sector; service sector*
Test *m test*
Testamentsnachtrag *m codicil*
Testdaten *ntpl test data*
testen *to test*
teuer *expensive; dear*
teures Geld *nt dear money*
Texteditor *m text editor*
Texterfasser(in) *m(f) keyboarder*
Textilindustrie *f textile industry; textiles*
Textteil *m body copy*
Textverarbeitung *f word processing*
Textverarbeitungsanlage *f word processor*
Tiefgarage *f underground car park*
Tieflader *m low-loader*
Tilgungsfonds *m sinking fund*
Time-sharing *nt time-sharing*
Tintenstrahldrucker *m ink jet printer*
tippen *to type*
Tischcomputer *m desktop computer*
Tischkalender *m desk diary*
Titel *m title*
Tochtergesellschaft *f subsidiary (company)*
Toilette *f toilet*
Toner *m toner*
Toningenieur(in) *m(f) sound engineer*
Totalschaden *m total loss*
tote Saison *f slack period*
totes Konto *nt dead account*
Touristenklasse *f economy class*
Tower *m tower; deskside computer*
Toxin *nt toxin*

tpi (Spuren *fpl* **pro Inch** *m***)** *tpi (tracks per inch)*

tragbare Entwicklung *f sustainable development*

Tragflügelboot *nt hydrofoil*

Tranche *f tranche*

Transaktion *f transaction*

Transitgüter *ntpl goods in transit*

Transitpapiere *ntpl transit papers; transit forms*

Transitstop *m transit stop*

Transport *m transport; haulage*

beim Transport *m in transit*

Transportkosten *pl haulage (cost)*

Transportschaden *m loss in transit*

Transportunternehmen *nt haulage contractor*

Transportverlust *m loss in transit*

Transportversicherung *f transport insurance*

Travellers Cheque *m traveller's cheque*

Treibgas *nt propellant*

Treibhauseffekt *m greenhouse effect*

Treibhausgas *nt greenhouse gas*

Trennwand *f partition wall*

Treppe *f stair; staircase*

Treppenabsatz *m landing*

Treuhänder(in) *m(f) fiduciary; trustee*

Treuhandverhältnis *nt trust*

Treu *f* **und Glauben** *m good faith*

trocken *dry*

Türsprechanlage *f entryphone*

Typenraddrucker *m daisy wheel printer*

U-bahn *f underground*

Überangebot *nt excess supply*

überarbeiten *to edit*

überbesetzt *overstaffed*

Überbevorratung *f overstocking*

Überbrückungskredit *m bridging loan*

überbuchen *to overbook*

Überdenkungsperiode *f cooling-off period*

Übereignungsurkunde *f bill of sale*

Übereinstimmung *f consensus; agreement*

Übergangsfinanzierung *f accommodation*

eine Übergangsfinanzierung *f* **gewähren** *to accommodate*

übergebucht *overbooked*

Übergepäck *nt excess baggage*

Überhang *m* **der Zahlungsausgänge** *mpl negative cash flow*

Überhang *m* **der Zahlungseingänge** *mpl positive cash flow*

überhitzte Konjunktur *f overheated economy*

überholt *out of date*

Überkapazität *f excess capacity; overcapacity*

überkapitalisieren *to overcapitalize*

Überliegegeld *nt demurrage*

Übernahme *f takeover*

Übernahmeangebot *nt takeover bid*

Übernahme *f* **der Gemeinkosten** *overhead absorption*

übernehmen *to take over*

Überproduktion *f overproduction*

überregionale Presse *f national press*

überschreiben *to overwrite*

überschreiten *to exceed*

Übersetzungsbüro *nt translation agency*

Überstunden *fpl overtime*

Überstundenverbot *nt overtime ban*

übertragen *to assign*

Übertragung *f assignment*

Übertragungsrechte *ntpl television rights*

überweisen *to transfer*

Überweisung *f transfer*

Überweisungsauftrag *m bank giro credit*

überzeichnet *oversubscribed*

Überziehungsgrenze *f overdraft limit*

Überziehungskredit *m overdraft*

Umbau *m conversion*

umbauen *to convert*

umformatieren *to reformat*

Umfrage *f survey*

umladen *to tranship*

Umladung *f transhipment*

Umlaufkapital *nt circulating capital;*

floating capital
Umlaufrendite *f current yield*
Umlaufvermögen *nt current assets*
Umsatz *m turnover; billing*
Umschlag *m envelope*
Umschlagzeit *f turnaround time*
umschulden *to reschedule*
Umschuldung *f rescheduling*
Umsetzung *f* (**der Arbeitskräfte** *fpl*) *redeployment*
Umwelt *f environment*
Umweltbewußtsein *nt environmental awareness*
Umwelteinfluß *m environmental impact*
Umweltfragen *fpl environmental issues; green issues*
umweltfreundlich *environmentally friendly; pollution-free*
Umwelt-Lobby *f environmental lobby*
Umwelt-Management *nt environmental management*
Umweltministerium *nt Department of the Environment*
Umweltschaden *m environmental damage*
Umweltschutz *m conservation*
Umweltschützer(in) *m(f) environmentalist*
Umweltschutzerklärung *f environmental statement*
Umweltschutzmaßnahme *f anti-pollution measure*
Umweltverträglichkeitsprüfung *f environmental assessment or audit*
Umzug *m relocation; removal*
Umzugskosten *pl relocation expenses*
unabhängig *independent*
unangefordeter Anruf *m cold call*
unangemeldeter Vertreterbesuch *m cold call*
unbeabsichtigt *accidental*
unbeglichene Schuld *f undischarged debt*
unbegrenzt *unlimited*
unbeschränkte Haftung *f unlimited liability*

unbeschränktes Monopol *nt absolute monopoly*
unbewohnt *unoccupied; vacant*
unbezahlt *unpaid*
uneinbringliche Forderung *f bad debt*
unerschlossenes Bauland *nt greenfield site*
unfaire Entlassung *f unfair dismissal*
Unfall *m accident*
Unfallversicherung *f accident insurance*
ungelernter Arbeiter *m,* **ungelernte Arbeiterin** *f unskilled worker*
ungerechtfertigte Entlassung *f wrongful dismissal*
ungeschützte Datei *f scratch file*
Unglück *nt accident; bad luck; unhappiness*
unkündbare Wertpapiere *ntpl undated stock*
unlauterer Wettbewerb *m unfair competition*
unmöbliert *unfurnished*
unredlicher Anspruch *m fraudulent claim*
Unredlichkeit *f dishonesty; fraudulence; bad faith*
unsichtbare Ausfuhren *fpl invisible exports*
unsichtbare Einfuhren *fpl invisible imports*
unsichtbare Vermögenswerte *mpl invisible assets*
(nach) unten *downstairs*
Unterbaugruppe *f subassembly*
Unterbeschäftigung *f underemployment*
unterbesetzt *short-staffed; understaffed*
unterbrechen *to interrupt*
unteres Management *nt junior management*
Untergeschoß *nt basement*
Untergrundbahn *f underground*
unterkapitalisiert *undercapitalized*
Unternehmen *nt business; concern; enterprise; undertaking; venture*
Unternehmensberater(in) *m(f)*

management consultant
Unternehmensführung *f management*
Unternehmensleitung *f management*
Unternehmensplanung *f corporate planning*
Unternehmensstil *m organizational culture; house style*
Unternehmensstrategie *f corporate strategy*
Unternehmergewinn *m profit*
unterschlagen *to embezzle*
Unterschlagung *f embezzlement*
Unterschriftsprobe *f specimen signature*
unterschwellige Werbung *f subliminal advertising*
Unterstützung *f backing; finance; support*
untervermieten *to sublet*
einen Untervertrag *m* **abschließen** *to subcontract*
Unterzeichner *m signatory*
unterzeichnet *undersigned*
Unterzeichnete(r) *f(m) undersigned; signatory*
Unterzeichnung *f endorsement; signing*
unverbindlich *not binding; recommended*
unverkauft *unsold*
unverlangte Waren *fpl unsolicited goods*
unwiderruflich *irrevocable*
Urkunde *f deed; document*
Urlaub *m holiday(s)*
Ursprungszeugnis *nt certificate of origin*
vakuumverpackt *vacuum-packed*
validieren *to validate*
variable Kosten *pl variable cost*
Vaterschaftsurlaub *m paternity leave*
Veranstaltungsräume *mpl function suite*
Verantreuung *f embezzlement*
verarbeiten *to process*
Verarbeitungsindustrie *f processing industry*

verbessern *to improve; to upgrade*
Verbindlichkeiten *fpl accounts payable*
als Verbindungsperson *f* **fungieren** *liaise*
verborgener Mangel *m latent defect*
verbrauchen *to consume; to use*
Verbraucher *m consumer*
Verbraucherkredit *m consumer credit*
Verbrauchermarkt *m consumer market*
Verbraucherschutz *m consumer protection*
Verbraucherverband *m consumers' association*
Verbraucherverhalten *nt consumer behaviour*
Verbrauchsgüter *ntpl consumer goods*
Verbrauchssteuer *f excise duty*
verderbliche Waren *fpl perishable goods*
Verdienst *m earnings*
vereinbarte Verfahrensordnung *f agreed procedure*
Vereinbarung *f agreement*
Vereinigung *f association*
Vereinigung *f* **südostasiatischer Nationen (ASEAN** *f)* *Association of South-East Asian Nations (ASEAN)*
Verfahren *nt procedure*
Verfahrensregeln *fpl code of practice*
Verfallstag *m expiry date*
verfrachten *to freight*
nicht verfügbar *down; unavailable*
verfügbarer Markt *m available market*
verfügbares Einkommen *nt disposable personal income*
vergeben *to award; to assign; to forgive*
Vergleichstest *m benchmark test*
Vergnügungsindustrie *f entertainment industry*
vergriffen *out of print*
vergrößern *to enlarge*
Vergrößerung *f enlargement*

verhandeln *to negotiate*
verhandeln mit *to deal with*
Verhandlung *f negotiation*
verhandlungsfähig *negotiable*
Verhinderung *f* **steuerlicher Belastung** *f tax shelter*
Verkauf *m sale*
Verkauf *m* **an der Haustür** *f door-to-door selling*
verkaufen *to sell*
zu verkaufen *for sale*
Verkäufer(in) *m(f)* *seller; salesman/woman*
Verkäufermarkt *m seller's market*
verkäuflich *saleable; marketable; for sale*
Verkaufsabkommen *nt agreement to sell*
Verkaufsabschluß *m completion of sale*
Verkaufsabteilung *f sales department*
Verkaufsbedingungen *fpl conditions of sale*
Verkaufsexperte *m,* **Verkaufsexpertin** *f merchandiser*
Verkaufskampagne *f sales campaign; sales drive*
Verkaufskurs *m asking price*
Verkaufsleiter(in) *m(f) sales manager*
Verkaufsoption *f put option*
Verkaufsort *m point of sale (POS)*
Verkaufsprospekt *m sales literature; brochure; prospectus*
Verkaufsstab *m sales force*
Verkaufsstelle *f outlet*
Verkaufstüchtigkeit *f salesmanship*
Verkaufsvorstoß *m sales drive*
Verkaufsziel *nt sales target*
Verkaufsziffern *fpl sales figures*
Verkauf *m* **und Rückmiete** *f sale and lease back*
verladen *to ship*
Verlag *m publishing house*
Verlagswesen *nt publishing*
verlängern *to extend; to renew*
Verlängerung *f renewal*
verlassener Grundbesitz *m vacant possession*

verlegen *to reschedule*
Verleger(in) *m(f) publisher*
Vermächtnisnehmer(in) *m(f) legatee*
vermarkten *to market*
Vermarkter *m marketer*
vermieten *to let; to rent*
zu vermieten *to let; for rent*
Vermieter(in) *m(f)* *landlord/landlady*
Vermittlung *f agency; switchboard; operator; placement*
Vermittlungsdienst *m operator service*
Vermögenssteuer *f wealth tax; property tax; ad valorem tax*
Vermögenswerte *mpl assets*
vernetzen *to network*
veröffentlichen *to publish*
Veröffentlichung *f publication*
verpachten *to lease*
Verpacken *nt packaging*
verpacken *to pack(age)*
Verpackung *f packaging; wrapper*
Verrechnungsscheck *m crossed cheque*
Verringerung *f reduction*
Versammlung *f* **des Verkaufsstabs** *m sales conference*
Versandabteilung *f shipping department; dispatch department*
Versandanzeige *f advice note*
Versanddokumente *ntpl shipping documents*
Verschiffung *f shipping*
verschleudern *to dump*
verschmutzen *to pollute*
Verschmutzung *f pollution; contamination*
verschwenden *to waste*
versenden *to dispatch; to consign*
Versender *m consignor*
Versicherer *m underwriter*
versichern *to insure; to underwrite; to cover*
versichert *insured*
Versicherte(r) *f(m) insured (party)*
Versicherung *f insurance; cover*
Versicherungsanspruch *m insurance claim*

Versicherungsbescheinigung *f insurance certificate*

Versicherungsgesellschaft *f assurance company; insurance company*

Versicherungshöhe *f extent of cover*

Versicherungsmakler(in) *m(f) insurance agent or broker*

Versicherungsmanager(in) *m(f) insurance manager*

Versicherungsmathematiker(in) *m(f) actuary*

versicherungsmathematisch *actuarial*

versicherungsmathematische Tabellen *fpl actuarial tables*

Versicherungsnehmer(in) *m(f) policy-holder*

Versicherungspolice *f insurance policy*

Versicherungsprämie *f insurance premium*

Versicherungsträger *m insurer*

Versicherungsverein *m* **auf Gegenseitigkeit** *friendly society; mutual insurance company*

Versorgungsunternehmen *nt public utility*

verspätet *delayed*

Versprechen *nt promise*

Versprechensurkunde *f deed of covenant*

verstaatlichen *to nationalize*

verstaatlichter Industriezweig *m nationalized industry*

Verstaatlichung *f nationalization*

Versteigung *f auction*

nicht zu versteuerndes Einkommen *nt non-taxable income*

Versuch *m trial; test; attempt*

vertagen *to adjourn*

Vertagung *f adjournment*

verteidigen *to defend*

Verteidiger(in) *m(f)* **der Anklager** *counsel for the defence*

verteilen *to distribute*

Verteiler *m distributor*

Verteilernetz *nt distributor network*

Verteilerpolitik *f distributor policy*

Verteilungszentrum *nt distribution centre*

vertikale Integration *f vertical integration*

Vertrag *m contract; agreement*

unter Vertrag *m under contract*

vertragliches Versprechen *nt covenant*

vertragliche Verplichtung *f contractual obligation*

Vertrag *m* **mit bestimmter Dauer** *fixed term contract*

Vertragsbruch *m breach of contract*

Vertragshaftung *f contractual liability*

Vertragskündigung *f termination of contract*

vertraulich *private*

vertreten *to represent; to stand in for*

Vertreter(in) *m(f) sales representative; travelling salesman/woman; agent; deputy; representative*

Vertreterbericht *m call report*

Vertreterprovision *f agent's commission*

Vertretung *f representation; agency*

Vertrieb *m distribution*

Vertriebskosten *pl distribution costs*

Vertriebsnetz *nt distribution network*

Vertriebsstelle *f outlet*

verunreinigen *to contaminate*

Verursachung *f causation*

Verwahrung *f bailment*

Verwalter(in) *m(f) administrator*

Verwaltung *f administration*

Verwaltungsgericht *nt administrative tribunal*

Verwaltungskosten *pl administrative expenses*

Verwaltungsrat *m directorate*

Verzögerung *f delay*

VGA *nt VGA (video gate array)*

Video *nt video*

Videokamera *f video camera*

Videokassette *f video (cassette)*

Video-Konferenzschaltung *f video conferencing*

Videorekorder *m video recorder*
Videospiel *nt video game*
Videotext *m teletext*
Vierteljahresschrift *f quarterly (magazine)*
vierteljährlich *quarterly*
vierzehntäglich *bi-monthly; twice a month; fortnightly*
Villa *f villa*
Virus *m virus*
vis-à-vis Verkauf *m face-to-face selling*
Visitenkarte *f business card*
Visum *nt visa*
Vizepräsident(in) *m(f) vice-president*
Vollbeschäftigung *f full employment*
Vollkaskoversicherung *f comprehensive insurance*
Vollkostenrechnung *f absorption costing*
Vollmacht *f authority; power of attorney*
Vollpension *f full board*
Vollstreckungsauftrag *m enforcement order*
vorankommen *to progress*
Voranschlag *m estimate*
Vorarbeiter(in) *m(f) foreman/woman; chargehand*
im voraus *in advance*
vorausberechnen *to forecast*
Vorausberechnung *f forecast*
Voraussage *f forecast; prediction*
voraussagen *to forecast; to predict*
voraussichtliche Ankunft *f estimated time of arrival (ETA)*
vorbehaltlich einer Bestätigung *f subject to confirmation*
vorbehaltlich eines Vertragsabschlusses *m subject to contract*
vordatierter Scheck *m post-dated cheque*
Vorderfront *f front*
Vorfertigung *f preproduction*
Vorführmodell *nt demonstration model*
Vorführung *f demonstration*
Vorgabe *f default*

Vorgabe- *default*
vorgeschrieben *required*
Vorhof *m forecourt*
vorläufig *provisional; subject to confirmation*
vorläufige Abrechnung *f draft accounts*
Vorort *m suburb*
vorrätig *in stock*
nicht vorrätig *out of stock*
Vorrichtung *f device*
Vorschau *f preview*
Vorschrift *f regulation; rule*
nach Vorschrift *f arbeiten to work to rule*
Vorsitz *m chair(manship)*
Vorsitzende(r) *f(m) chair(person); chairman/woman*
Vorspeise *f starter; hors d'œuvre*
Vorstand *m board (of directors)*
Vorstandssitzung *f board meeting*
Vorstellungsgespräch *nt interview*
vorübergehend *temporary*
vorübergehende Stillegung *f temporary shut-down*
vorzeitig *early*
Vorzugsaktien *fpl preference shares*
Wache *f security guard*
Wachstumsindustrie *f growth industry*
Wachstumsrate *f growth rate*
Waffenhandel *m arms trade*
wählen *to dial*
wahlfreier Zugriff *m random access*
Währungskorb *m basket of currencies*
Währungspolitik *f monetary policy*
WAN *nt (Weitverkehrsnetz nt) WAN (wide area network)*
Wand *f (inside) wall*
Wanze *f bug*
Ware *f commodity*
Warenabnahme *f acceptance of goods*
Warenbestand *m stock(s); stock-in-trade*
Warenbestandsaufnahme *f stocktaking*
Warenbörse *f commodity exchange*
Wareneingangsbescheinigung *f*

goods received note

Waren *fpl* **unter Zollverschluß** *m* *bonded goods*

Warenzeichen *nt* *trademark*

Waren *fpl* **zur Ansicht** *goods on approval*

Warteraum *m* *waiting room; transit lounge*

Wartungsschicht *f* *maintenance shift*

Wäscherei *f* *laundry (service)*

Waschmittel *nt* *detergent*

Wasseranschluß *m* *mains water*

wasserdicht *waterproof*

Wasserverschmutzung *f* *water pollution*

Wechsel *m* *charge; exchange; rotation; bill of exchange*

Wechselforderung *f* *bill*

Wechselkurs *m* *exchange rate*

Wechselkursmechanismus *m* *Exchange Rate Mechanism (ERM)*

Wechselmakler(in) *m(f)* *bill-broker*

Wechselverbindlichkeiten *fpl* *bills payable*

Weckruf *m* *alarm call*

Weinherstellung *f* *winemaking*

weiße Tafel *f* *whiteboard*

weiße Waren *fpl* *white goods*

Weltbank *f* *World Bank*

Welthandelskonferenz *f* **(WHK** *f)* *UN Conference on Trade and Development (UNCTAD)*

Welthandels- und Entwicklungskonferenz *f* **der Vereinten Nationen** *UN Conference on Trade and Development (UNCTAD)*

Werbeagentur *f* *advertising agency*

Werbegeschenk *nt* *free gift; freebie*

Werbekampagne *f* *advertising campaign*

Werbeleiter(in) *m(f)* *advertising manager*

Werbematerial *nt* **am Verkaufsort** *point-of-sale material*

Werbemelodie *f* *jingle*

werben *to advertise; to publicize; to canvass*

werben für *to promote*

Werbeschrift *f* *brochure; prospec-*

tus

Werbesendung *f* *commercial*

Werbespot *m* *spot*

Werbestrategie *f* *advertising strategy*

Werbetext *m* *copy*

Werbetexter(in) *m(f)* *copywriter*

Werbeträger *m* *inv* *advertising media*

Werbung *f* *advertising; promotion*

Werbung *f* **am Verkaufsort** *m* *point-of-sale advertising*

ab Werk *nt* *ex factory; ex works*

Werkstatt *f* *workshop; shop floor*

Werkzeug *nt* *tool; toolkit*

Werkzeugmaschine *f* *machine tool*

Wert *m* *value*

im Wert *m* **sinken** *to depreciate*

unter Wert *m* **verkaufen** *to undersell*

Wertbescheinigung *f* *certificate of value*

Wertbestimmung *f* *valuation*

Wertminderung *f* *depreciation*

Wertminderung *f* **der Ressourcen** *fpl* *waste of resources*

Wertpapier *nt* *stock; security*

sichere Wertpapieranlage *f* *blue-chip investment*

Wertpapierportefeuille *nt* *investment portfolio*

Wertsteigerung *f* *appreciation*

Wertsteigerung erfahren *to appreciate*

Wettbewerb *m* *competition*

wettbewerbsbeschränkende Abmachung *f* *restrictive trading agreement*

Wettbewerbsvorteil *m* *competitive advantage/edge*

Widerruf *m* *revocation*

wiederausführen *to re-export*

Wiederbeschaffungskosten *pl* *replacement cost*

Wiederbeschaffungswert *m* *replacement value*

wiedereinstellen *to reinstate*

Wiedereinstellung *f* *reinstatement*

wiederhergestellt *restored*

Wiederinbesitznahme *f* *reposses-*

sion
wiederverwendbar *reusable*
wiederverwertbar *recyclable*
wilder Streik *m wildcat strike*
Wirtschaft *f economy*
Wirtschaftsentwicklung *f economic development; economic trend*
Wirtschaftsklima *nt economic climate*
Wirtschaftskrieg *m economic warfare*
Wirtschaftskrise *f depression*
Wirtschaftsprüfer(in) *m(f) auditor; accountant*
Wirtschaftsprüfung *f audit; accounting*
Wirtschaftsteil *m business section*
Wirtschaftswachstum *nt economic growth*
Wirtschaftswissenschaften *fpl economics*
Wirtschaftswissenschaftler(in) *m(f) economist*
wissenschaftlich *scientific*
wöchentlich *weekly*
Wochenzeitschrift *f weekly (magazine/newspaper)*
Wohnblock *m apartment building*
Wohngebäude *nt residential building*
Wohngegend *f residential area*
Wohnung *f apartment; flat*
Wohnzimmer *nt lounge*
für Wohnzwecke *mpl for residential use*
Workshop *m workshop*
Wörterbuch *nt dictionary*
Wörter pro Minute *ntpl (WpM) words per minute (wpm)*
Wortzählung *f wordcount*
Wühltisch *m dump bin*
Wurfsendung *f cicular*
WYSIWYG *nt WYSIWYG (what you see is what you get)*
zahlbar (an) *payable (to)*
zahlbar bei Sicht *f payable at sight; payable on demand*
zahlen *to pay*
Zähler *m meter*
Zahlung *f payment*

Zahlung *f* **bei Rechnungsvorlage** *payment on invoice*
Zahlungsaufforderung *f default notice*
Zahlungsbedingungen *fpl terms of payment*
Zahlungsbilanz *f balance of payments*
Zahlungsempfänger(in) *m(f) payee*
Zahlung *f* **stoppen** *to stop payment*
zahlungsunfähig *insolvent; unable to pay*
Zahlungsunfähigkeit *f insolvency*
Zahlungsverrechnung *f payment clearing*
Zahnarzt *m,* **Zahnärztin** *f dentist*
Zedent *m assignor*
die Zehnergruppe *f* **(G10** *f)* *Group of 10 (G10)*
Zeichen *nt character; sign; symbol*
Zeichenfolge *f string*
Zeichensatz *m character set*
Zeichner(in) *m(f) subscriber*
Zeichnung *f subscription*
Zeiger *m pointer*
Zeilenabstand *m line spacing*
Zeilenumbruch *m wordwrap*
Zeilenvorschub *m line feed*
zeitliche Begrenzung *f time limit*
Zeitplan *m schedule*
Zeitpunkt *m* **des Inkrafttretens** *f effective date*
Zeitschrift *f magazine; periodical*
Zeitung *f newspaper*
Zeitvorgabe *f timescale*
Zentralbank *f central bank*
Zentrale *f head office*
Zentraleinheit *f central processing unit (CPU)*
zentral gesteuerte Wirtschaft *f centralized economy*
Zentralheizung *f central heating*
zentrieren *to centre*
zerstören *to destroy; to spoil*
Zessionar *m assignee*
Ziel *nt target; objective; goal*
Zielgruppe *f target audience*
Zielmarkt *m target market*
Zielsetzung *f targeting*
ziemlich *quite; rather*

Ziffer *f digit; figure; number*
Zimmer *nt room*
Zimmermädchen *nt chambermaid*
Zimmerpreis *m room rate*
Zimmerservice *m room service*
Zinsen *pl interest*
Zinsenkonto *nt interest-earning account*
Zinseszins *m compound interest*
zinslos *interest-free*
Zinssatz *m interest rate*
Zivilluftfahrt *f civil aviation*
Zivilrecht *nt civil law*
Zoll *m duty; customs*
Zollabfertigung *f customs clearance*
Zoll(abfertigungs)hafen *m port of entry*
Zollamt *nt customs house*
Zollbeamter *m,* **Zollbeamtin** *f customs official; customs officer*
Zollbescheinigung *f clearance certificate*
Zollbestimmung *f customs regulation*
Zolldeklaration *f bill of entry*
Zollerklärung *f customs declaration*
Zollformular *nt customs form*
zollfrei *duty-free*
Zollgebühr *f customs duty*
Zollgutlager *nt bonded warehouse*
Zollmakler *m customs broker*
Zollquittung *f customs receipt*
Zollregistriernummer *f customs registered number*
Zollschranke *f tariff barrier*
Zollunion *f customs union*
unter Zollverschluß *m in bond*
unter Zollverschluß *m* **nehmen** *to bond*
zuerkennen *to award*
Zuerkennung *f award*
zuerst *first*
Zug *m train*
Zugabe *f extra; bonus; free gift*

Zugabeangebot *nt premium offer*
Zugang *m access*
zugelassenes Gepäck *nt baggage allowance*
zugestehen *to allow*
zugreifen auf *(+acc) to access*
Zugriff *m access*
Zugriffszeit *f access time*
Zuhörer *mpl audience*
Zulage *f increment; bonus*
zulässig *permissible; allowed*
zuletzt *last*
zunehmend *increasing; growing*
zurückstufen *to demote; to downgrade*
Zurückstufung *f demotion; downgrading*
Zusammenfassung *f summary; synopsis; abstract; combination; concentration*
Zusatz *m additive; codicil; appendix; rider*
Zusatzstoff *m additive*
Zuteilung *f allotment*
zuviel *too much; too many*
Zwangsvollstreckung *f foreclosure*
Zwangsvollstreckung *f* **betreiben** *to foreclose*
Zweigstelle *f branch*
Zweigstellenleiter(in) *m(f) branch manager*
zweimal jährlich *bi-annual; bi-annually*
zweimonatlich *bi-monthly; every two months*
zweite Klasse *f second class*
Zwischenablage *f clipboard*
Zwischenkonten *ntpl interim accounts*
Zwischenlandung *f stopover*
zwischenstaatlicher Tauschhandel *m countertrading*
Zyklus *m cycle*